Famo

"An intimate look at the famous, and famously private, musician, whose seven Emmys only begin to scratch the surface of his musical achievements."　　　　　　　　　　　*—Vanity Fair*

"Readers are taken behind the scenes into what most would consider a fantasy life. There were vacations, Beatles concerts, luxury apartments, and dinner parties with famous guests. To many readers, Jamie Bernstein's childhood will seem charmed. Alas, the family has its issues. Readers may find interesting the (largely) bygone era of extravagance."　　　—Associated Press

"Film documentarian Bernstein (*Crescendo: The Power of Music*), the oldest of three children of conductor and composer Leonard Bernstein, presents an in-depth, intimate view of her father, juxtaposed with her own upbringing in his shadow. . . . Bernstein paints a fascinating picture of the dizzying magic that Leonard Bernstein brought to his music—and the complexity to his home life."　　　　　　　　　　　*—Publishers Weekly*

"Yes, *Famous Father Girl* is a love letter. It is also honest."
　　　　　　　　　　　—WOSU Radio

"Jamie Bernstein has taken on perhaps the hardest task in literature, writing a memoir about a famous parent which manages to be both honest and tender. Semimiraculously, she's pulled it off, and *Famous Father Girl* both paints a winning picture of the Bernstein family, especially her parents, the much-celebrated Lenny and the much-loved Felicia, while offering a poignant take on the complexities of growing up as the child of a legend—or, for that matter, as anybody's child."　　　　　—Adam Gopnik

"Jamie Bernstein's book about her fabled father not only takes us closer to Leonard Bernstein than anything yet published but stands by itself as a beautifully written and unflinchingly courageous expression of love, exasperation, amazement, and forgiveness."

—Tim Page, professor of journalism and music at the University of Southern California

"Jamie Bernstein's compulsively readable adventure tale, *Famous Father Girl*, tells of her growing up under the seductive spell of her father, the composer, the conductor, the true legend who needed the sustenance of a bourgeois life, upholstered with adoring wife and three perfect kids, as much as he needed the untrammeled chaos his genius compelled him to pursue. For Leonard Bernstein, the chaos won. Bernstein's jaw-dropping honesty and humor give us the best example of the 'growing up famous' genre since Brooke Hayward's classic *Haywire*."

—John Guare

"You think you had a complicated father? In this wry and clear-eyed, ardent and altogether terrific memoir, Jamie Bernstein lets us in on what it's like to have a childhood as fraught as it was charmed. Plus, great gossip! (I've run out of friends to share the Michael Jackson anecdote with—so I'm going to meet more people.)"

—Patricia Marx

"Growing up in the presence of a superfamous parent is no easy thing. Jamie Bernstein presents an undisguised and understanding picture of her father, family, and friends. She chronicles her emergence as a partisan of ideals in which they believed. The book is full of inside stories and personal perspectives on the inspiring, spontaneous, and often no-holds-barred challenges of Bernstein's multiple worlds."

—Michael Tilson Thomas

Famous

Father

Girl

A MEMOIR OF
GROWING UP BERNSTEIN

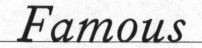

Jamie Bernstein

HARPER

NEW YORK · LONDON · TORONTO · SYDNEY

HARPER

FIRST HARPER PAPERBACKS EDITION PUBLISHED 2019.

Designed by Leah Carlson-Stanisic

Library of Congress Cataloging-in-Publication Data has been applied for.

ISBN 978-0-06-264136-6 (pbk.)

24 25 26 27 28 LBC 11 10 9 8 7

To my beloved, delicious family: in every generation.

"I feel like it didn't really happen until I tell someone the story."

—DICK AVEDON

Contents

Famous

Father

Girl

I

The Osborne

LB, Jamie, and Henry the dachshund, 1953.

The story goes that when my brother was born, Henry the dachshund and I were both so outraged by the intrusion that we jointly peed on my mother's pillow. Nor was I consoled a year later, as I warily watched Alexander pull himself to his feet; was this little interloper going to walk now, too?

But as soon as Alexander could talk, I realized what the point of a brother was. We became coconspirators, eventually expanding into a trio with our younger sister, Nina. Together we created a force field around ourselves, a layer of insulation from the raucous, confusing world of our parents. But there was something seductive about that world, too, with its laughter and teasing; its music, theater, and books; the screaming parlor games; the elegance of smoking.

We lived in a duplex in the Osborne, a nineteenth-century apartment building on West 57th Street that had, by the 1950s, acquired a patina of sooty grandeur. Alexander and I spent little time in the downstairs spaces: the living room, with its wall of smoked mirrors and pair of nested brown pianos; the connecting library, with its clunky television console; or the studio off the front hall, where Daddy worked. We never ate dinner with the grownups in the formal dining room. Our domain was in the kitchen, where we had all our meals, and in our bedroom upstairs, with our toys and games, and our record player with the fuzzy animal decals on the sides.

In the evenings, after Rosalia, the cook, gave us dinner and our nanny, Julia, bathed us upstairs, my brother and I were brought in our bathrobes to the library, where our parents would be having before-dinner drinks with their friends. All the grownups would make a lovely fuss over us. Daddy would let Alexander open and close his Zippo lighter: *shhhuppp, shhhuppp*; Mummy would peel the thin red cellophane ribbon off her fresh pack of Chesterfields, expertly zip the ribbon between her thumb and fingernail, and crimp it into a little corkscrew to tuck behind my ear. Alexander would perform silly dances, while I stood on the arm of the sofa giving loud, arm-waving speeches in gibberish—imitating the man with the brushy little moustache and plastered-down hair whose occasional appearances on the library TV always wiped the smiles off the grownups' faces. They would explain to me in oddly tense tones that he was "a very bad man." But they enjoyed my impersonation, cheering lustily after each of my fiery cadences.

Too soon, Julia's starched white uniform would materialize in the doorway, signaling it was time for us to go to bed. "Kisses all around, good night, good night!" our mother would trill. But we never wanted to leave. Finally, Mummy would warn us that if we didn't cooperate, we'd have to be taken "*a la fuerza,*" by force. I thought the phrase meant that I'd be sent to a hellish place of punishment: "I don't want to go to the fuerza!" I would scream, kicking Julia's shins as she dragged me upstairs. (The next day, she'd point accusingly at her bruises: "Look what you did to me!")

In the glow of the nightlight, Alexander and I lay in our beds, listening to the grownups carrying on downstairs. We sailed into slumber on the waves of their revelry: the tinkling of ice plopping into glasses, the roaring of songs around the piano. We knew it had to be our father at the piano, with the others clustered around him.

"Don't drop him!" The family in the Osborne.

It seemed as if all grownups ever did was have fun, with Daddy as their audible ringleader.

Our mother, Felicia, would be right beside him at the piano. Petite and elegantly beautiful, with a long, swan-like neck, she had grown up in Chile, the middle daughter of Chita, an aristocratic Costa Rican, and Roy Cohn, an American mining engineer. (No relation to the nefarious Roy Cohn of the McCarthy hearings.)

Felicia Cohn was a wild spirit; Chile was too small and provincial to contain her. In her twenties, she was allowed to move to New York to study piano with her fellow Chilean, the eminent pianist Claudio Arrau. But upon arrival, Felicia shifted to an acting career, which likely had been her plan all along. She lived in a basement apartment in Greenwich Village with her dog, Nebbish. It was 1946, Felicia was twenty-four—and that's when she met Leonard Bernstein.

We often heard the story: There was a joint birthday celebration for Felicia and Claudio Arrau. Lenny Bernstein, the brash, handsome young musician everyone was talking about, showed up at the party. Bernstein had been in the news ever since his nationally broadcast conducting debut with the New York Philharmonic three years earlier: at age twenty-five, he'd stepped in for the flu-stricken maestro, Bruno Walter, in Carnegie Hall—an event that made the front page of the *New York Times*. Soon after, Bernstein made a double splash as a composer: first with his ballet *Fancy Free*, about three sailors on the loose in New York City, and then with *On the Town*, the hit Broadway show inspired by the ballet. Leonard Bernstein was young, American-born, Jewish, Harvard-educated, matinee-idol handsome, madly charismatic: a superstar. The press lavished its attentions on him, as did the women, and men, in every room he entered. This was the man Felicia met that night in 1946. As the story came down to us,

Lenny sat on the couch while Felicia curled up at his feet and fed him shrimp, one by one.

They became engaged; there was even a notice about it in a gossip column. But then they broke it off. There were complications; they just couldn't make the leap. Felicia went off to be Eva Gabor's understudy in a Broadway play, where she fell in love with the leading man, Richard Hart. He was a hopeless alcoholic, abusive when drunk, but she loved him. She told us that Hart died in her arms, of liver failure. A couple of years later, sadder but wiser, or something, Felicia and Lenny decided to make a go of it after all. They married in September of 1951, flooded with nerves. On the drive from Massachusetts to Mexico for their honeymoon, Lenny—possibly out of pure suppressed panic—drilled Felicia on the rules of English grammar. Each morning, they would climb back into the car and Daddy would say, "You remember in yesterday's lesson . . ." It's a miracle the marriage even made it to Mexico.

They spent their honeymoon in a cheerful villa in Cuernavaca, spending much of their time with the writer Martha Gellhorn, who would become a lifelong friend. She may well have saved the shaky new marriage by toggling back and forth between the anxious newlyweds, lending each a sympathetic ear. I was born exactly one year later.

When I was little, my mother was a steadily working stage actress, using her mother's maiden surname: Felicia Montealegre. She also acted in live television dramas, winning awards for her performances on shows like *Playhouse 90* and *Kraft Theatre*. And she did concert narrations, as well. In our living room, there was a framed photograph of Mummy as Joan of Arc, her eyes looking heavenward as she is consumed by a backdrop of flames. Alexander and I loved that picture. We had no idea she was narrating

Honegger's oratorio; as far as we were concerned, our mother simply *was* Joan of Arc.

But there was so much more to Felicia. She was witty and well-read; she could fix lamps, paint windowsills, perform flawless manicures. She was even an expert hair cutter. We thought she looked so professional, snipping away at our father's head, occasionally leaning back to assess her handiwork, the comb gripped between her teeth.

One area where Felicia's expertise did not extend was in the kitchen. She could make one dish—baked eggs with béchamel sauce—but was otherwise happy to turn the proceedings over to Rosalia, her fellow Chilean. My mother had solved a uniquely personal puzzle when she decided that "the kitchen of life," as she

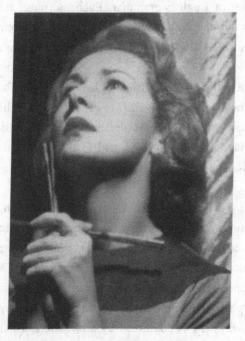

Felicia in the role of Joan of Arc.

called household matters, would be conducted entirely in her native Spanish. My father spoke several languages and could fake his way through Spanish, but he was far from fluent. The South American staff gave my mother a comforting balance in that Bernstein-heavy universe. As for us three kids, we received the priceless, wholly unearned gift of growing up bilingual.

(The only drawback was my constant childhood language mix-ups. Not only was I sorting out two languages at once; I was also coping with my father's vaguely Boston Brahmin accent, as well as the perfumed diction of my mother's stage voice. So I grew up thinking we traveled to Cape Card in the summers, and that everyone prayed to Guard—which, after all, made a kind of sense.)

Julia Vega (pronounced the Spanish way: "Hoo-lia") was our Chilean nanny. Organized, dependable, and willing to enforce the rules, Julia was utterly devoted to our mother and soon became the housekeeper, in charge of the whole domestic scene. Her English was strong enough to order the groceries over the phone, and accompany Alexander and me to Bloomingdale's to buy shoes. Julia's room contained the only other television in the house. When Alexander or I got sick, we were allowed to spend the whole day in Julia's bed, drinking warm ginger ale in a fervid daze while watching the weekly feature on *Million Dollar Movie* over and over again.

But Julia was also irascible, and she shamelessly favored her "*niñito*," my baby brother. Rosalia, the cook, by contrast, was sunny and relaxed, and her affections helped offset Julia's wounding favoritism. The best day of the week was Friday, Julia's day off, when Rosalia was put in charge of us. She was far less interested in rules, even going so far as to indulge us in the ultimate transgression: dinner in front of Julia's television.

Supplemented with an ever-shifting series of South American

maids, this staff of two was the engine of the safe and nurturing household Alexander and I inhabited in our early years. The staff referred to our mother as La Señora, and to our father as El Caballero: the Cavalier, literally—a rather archaic honorific. But it became somewhat more fitting in 1958, when he became the principal conductor of the New York Philharmonic, right across the street at Carnegie Hall.

As kids, we had no idea that our father's background among striving Jewish immigrants in the Boston suburbs might be incongruous with being called a caballero. Nor did it seem odd for this Daddy of ours, who played on the floor with us and loved jokes about bodily functions, to wear tails and a long black cape to work, to tour the world for weeks at a time, and occasionally even to materialize on the screen of that clunky black-and-white television in the library. El Caballero worked hard, and was always hungry. Rosalia would prepare him special lavish breakfasts every day, featuring eggs with bacon or sausage—or sometimes, to our disgust, kippers. The combined morning smells on Daddy's breath of orange juice, coffee, L&M cigarettes, and kippered herring made for a revoltingly heady mix.

Another characteristic Daddy smell was the blend of cigarette smoke and flatulence, which would commence at the breakfast table, once the nicotine and coffee had achieved their combined effect. "I'm getting stinky," he would announce, and soon he was off to the bathroom with an as-yet-unread section of the newspaper, or perhaps one of his beloved, bedevilingly hard British crossword puzzles. Sometimes he would bring along symphonic scores to study. El Caballero would sit contentedly on his porcelain throne for long periods: smoking, reading, puzzling, studying, stinking. He almost always left the door open, and was not averse to being interrupted.

One morning I had to show Daddy something important and

Jamie and Alexander hugging Julia.

ran into his studio, where I found him sitting in his bathroom there, smoking away with a score on his lap. I begged him to look at whatever it was I was so excited about, and he replied, "Oh, I'll be with you in a minute, darling—let me just finish this movement." Then he exploded in laughter, which culminated in the usual coughing fit, and after pulling himself together, he explained to me why what he'd said was so funny. There simply was no moment when Leonard Bernstein wasn't being a teacher.

It was words, above all, that he shared with us in all their glorious incarnations. He was reciting Lewis Carroll, and telling me the difference between nouns and verbs, before I could write my name. The summer when I was six, as we gazed out on a placid lagoon, Daddy explained that if we said it looked *like* a mirror, we were using a figure of speech known as a simile. But if we said the lagoon *was* a mirror, then the figure of speech was a metaphor. For the rest of that summer, on every windless day, we'd all tell one another, "The lagoon is a figure of speech today."

He treasured jokes. Jewish jokes, vaudeville routines, old-time radio gags—Daddy knew them all, and told them with unalloyed gusto. By age seven, I already knew the running vaudeville gag where a rumpled old salesman crosses the stage after every act, holding a bunch of multicolored balloons and intoning, "Rubber balloons . . . rubber balloons . . ." Later in the show, Daddy explained, a chorus girl faints and crumples to the floor, creating a ruckus as the other performers rush to her side, shouting out suggestions: "Rub her ankles!" "Rub her forehead!" "Rub her wrists!" Along comes the rumpled salesman: "Rub 'er balloons . . ."

In my mind's eye, my father is always in a scruffy brown wool bathrobe; my cheek still prickles at the memory of his scratchy morning hugs. He was frequently away on conducting tours; we never felt we got enough of him. When he'd suddenly rematerialize at the front door, putting down his soft leather suitcase and squatting down to enfold us in his arms, Alexander and I would tumble all over him like puppies—"*Daddy Daddy Daddy Daddy*"—mad with joy, and hungry for the presents he'd brought us from those faraway lands. Mummy stood to the side, grinning, waiting her turn for the deep, tender kiss her husband would give her.

One Christmas morning, Alexander and I were watching television in Julia's bedroom, waiting interminably, it seemed, for our parents to wake so we could open our presents. At last, Daddy appeared at the door, all tousled and sleepy. "Merry Christmas," he croaked in his precoffee voice, with an especially bright smile—whereupon there was a stirring under the brown wool, and up from the bathrobe wriggled . . . a dachshund puppy: our brand-new Henry, squirming upward to lick Daddy's chin.

But this new Henry was a very bad dog. He simply would not be housebroken—and he seemed especially to enjoy peeing in Alexander's and my room. Daddy sat on the edge of my bed, despairing. "But *why?*" he said to us. "*Why* does Henry keep peeing in here?" I thought about it. "Maybe," I ventured, "maybe it's because it's so sunny in this room that he thinks he's outside, and so he thinks he's peeing outside, like he's supposed to."

Then four-year-old Alexander said, "Maybe he *likes* to be bad."

Daddy straightened up with new interest. "Hmm . . . he *likes* to be bad! Maybe you're onto something there." I was stung that my scientific theory had been ignored in place of my baby brother's ridiculous suggestion.

There were always people, so many people, drifting in and out of our house. The most frequent visitors were Daddy's two siblings: his sister Shirley and brother Burton. Shirley, who was also my godmother, was a vivacious, excitable, attractive woman, with a big ringing laugh. She would take me on special dates to Rumpelmayer's for cake and ice cream—grateful, I suspect, to have me along as an excuse to indulge in those treats.

As a baby, I called my father's brother Uncle BB, and it stuck. He was thirteen years younger than our father, and barely in his twenties when I was little. BB was pure fun. He could run straight up the trunk of a tree to rescue our snarled kite. He introduced us to the joys of practical jokes: dribble glasses, whoopee cushions, plastic ice cubes with a housefly trapped inside. His best audience was his own brother and sister, who roared over his hijinks.

After our own parents and the Spanish-speaking staff, those

three Bernstein siblings were the most stable human structure in our universe. They were devoted to one another; during the Second World War they'd even referred to themselves as the Impenetrable Bernstein Front. As a trio they could be exhausting, but our mother was exceptionally patient with their endless in-jokes and teasing. She even learned their private language, Rybernian; she was one of the very few non-Bernsteins who did.

Daddy had created the language with his childhood neighbor Eddie Ryack (hence its portmanteau name). It wasn't a comprehensive language, but rather the saying of certain words or phrases in funny ways, based on a mash-up of pronunciations and sonorities produced by the boys' older immigrant relatives. My father's Rybernian name was Lennuhtt. "Do it" or "did it" was "didduhtt." Shirley was Hilee (rhymes with "smiley"). "I love

Lenny, Shirley, and BB on Martha's Vineyard.

you" was "Me laudü." And BB was Baudümü. It was entirely rude and peculiar, and *loud*; shouting was one of the attributes of that older generation that Rybernian was mimicking.

Shirley and BB were the most constant presences, but our house was continually full of our parents' friends. Only much later did I realize how extraordinary it was to be surrounded on a regular basis by (let the name-dropping begin) Dick Avedon, Mike Nichols, Betty Comden and Adolph Green, Lillian Hellman, Steve Sondheim, Jerry Robbins, Sidney Lumet, Betty (Lauren) Bacall, Isaac Stern . . . Their luminosity meant nothing to Alexander and me.

It made sense that so many of these friends were also our father's work colleagues; the membrane between work and play was, for him, virtually nonexistent. When Alexander and I would peek into Daddy's studio and see him through a bluish haze of cigarette smoke, pounding away at the piano surrounded by Betty and Adolph, or by Jerry Robbins, Arthur Laurents, and Steve Sondheim, it was hard to distinguish that scene from the one around the living room piano after dinner, when those same pals all clustered around our father to bawl out silly songs and make one another laugh. Daddy effortlessly and inevitably became the center of attention; he never seemed to tire of it.

But Mummy could get tired. Over time, she developed a habit of "slipping away," as she put it, without saying good night. Daddy was always the last one standing. He couldn't sleep anyway; his was an engine that would not, could not shut itself off. He had terrible insomnia, and in my early years he was already well into his lifelong dependence on sleeping pills. But then, all the grownups took sleeping pills in those days.

Daddy did most of his composing during his sleepless night hours. I wasn't born yet when he wrote *Fancy Free*, which led to *On the Town*; nor was I around for his first two symphonies or his one-act opera, *Trouble in Tahiti*. And I was unaware of the pieces he was writing during the first few years of my life: his concert work *Serenade*; his second Broadway show, *Wonderful Town*; the score to the film *On the Waterfront*; his jazzy piece *Prelude, Fugue, and Riffs*. The first works I was just barely conscious of Daddy composing were two musicals he was writing simultaneously: *Candide* and *West Side Story*.

Candide opened first, in 1956. I was four. I remember my parents all dressed up one night; clearly they were about to do something exciting. "Where are you going?" I asked. "We're going to see *Candide*!" Mummy said, with a little shiver of anticipation.

They were going to see candy? That sounded wonderful. "I want to go, too!" I said. "No, darling, this is for grownups." Candy—for grownups? Impossible. "But I want to see the candy! *I want to see the can-deee . . . !*" I was still kicking Julia's shins in the throes of my tantrum as my parents scurried out the door in their opening-night finery.

The following summer, while Daddy was working feverishly to finish the *West Side Story* score, Mummy escaped the heat of the city (and the show) by taking me down to Chile to visit her family. While I played with my cousins, Lenny and Felicia kept in touch through letters. One of them that arrived was addressed to me.

July 23: DERE JAMIE: IT IS VERY HOT HERE AND HUMIT AND I SURE WISH WE WERE ALL SKI-ING IN THE ANDEES MOUNTINS, INSTED OF WRITING THIS *FUKING SHOW. I DON'T LIKE JERY ROBINS. YESTERDAY WE HAD OUR FURST READING AND EVERYONE IS HISTERICAL. I HOPE AFTER YOU GO TO BREERLY YOU CAN SPEL BETER THAN THIS. KIS MUMMY A LOT FOR ME . . . I ADORE

YOU. WRITE TO ME! YOUR LOVING, LONELY FA-
THER, LENNUHTT.
 *censored

I was too young to see *West Side Story* on the Broadway stage,
with its knife fights and scary gunshot at the end. But Alexander and
I listened constantly to the recording on the little record player in our
bedroom. We listened to all Daddy's shows. I loved *On the Town*,

Jamie holds Henry's leash at the stage door of Carnegie Hall.

with its goofy "Taxi Number" and the dreamy, melancholy "Lonely Town" ballet music that spoke to a place inside me no one knew about. *Wonderful Town* featured the song "A Quiet Girl," which I was told my father had originally written as a lullaby to me—a delightfully inapt dedication as I was, by all accounts, the noisiest girl in the world. *Candide* had a thousand words we couldn't follow, but the tunes were irresistible. Were we putting on the records, or was someone else putting them on for us? Either way, we came to know those scores by heart.

West Side Story was a Broadway hit and Leonard Bernstein's fame increased—but later that same season, something else happened to him that I found far more impressive: not his first season as music director of the New York Philharmonic, but rather his presenting the orchestra's traditional Young People's Concerts, live, *on CBS network television*. As far as Alexander and I were concerned, nothing was more magical than being on TV.

"Don't step on the cables," warned whoever was holding my hand backstage at Carnegie Hall for the first live broadcast of a Young People's Concert. I carefully lifted my party shoe over the anaconda-sized wires. Of the concert itself, I remember nothing, except that it began with the *Lone Ranger* theme, followed by Daddy explaining that the music had nothing to do with the Lone Ranger, at which point I stopped listening. Afterward, a lady kneeled down in front of me and asked brightly, "Did you understand what your father was talking about?" "No," I replied.

2

The Vineyard and Redding

It was in the summers that we came alive as a family. In those early years before Nina was born, we spent the summer months on the island of Martha's Vineyard, off the coast of Cape Card.

But first we had to get there. It was a quasi-military operation, involving my mother driving the station wagon with Julia, Rosalia, and the maid; plus all of Rosalia's cooking utensils, which she insisted on bringing; plus duffel bags full of sheets and towels; plus the canary and the fish and the turtles and, of course, Henry the dachshund. Plus Alexander and me. The spillover went into Daddy's gray, yacht-sized Lincoln Continental convertible, a present from the car company that sponsored his television shows. The car was all button-operated—one of the first of its kind—and the buttons were always jamming and short-circuiting. But it was exceedingly glamorous.

One summer, we had so much stuff to transport to the Vineyard that a U-Haul trailer was affixed to the rear of the Lincoln. I rode along with Daddy, just the two of us: a treat. (I was still too young to fret over the fact that Leonard Bernstein was the most terrible, erratic, reckless driver on the planet.) We should have set out on the Connecticut Turnpike, which permitted our multiple-axled vehicle, but Daddy preferred the bucolic, truck-free serenity of the Merritt Parkway. So we took the Merritt, and were soon pulled over by a trooper. He pointed out that we were breaking the law, no trailers allowed, and asked for my father's license and registration. "Oh—you're the conductor? I saw you on the television!" On came the dazzling Lenny smile, the laser-beam charm.

Pretty soon the trooper was reminiscing about his violin lessons in elementary school, and shaking Daddy's hand, and oh, forget the ticket, Maestro, just take the next exit to the Connecticut Turnpike. A pleasure to meet you, sir! And off we went.

But the Maestro liked it on the Merritt, so we stayed on the Merritt. "Daddy, they're gonna arrest you! We're gonna be in trouble!" "Naw, it'll be fine, you'll see!" Soon enough came the siren and the flashing light, and once again we were getting pulled over.

Trooper, license, registration, Lenny laser beam, handshake, just take the next exit, Maestro—a pleasure to meet you, sir!

The man was blessed. But I was a shrunken ball of mortification—not for the first time and not for the last, by many a country mile.

The Weaver house, our rental on the figure-of-speech lagoon,

The family on the figure-of-speech lagoon, Martha's Vineyard.

was a paradise for Alexander and me. We shared endless make-believe games, indoors and out. Somehow I'd gotten the impression that "Casino" was a normal part of a restaurant name, so I invented a game where the house had three restaurants: Casino Fancy, Casino Medium, and Casino Sloppy. At Casino Fancy, in the dining room, you used supergood manners, and everything was just so, and you spoke with a fancy accent about fancy things. Casino Medium was so boring that we never went there. Casino Sloppy, outside the kitchen door, was the most fun: you could eat chicken with your fingers, wipe your mouth on your sleeve, and talk like a cowboy. Years later, we came to understand that these two restaurants were perfect manifestations of our parents: Casino Fancy was elegant and well behaved, like our mother, while Casino Sloppy was messy, spontaneous, a little naughty, and (we had to admit) more fun, like our father.

Actually, our father wasn't sloppy so much as clumsy. His siblings teased him about his "*lappes*"—Yiddish for paws. He spilled things; he forced objects and broke them; he never owned an audio system he didn't bust. And despite his prodigious gifts, he had no visual sense at all. He'd sported many god-awful, garish outfits until Felicia came along to civilize him. She bought many of his clothes, and surreptitiously hid or threw away the ones she disapproved of. Years later, we would open a blanket chest to find it stuffed with things like flocked orange sweaters and black leather bathing trunks: we'd accidentally discovered Felicia's burial ground for her husband's sartorial atrocities.

The Weaver house was full of guests, just as the Osborne always was. Betty Comden and Adolph Green would make their way up to the Vineyard every summer. *BettyandAdolph*: they were a crucial presence in our collective lives. Theirs was not a romance, in the traditional sense—they each married other people and raised

Adolph, Betty, and Lenny in *On the Town* days.

their own families—but it was a lifelong partnership. They wrote screenplays, they wrote lyrics and dialogue for musicals, and they amused and inspired each other for over half a century.

Back in the 1930s, Betty and Adolph had paired up in a sketch comedy group called the Revuers, which also included the young actress Judy Holliday. Our father had gone to all their gigs at the Village Vanguard, sometimes accompanying them on piano. He taught us all the Revuers' sketches by heart; they became part of the family DNA.

We also knew about Lenny and Adolph's memorable first encounter, at a summer camp where nineteen-year-old "Uncle Lenny" was the music counselor and Adolph had been imported from the Bronx to play the Pirate King in a production of Gilbert and Sullivan's *Pirates of Penzance*. Upon Adolph's arrival, Lenny began quizzing him on musical pieces, and rapidly discovered that *he could not stump Adolph*. Adolph knew everything—by heart, and all by ear—and he could sing anything from Tchaikovsky to Sibelius to a virtuosic, tongue-twisting rendition of "Flight of the Bumblebee." Adolph was zany, quick on the trigger, deeply intellectual, and utterly unique. Lenny and Adolph became friends at that deep, mysterious level where humor, intellect, and aesthetic instinct all meet. It was a kind of true love that lasted all their lives.

As for Betty, she struck me as the last word in female self-possession. Whip-smart, with her glossy hair and stylish outfits, Betty was a true career girl who could crack wise like a living screwball comedy heroine. From my listening post in bed at night, I could hear how often Betty's voice generated the gales of grownup laughter. She could play word games with Steve Sondheim, and not quaver. She could quote Shakespeare and Ibsen and Bugs Bunny. I wanted to be just like her.

A piano was set up for Daddy in a big airy room above the Weaver house garage. (In exchange for Leonard Bernstein's endorsement of Baldwin Pianos, the company provided him with a piano wherever he went in the world.) Daddy announced that Alexander and I were going to help him write a show. We didn't get far in the collaboration, but I remember my father at the piano, playing something we were "working on," and as I casually leaned my little elbow into the crook of the piano in that room above the garage, I felt—oh, I felt just like Betty Comden!

Mike Nichols would also visit every summer. He was a family favorite: witty and hilarious with our parents, warm and amusing with us kids. Once, when we were devising awful, imaginary ice cream flavors, Mike came up with the yummiest one of all: "liver ripple."

One weekend, I was going around the room offering all the grownups scalp massages. When I got to Mike, he demurred. I insisted, telling him he'd really like it. He said no, thanks. I continued insisting until Daddy suddenly raised his voice sharply: "*JA-MIE! He says he doesn't want a scalp massage!*"

Daddy never yelled at us; Alexander and I were horrified. We ran upstairs and cried in our room. Daddy came up a few minutes later, sat on Alexander's bed across from mine, and explained to us that when Mike was a little boy, he got a bad disease that caused all the hair on his body to fall out and never grow back. So he wore a wig and false eyebrows. And he had no eyelashes—which, we then understood, gave him that slightly peculiar gaze.

I was mortified at what I'd done: the kind of mortification that makes you moan involuntarily every time you recall it. It took me a while to feel comfortable again in Mike's presence, but his calm, affable ways and irresistible hilarity nudged me past my embarrassment.

Another frequent guest was the playwright Lillian Hellman, who had her own house on the Vineyard. It was in those years that she and my father were collaborating on *Candide*. The idea for the musical was Lillian's; she'd suggested using Voltaire's eighteenth-century satirical novella to mock the House Un-American Activities Committee's Spanish Inquisition–like persecution of left-leaning artists. The collaboration was a lengthy torture, but Lillian and my father managed to stay friends mostly due to Mummy, who adored Lillian and put up with her brusque, growling ways.

Henry the dachshund hated Lillian; the minute she stepped through the door he'd lunge for her ankle, a reaction Alexander and I viscerally understood. Everything about Lillian Hellman was scary: her craggy face with the big, irregular teeth; the way her mouth turned down at the corners when she let loose with her gravelly laugh, "HAWWW, HAWWW, HAWWW." It was enough to make you jump out the window. Upstairs in the Weaver house, Alexander and I would sit opposite each other on our bedroom floor, look at each other intensely, and whisper the dreaded words, *"Lillian Hellman!"*—triggering a mutual laughing fit that would leave us clawing the floorboards, gasping for breath.

Jamie with Lillian Hellman, Martha's Vineyard.

Some years later in New York, Nina was in the library with our mother and Lillian while the two ladies were having tea. Mummy told Nina that Lillian had been appointed her godmother. "That's right, kid," Lillian told my five-year-old sister. "When the plane goes down, I getcha." Imagine Nina's alarm.

The whole business of godparents was decidedly unofficial; it mainly served as a way for our parents to honor those closest to them. My own appointed godfather, composer Marc Blitzstein, had bonded with my father years earlier over music and politics; both were composers and confirmed lefties. (Harvard senior Lenny Bernstein had made a name for himself by presenting Marc's inflammatory musical *The Cradle Will Rock*.) Bald, spry, and twinkly-eyed, Marc showed up in the Vineyard one summer in time to participate in an elaborate home movie my parents and Uncle BB were devising, entitled "Call Me Moses." Marc played the Egyptian slave driver who whipped the Jewish slaves into building the pyramids—all of this being filmed on the beach by cinematographer Uncle BB using his 8-mm movie camera. Lenny took over as the shaky cameraman for the scenes in which his brother played the starring role of Moses, in full Orthodox Jewish regalia, *payis* included. On-screen, Lenny played the cruel pharaoh, in a regal lampshade crown, lusting after Moses's girlfriend, played by Uncle BB's actual girlfriend (and eventual wife) Ellen, all be-robed in white sheets. Felicia, in a Cleopatra-style wig, played the pharaoh's wife, who lusted after Moses. Felicia masterminded these complex home movies, devising the shooting script and collecting all the props. On-screen, she was riveting; with her Chaplin-grade talent for body language and exaggerated facial expressions, Felicia Montealegre was born to play silent films.

Alexander and I got bit parts as Daddy-the-cruel-pharaoh's children. In our big scene, he was distractedly playing cards with us until, spying the nubile Ellen, he knocked us kids unceremoniously to the side (a little too vigorously: Alexander cried). The climax of the film, the Red Sea chase, was filmed on the lagoon, with the two brothers taking turns filming from the motorboat while each of the characters made it across the Red Sea—or didn't—on water skis.

Steve Sondheim directed several of our Vineyard home movies, the greatest of which was an excerpt from the opera *Tosca*, in which Tosca (Mummy) murders the wicked Scarpia (Daddy, sporting a dastardly mustache applied with a burned cork). The innovation on that film was the addition of sound: our parents lip-synched to the Maria Callas and Tito Gobbi recording.

Steve visited every summer. He had been the "kid" collaborator on *West Side Story*: a mere twenty-seven to Lenny's and Jerry Robbins's thirty-nine and Arthur Laurents's forty. But Steve held his own. His powers of wordplay were prodigious, and he was madly witty at every party, often slouched on a couch, squinting through his cigarette smoke and making cutting remarks. With his slightly disheveled way about him, he was not exactly cuddly.

There was an enormous party at the Weaver house when Daddy turned forty. Steve devised a complex treasure hunt; all the grownups were outside, dashing around in the dusk, screaming with laughter. Daddy also received a birthday song from Steve, with the lyric: "You're only as old as you look—and you look . . . forty."

* * *

My father loved the water: swimming in it, water-skiing over it, or steering a boat across it. He was particularly fond of sailing. One Vineyard afternoon it was just him and me on the *Janie*, a little sailboat that came with the house. As we drifted across the lagoon in figure-of-speech conditions, Daddy said, "Isn't it marvelous out here, just the two of us? Oh, I can just imagine, though, when you're a teenager, I'll say, 'Would you like to go for a little sail with your old pappy?' And you'll say, 'Oh, but *DAD*-dy, Jim's invited all the kids on his yacht, and I really want to go!' And I'll say, 'Aw, but don't you want to go for just a little spin with your old, old pappy?' And you'll say, 'Oh, but *DAD*-dy, *all* the kids are going on Jim's yacht!' And away you'll go, leaving your poor old pappy all alone."

I thought about this for a moment, then replied, "Well . . . let's make the best of it now." My father roared with laughter and gave me a suffocating hug. I wasn't sure why what I'd said was so funny; was he hoping I'd reassure him that I'd never act that way as a teenager? But how could I know what life would be like in that remote future? I figured he had to know more about it than I did.

He knew more than I did about everything, of course—especially music. But music was something he wanted me to learn. I understood that it was my fate to take piano lessons, which commenced that very summer. My teacher was Shirley Gabis, a friend of my father's from his student days at the Curtis Institute. After one of my early lessons, my father sat me on his lap and said, "Well, you'll never be a great pianist." Shirley was appalled; why did he say that—even as a joke? Still, I blundered along with my lessons: not particularly enjoying them, but with a docile acceptance that it was something I had to do, like brushing my teeth or going to the doctor.

One summer when our father had to leave the Vineyard early and go conduct somewhere, he wrote a song to remind us of him. Mummy was at the piano, while Alexander and I sang the words, and we would perform it for all the visiting houseguests. Daddy's lyrics went:

Evening, when it's booze time
That's the time we think of Daddy
Nighttime, when it's snooze time
That's the time we dream of Daddy

Where is that funny face
Where is that fatty

Soon, soon, in September
We will booze again, we will snooze again
With Daddy . . . Daddy . . . Daddy . . .

In the last Vineyard summer, just before I turned nine, there was a scary moment when Mummy was overcome with a terrible stomachache and had to be taken to the hospital in Oak Bluffs. Alexander and I weren't allowed inside her room, but we could wave at her through a window. We were frightened at the time, but a few weeks later we found out, to our delight, that she was pregnant.

Nina was born in New York City the following February. I'd had my piano lesson that afternoon, and Shirley Gabis stuck around to count the contractions. When our mother left for the hospital around nine p.m., I made Julia promise to wake me up if the baby was born during the night. Sure enough, Julia opened my door at about one in the morning. I sat right up in bed and asked hopefully, "Is it a girl?" Julia's face darkened, and she mimicked back at me, "*Is it a girl??*" and slammed the door. In true Latin American form, she'd been hoping for another *niñito*.

*   *   *

The next summer, our family had a little country house of our own in West Redding, Connecticut. Daddy named the house the

Apiary—a reference not to bees but to the Bernstein siblings'
lifelong obsession and identification with apes. They called
themselves the Apes, and "Don't be an ape!" was a common saying in our house. Uncle BB often made reference to that under-
appreciated baroque composer A. P. E. Bach. And we called Ed
Sullivan, the TV variety show host, Ape Solomon. (That last one
was also an homage to our grandpa Sam, who managed to ren-
der every notable person Jewish: he referred to Adlai Stevenson
as "Steve Adelman"; even President Eisenhower became "President Eisenberg.")

The Apiary was on a steep, wooded hill where Alexander and I
devised make-believe games using the trees, the rocks, the brook

Felicia in curlers, in the days before her sun allergy.

down the hill as the scenery and props of our inventions. Most of our fantasies were about life in a small town, where we ran little stores or walked to work, waving genially to each other along the way. In our real life, we felt some vague differentness: we knew our parents weren't quite like other parents. What was more, we lived in the city, not in the suburbs, where the families on our favorite TV shows resided. We longed to be like the "normal" people we saw on TV; so Alexander and I created that illusion for each other in the woods.

One afternoon, Daddy hauled his portable record player down the rocky path to the swimming pool so he could listen to a recording of Mahler's Fourth Symphony while he studied the score. He was planning to reintroduce the long-neglected music of Gustav Mahler to his New York Philharmonic audiences in the fall. The conductor on the recording was Bruno Walter—the very maestro who had conveniently caught the flu and given Leonard Bernstein his big conducting break back in 1943. Now, nearly two decades later, Daddy sat in the sun in his bathing suit, with a fresh pack of L&M's on the little table next to his lounge chair, following the recording with the score in his lap while his children splashed in the pool. As the record played, Daddy pointed out the kid-friendly features of the symphony to Alexander and me. "You hear that jingling? That's sleigh bells! Listen—here they come again!" In the last movement, he told us that the soprano was describing a child's vision of heaven.

Meanwhile, up the hill in the house, Mummy was performing her magic trick of silencing baby Nina's cries by playing a Brahms intermezzo on the piano. She looked so beautiful while playing those swoony, melancholy pieces by Chopin, Schumann, and Brahms. But her visits to the piano had been dwindling. She used to play duets with Daddy, but Mummy told us it now made her too nervous.

We'd begun to understand that our mother harbored fear. She told us she suffered from stage fright, and that was why she'd been turning down acting jobs recently. She was afraid of heights; she nearly expired over Daddy's prank of balancing four-year-old Alexander on an overhanging gargoyle at the top of Notre-Dame Cathedral. Mummy was terrified of airplanes; she crossed herself on takeoff and landing, and in between she clutched the armrests in a grim panic. There was a strange new darkness hovering at the edges of our mother's demeanor and we avoided inspecting it too carefully.

That summer in Redding, Mummy played the piano more than usual: not just to soothe baby Nina, but also because Daddy was away at the MacDowell Colony, the artists' retreat in New Hamp-

Just a normal pair of parents.

shire, working on his third symphony. When he drove back down to Redding, he arrived with not one but *two* puppies in his car! (By then, Henry the Second was no longer with us.) Daddy explained that they were "mongrels"—a nice new word—and that their names were Franny and Zooey, siblings from a book. We were besotted with our beautiful new puppies: Zooey for Alexander and Franny for me. Our mother was considerably less enthusiastic.

The "mongrels" turned out to be part German shepherd, and before you could say J. D. Salinger, Franny and Zooey got really, really big. When it was time to return to the city in the fall, our mother announced that Franny and Zooey were not coming with us. This was increasingly the pattern: Daddy would do something impulsive that got us all excited, and then Mummy felt compelled to be responsible and ruin the fun. Alexander and I were heartbroken, but now I can well imagine what was going through our mother's mind as her husband pulled that pair of energetic creatures out of the back seat of his car.

*   *   *

Aunt Shirley got me hooked on reading. She'd drive me to the little Mark Twain Library a few miles away, where I'd replace the three Nancy Drew books I'd devoured over the past few days, and pull out the next three from the shelf. But on the way home from the library, Shirley often took us on a detour to the general store, where Alexander and I were permitted to assemble a magnificent pile of penny candy for what she dubbed our Cavity Party. Back at the house, the three of us would sit in a circle on the living room floor with the candy in the middle and eat it all. Shirley wasn't entirely like a grownup.

At the end of that summer Daddy turned forty-four—and to celebrate the occasion, Shirley helped Alexander and me cook up a birthday entertainment in Redding. (She was no doubt remembering her own childhood summers, when Daddy conscripted Shirley and all the neighborhood kids into ambitious productions of *Carmen* and *The Mikado* at their lakeside community in Sharon, Massachusetts.) Our presentation was to be a takeoff on our favorite Sunday night TV program: *The Ape Solomon Show*. Alexander played Ape himself; I played guest star Jimmy Durante, sporting a big rubber schnozzola and performing a song I'd made up, affecting Durante's signature rusty Lower East Side voice. We persuaded Rosalia, the cook, to come out and do the commercial for Helena Rubinstein hand cream; she gleefully recited our purple-prosed ad copy with her outlandish Chilean pronunciation. Rosalia was a good sport; Julia wouldn't have dreamed of participating in such antics. (Daddy was such a big Rosalia fan that he christened a ship in *Candide* after her—the *Santa Rosalia*—and named a Sharks girl Rosalia in *West Side Story*.)

Our show concluded with Alexander and me singing lyrics I'd written to the tune of "Hey, Look Me Over":

> *Oh, happy birthday, dear Daddy-O,*
> *I guess that life just doesn't go so slow.*
> *'Cause you're already forty-four years old,*
> *But you can conduct, and you can compose,*
> *And you can still be bold! [arrghh]*
>
> *And you'll grow like a beanstalk, high on a vine*
> *Don't work so hard but take a tip from mine [sic]:*
> *Way down deep in your heart you're not growing old,*
> *So listen to our words:*
> *Happy birthday . . . happy birthday, Daddy-Ooooo!!!*

3

Park Avenue and Fairfield

Lenny and Felicia on their way to something elegant, vamping it up
in the elevator vestibule for Jamie's Instamatic camera.

Between the birth of our baby sister and Daddy's high-profile
job as conductor of the New York Philharmonic (about to
become even higher-profile upon the orchestra's move to its new
home in Lincoln Center), it was time for our family to move to a
bigger, fancier apartment.

When school began in the autumn of 1962, Alexander and I
were newly residing in a penthouse duplex at 895 Park Avenue.
We had our own rooms now, while Julia and baby Nina shared
a third bedroom. The bedrooms, plus Daddy's studio, were all

downstairs, while the living room, library, dining room, and kitchen were upstairs: an upside-down house. My bedroom had three windows facing west, offering me a sunset over Central Park every single day—plus, I had one window facing south, where I could look straight down Park Avenue. There was so much light drenching the enormous apartment, it felt as if an intensely bright beam were being trained upon us. Our whole family life seemed somehow ratcheted up.

We sensed that Mummy was taking her role of Mrs. Maestro much more seriously. Her new walk-in closet was a marvel of treasures: Chanel suits, Dior evening dresses, a parade of elegant shoes and purses—all that glittering armor for the myriad events she attended and hosted. Even her hairdo from the Kenneth salon seemed blonder, the swept-up French twist somehow more regal. When she sat at her desk, immaculately dressed, one hand holding

Felicia on the phone in her bedroom on Park Avenue.

the phone receiver to her ear, the fingers of the other hand extending her cigarette ceilingward as she intoned, "Hello, this is Mrs. Leonard Bernstein calling . . . ," well, she was formidable. (Years later, I gasped in recognition to see Betty Draper on *Mad Men* assume this exact posture.)

Mummy seemed invincible to me, but maybe she was having some pangs of insecurity—for despite her unerring eye for design, she sought professional assistance in raising penthouse A to a higher level of grandeur. We always had to shake hands and be very polite to Mr. Irvine, who was stuffed into his pin-striped suit like a sausage into a casing. A noted interior designer, Keith Irvine talked our mother into some uncharacteristically flamboyant decisions. The dining room had Clarence House wallpaper and matching drapes depicting birds of paradise perched along vivid floral braids. The dining table was made entirely of mirrors, surrounded on two sides by a claret-toned corduroy banquette, itself backed by a mirrored shelf holding crystal candelabras and a collection of antique mercury glass orbs. The walls behind the banquette were mirrors, reaching all the way to the ceiling. At a dinner party, amid the dazzle of crystal, the gleaming silverware, the flowers and mercury glass and vaulting birds of paradise, all multimirrored in candlelight—the effect was downright magical. That dining room really *was* Casino Fancy.

By now, our parents had become socially beholden to many people who were not close friends. To erase all the pesky obligations at a single blow, Mummy came up with a solution she dubbed "monster rallies": large dinner parties, with extra tables set up in the Casino Fancy dining room. Alexander, Nina, and I steered clear of those events, hiding downstairs throughout. But there was one monster rally we heard about at dinner the next day.

Herman Shumlin, a theater producer of fidgety disposition, was already a sort of verbal family mascot. Uncle BB loved the name so much that he took every opportunity to shoehorn it into the conversation: "I'll be back before you can say Herman Shumlin." At this particular dinner party, Mr. Shumlin was seated with three other people at a small, elegantly arrayed table that was actually a very humble folding card table underneath. Mr. Shumlin had been unwittingly kicking at the butterfly wing nut that set the table at its higher-up position. He eventually managed to kick the wing nut all the way around, whereupon the table abruptly and deafeningly

Felicia lights the candles in the Casino Fancy dining room.

crashed down to its lower position, dumping Mr. Shumlin's entire dinner onto his lap. There was a great commotion, and while the serving staff cleaned everything up, Mummy took her guest downstairs and lent him a pair of Daddy's trousers. Mr. Shumlin reentered the dining room to general applause from the other guests, and he sat down to a nicely reset table and a fresh plate of food. This was a pretty great story to hear about the next day—and too good to be true that this festive calamity had happened to *Herman Shumlin*! But the best part, the part that still brings tears of joy to our eyes, the part that enshrines the story forever . . . is that ten minutes later, fidgety Herman Shumlin kicked the table down *again*.

One keen advantage for Mummy in the move across town was that Helen Coates, our father's secretary, now had to make distinct appointments to come over to our house, to deal with his correspondence and "have him," as she would put it, for a few hours.

"Nanny" Helen lived in an apartment on the other side of the Osborne building and used to spend some hours at Daddy's desk nearly every day. She had been one of Daddy's first piano teachers, eventually turning her life over to him with the fervor of a nun devoting herself to God. She was prissy and persnickety, with an odd little nervous whinny peppering her speech. She kept every Lenny-related letter, photo, article, and concert program, inserting them all into tidy, labeled albums. Today they comprise a priceless trove, lovingly preserved at the Library of Congress. But she was terribly possessive of her Lenny; not surprisingly, she'd advised him against marrying Felicia. Now, with our move to Park Avenue, Helen was considerably less underfoot, much to our mother's relief.

Helen was but one of the many people looking after Leonard Bernstein. He had a tailor named Otto Perl, a spry Viennese who

Baby Jamie with Helen Coates.

made house calls for fittings of suits and concert tails. (I found out he was a survivor of Dachau *and* Buchenwald—yet such a jolly man.) There was Dr. Z, a chiropractor for Daddy's chronic bad back. During the session, we kids played under the folding massage table, flinching each time Dr. Z got a resounding *crack* out of Daddy's vertebrae.

And there was Rita the Popper. Her job, and skill, was to twist one little hank at a time of Daddy's hair around her forefinger and yank it suddenly, which would pull the scalp away from the skull with a sickening little *pop*. Daddy grimaced with every pull, but he put up with Rita the Popper's visits; her treatment, which helped circulate the blood between skull and scalp, was supposed to help keep his famous hair on his head. (And since he kept some hair on his head to the very end, Rita the Popper may as well get the credit.)

Our father also had a colorful assortment of valets and chauffeurs. There was Luis, who affixed little organizing signs onto Daddy's closet shelves. Alexander and I were enchanted by "fancy dress shirst" [*sic*]. There was a chauffeur with the august name of Frederick Stammers, who was so handsome that when he drove the convertible, he got more attention than Daddy did. Stammers was soon dismissed. Then there was "Lucky" Bob Beckwith, who stole Daddy's Lincoln—and cuff links—until he was stopped for a routine speeding violation in Florida, where it further emerged that he was AWOL from the army. By comparison, Michael, the jovial Cockney from England, seemed like an elder statesman. We loved when he talked about the "wheews" of the car. And we were all willing to overlook the fact that during his off-hours, in a squalid storage room off the back hall, he would spy on neighbors using the powerful stargazing telescope Steve Sondheim had given our parents for Christmas.

Another Daddy helper—albeit an inanimate one—was his sunlamp. He would lie under it on the floor of his bathroom, chatting with us while he cooked himself in that strange, smelly, violet light.

*   *   *

Our move across town coincided with my move from Lower School to Middle School. By now I was in fifth grade at the Brearley School, a rigorous private school for girls way over on East End Avenue. Middle School featured homework: lots of it. And life was no longer just about pleasing your teachers, which had been my specialty in Lower School. Now it was important to stay on the right track with your friends.

Back in second grade, it hadn't bothered me too much when my classmate Lisa dubbed me "famous father girl"—which devolved a week later into "famous monkey face." But now, in fifth grade, I became self-conscious about my famous father. I didn't want to be singled out; I just wanted to be *normal*—that elusive condition to which Alexander and I perpetually aspired.

That spring, it got even tougher to be normal, when the movie of *West Side Story* came out. It was an enormous hit, winning ten Academy Awards. I was finally old enough to see it, and fell in love with the film. "I'm gonna see this movie ten times!" I vowed. I even managed to work up a crush on Richard Beymer, which took a little doing.

I was disappointed that my father himself wasn't fonder of the movie. He was particularly unhappy with the musical arrangements—but he'd been too busy with his conducting career to deal with the issues of adapting his score to the film. Having ceded that responsibility to a fellow named Johnny Green, the composer kept his cavils mostly to himself.

Anyway, Leonard Bernstein was now more famous than ever, and we lived on Park Avenue. Did that mean I was rich? I had no idea. In our house, no one ever talked about money. Nanny Helen paid all the bills, and it was clear that both our parents were delighted not to have to discuss financial matters. I had no sense of where we sat on the scale of moniedness.

Daddy often told us how his parents had fought about money; it was one of the blights of his childhood. Sam Bernstein tormented his wife, Jennie, by withholding money until she had to beg miserably for it; then he excoriated her for being a spendthrift. Sam was one of those fathers who withheld love by withholding money. He even resisted paying for Daddy's piano lessons, to discourage his son from pursuing such an unlucrative career. He'd fully expected to pass his hard-won, successful hair and beauty supply business along to his eldest son: this was, after all, the immigrant dream come true. (Years later, after Daddy's magical overnight success at Carnegie Hall, some journalist got wind of Sam's behavior and confronted him: "Mr. Bernstein, is it true you wouldn't pay for your son's piano lessons?" Sam's immortal reply: "Well, how was I supposed to know he'd turn out to be Leonard Bernstein?")

My father had clearly organized his home life to spare his children his own damaging childhood experience. We never saw our parents fight—and the subject of money never came up. We didn't even have regular allowances; if we needed money, an appropriate amount was given to us.

In those days, it was normal for schools like ours to have parents who didn't get particularly involved in their children's education; they just assumed the school would take care of everything. So it was unusual—alarming, actually—when Daddy showed up on Parents' Day. There was a general tremor of awe when he slipped, not quite unobtrusively, into the classroom, making the teacher visibly nervous. I felt more than heard the whispering around me, while inside my head there swarmed a hive of self-consciousness.

But nothing was worse than the Brearley Christmas Assembly Fathers' Chorus, a scarring experience for Nina and myself. The music teacher, Mr. White, was in a dither, having the Maestro in his midst. At the assembly, when it was the fathers' turn to perform their carol, Daddy felt compelled to sing not the tune but *the descant*, in his loud, tuneless voice: "Nowell, *NO-WELLL* . . ." You could hear him above everyone else. Mummy's favorite Chilean expression was invented for moments like this: "*Tierra, trágame.*" Earth, swallow me.

*   *   *

When I turned ten, we said good-bye to the poky little Redding house and got a much bigger country house in Fairfield, Connecticut. Mummy told us about it one afternoon after school. She said it used to be a horse farm in the 1870s, and it had barns and stables, meadows and woods. It also had a swimming pool (which Redding had) and a tennis court (which Redding did not have). "How much did it cost?" we wanted to know. "Oh, I can't tell you, it's too horrifying. It was terribly expensive!" "Tell us, tell us!" "Oh, I can't even say it out loud!" "Tell us! Tell us! Tell us!" Finally Mummy whispered, "Eighty." "What? Eighty dollars? The house

The Fairfield house in spring.

cost eighty dollars?" "No, no . . . eighty . . . [she could only mouth the word silently] . . . *thousand*."

"WOW, eighty *thousand* dollars? That's so much money! This must be the biggest house in the world!" "Shh, shhh!" our mother begged. She hated speaking aloud of money.

(Today, of course, $80,000 would not buy you a pup tent in Fairfield, Connecticut.)

The house was indeed wonderful, and not fancy at all: it was basically an old-fashioned New England saltbox onto which additions had been built over the years, giving it a charmingly meandering shape. Around the grounds, there were mighty trees of many varieties, including an enormous, invitingly climbable copper beech and a giant ginkgo, which, we would discover in the fall, dropped all its leaves at once overnight, leaving a bright yellow carpet on the driveway for us to find the next morning.

The pool's concrete foundation was covered in a turquoise blue plastic lining, with a logo at the shallow end showing the silhouette of a woman diving and the legend "An Esther Williams Swimming Pool." This particularly delighted Aunt Shirley, who had been a big fan of the Esther Williams swimming movies. When Shirley wore her white bathing cap and launched herself sportily off the diving board, we thought she looked exactly like the lady on the logo.

Our mother loved the new house, and relished fixing it up. She trolled the antique stores and junk shops along Route 7, often taking us along with her, to our desperate boredom. She found things made of wicker or murky brass, funny old paintings and eccentric lamps. Then she would set about restoring the stuff. Under a tree, she would scrape the old paint off the wicker furniture using dental instruments. Then she'd repaint. We grew accustomed to the rattle of those spray-paint cans being shaken, and the terrible fumes that pursued us right into the house.

Also, Mummy obsessed over her flower garden, spending long hours weeding and pruning in her broad-brimmed straw hat. She had strong opinions about flowers. Gladioli—bad: too funereal! Petunias—bad: too suburban! Zinnias, peonies, rambling roses— all good.

Aunt Shirley replicates the logo in the Esther Williams swimming pool in Fairfield.

During the school year, the routine became that Mummy would drive us kids, Julia, and the dog up to Fairfield after our half day of school on Friday afternoons, and we'd spend the weekend up there. If Daddy joined us, he'd drive up later in the other car. Mummy was an excellent driver: a bit on the fast side, staying mostly in the left lane, but steady as a rock. It galled her to no end, therefore, that *she* was the one who always got the speeding tickets, while Daddy—who drove with the attention span of a puppy, paid minimal attention to lane dividers, and turned around to face anyone he was addressing in the back seat—somehow never got a ticket. His automotive invulnerability was all part of the Lenny magic.

Our drives were fairly peaceable, but there was one part of the drive I hated, particularly in the cold months, regardless of which parent was at the wheel: the smoking. As a grand gesture to whoever else was in the car, Mummy and Daddy would crack the driver's window one inch when they lit up, which would do virtually nothing to dissipate the noxious clouds of smoke that accompanied the first moments of lighting a cigarette. My stomach lurched with trepidation when they pushed in the car lighter, which popped out a few seconds later, glowing red within, ready to do its job. As the driver's hand raised the stubby car lighter toward the cigarette waiting between his or her lips, I'd take as deep a breath as I could, and try to hold it until that first ghastly burst of smoke had subsided. But I could never hold my breath long enough, and inevitably I had to gulp down that heavy gray stink.

The cigarette-lighting ritual was less odious in warm weather because we could crank down the car windows. In the summers, Mummy moved the entire household to Fairfield for the season: cook, maid, and all. Daddy's favorite thing in those golden months was to go straight to the vegetable garden when he woke

up. Wearing a terrycloth bathrobe over his bathing suit and carrying a saltshaker, he'd shuffle to the vegetable garden, pick a tomato, lick it so the salt he sprinkled there would stick to the skin,
and take a big bite. "Heaven!" he'd gurgle through a mouthful
of tomato pulp. After that, he'd shuffle back to the pool and take
a swim. Then came breakfast under the poolside umbrella—the
usual eggs and bacon and all the rest—and he'd read the paper
until he got stinky. Then he would head up to his studio to attend
to his various movements.

The studio, a short way up the driveway (or even shorter, by
way of the lawn), was a little two-room house attached to the old
stables. Mummy had found Daddy a huge wooden stand-up desk;
because of his back problems, he liked to work standing up. On the
wall behind the stand-up desk, and all around the room, Daddy had
a display of endlessly fascinating photos, many signed, of everyone
from Carl Nielsen to Gustav Mahler to Aaron Copland to Darius
Milhaud (who drew a mustache on his image with a ballpoint pen)
to John F. Kennedy to a particularly mournful Abraham Lincoln.

An interesting offer came my father's way that first summer in
Fairfield. The Gas Company (or, as they called themselves on the
TV commercial, "Your Gas Company") offered him a staggering *one million dollars* to write—I can still hardly believe this—
the Gas Symphony. These were the golden years of corporations
underwriting cultural projects; evidently a piece by Leonard
Bernstein was an extra-illustrious proposition, worth the grand
expense. With our family's devotion to the execution and perennial discussion of all personal gaseous emissions, the Gas Symphony was our favorite topic for several weeks. We fantasized
about the tuba effusions, the trombone reports, the intestinal
rumbles of timpani . . . And—a million dollars! "C'mon, Daddy,
do it! We'll be so rich!"

Our father was tempted to take the offer; he was always longing for more composing opportunities, and that symphony he'd been working on at the MacDowell Colony was taking him forever to finish. So he strung along Our Gas Company long enough to accept their offer to fly him, Alexander, and me by helicopter from Bridgeport, Connecticut, to the New York World's Fair, where we were treated to a lavish lunch at the Festival of Gas Pavilion(!). We were then escorted to all the most popular presentations without having to stand on the two-hour lines. General Motors, IBM, Ford, and General Electric had up-to-the-minute multiscreened films and animatronics; Alexander and I were enthralled. At sunset, the three of us were helicoptered back over Long Island Sound to Connecticut. Soon after, Daddy gave Our Gas Company the bad news: he wouldn't be writing Their Gas Symphony after all. But hey—thanks for the ride, fellas!

He went back to work on his symphony.

One day in August, Alexander and I were sitting by the Esther Williams swimming pool with Mummy, while she had her end-of-the-day vodka. We heard the screen door slam shut in Daddy's studio. We turned around to see him walking toward us across the lawn, waving a thick sheaf of paper over his head. "*I didduhtt!*" he crowed in Rybernian. "I finished my symphoneee!"

"Hooray!" Mummy yelled. She leaped out of her chair and, to our everlasting astonishment, jumped into the pool with all her clothes on.

4

The First Shadows

So, all the pieces were in place. Daddy had his job at the New York Philharmonic, newly relocated to Lincoln Center. We had our own new homes, on Park Avenue and in Fairfield. Mummy was the beautiful, gracious, witty wife and mother. Nina was the adorable toddler, always saying clever things. I was in sixth grade at Brearley, and Alexander was in third grade at the Collegiate School, just across the park. Julia kept things running on an even keel while doting on Alexander, fussing over Nina, and squabbling with me. Alexander and I had our weekly piano lessons; we loathed them, and never practiced. We had Aunt Shirley and Uncle BB and all the friends, who came over to the house for dinner and out to Fairfield on the weekends. It was a happy, noisy, busy pair of households. If there were any shadows, I didn't see them.

The 1960 presidential election was the first one to which I paid any attention. Julia wasn't a US citizen yet, but she said that if she could vote, she'd cast her ballot for Richard Nixon, because "he has his hair combed." She thought John F. Kennedy had an unruly look about him. (How right she was.) But my parents and all their lefty friends were thrilled when Kennedy won. Daddy even got to perform at JFK's inaugural and came home with a delightful tale about getting caught in the epic blizzard while traversing Washington in a limo with Bette Davis. Because he couldn't make it to his hotel, he conducted his specially composed presidential fanfare dressed in a Caribbean shirt, several sizes too big, lent to him by Harry Belafonte.

Our parents were in love with the Kennedys. The feeling was

mutual enough that they were invited to the White House several times. Once it was just the four of them: Lenny and Felicia dining in the family quarters with Jack and Jackie. Our parents' eyes were shining as they told us the next day about how the president's sisters, Eunice and Pat, called after dinner, asking what was going on over there. Jack told his sisters over the phone that Lenny and Felicia had joined them for dinner, and then reported Eunice's reply: "You have all the fun! Why weren't we invited?" Daddy loved the dynamic between the Kennedy siblings; he felt right at home. In fact he felt so at home that after dinner, according to Mummy, Daddy went and sat in the president's very own iconic rocking chair. "*Lenny!*" she hissed. "*Get up from there!*"

Another time, when our father was attending an event at the White House while a Young People's Concert was being broadcast, he asked (rather impertinently) if there was a television where he could watch a bit of his show. He was taken up to the nursery, where he sat down on a chair behind the president's four-year-old daughter, Caroline, who was sitting cross-legged on the floor, huddled close to the screen. She watched the program intently for a few minutes, impressing our father with her concentration. Suddenly she turned around to him and announced, "I have my own pony!"

This was why we loved Daddy: because he would tell this story on himself, giving his family the gift of a chance to tease him. His endless parade of triumphs and that blazing energy that overtook every situation could be exhausting to live with, especially for our mother. She was particularly appreciative of any opportunity to tease her Lennuhtt—and Lennuhtt knew it.

Our most-played record in the Park Avenue living room was Vaughn Meader's *First Family* album, a bestselling collection of comedy sketches poking fun at the Kennedy family. Alexander and

I knew all the routines by heart. Daddy had been at Harvard just a year behind Jack, and he really identified with those rambunctious, affectionate Kennedy siblings. When Daddy was horsing around with Shirley and BB, we imagined him feeling a bit like the Semitic counterpart of Jack: the illustrious head of a parallel Jewish Kennedy clan.

One Friday in late November, I was eating lunch in the kitchen when the news came over the TV that President Kennedy had been shot while in a motorcade in Dallas.

Mummy tried to keep herself together for Alexander's and my benefit, but finally crumpled onto her side of the bed and sobbed. Daddy came rushing home from his Young People's Concert production meeting. He was crying, too. Shirley came over, crying. The grownups drifted in, sat together in the library with the shades drawn: watching TV, drinking, chain-smoking, and crying. I had never seen the grownups cry before.

The gloom persisted for days. Our father conducted Mahler's Second Symphony in the president's honor, and it was even broadcast on TV—but for once Alexander and I didn't watch; it was too serious for us. We had never seen the grownups watch so much television. We were all in the library with the TV on when Jack Ruby shot Lee Harvey Oswald. Everyone seemed thunderstruck by the events toppling over us, bursting right out of that little gray screen. We watched the funeral together: the skittish, riderless horse with the boots turned backward in the stirrups; Mrs. Kennedy in her black veil; little Caroline, dressed just like me at that age in the velvet-collared Chesterfield wool coat with the matching leggings; tiny John-John Kennedy saluting as the coffin went by.

Daddy decided to dedicate his new symphony to his beloved slain president. It was eerily appropriate: the symphony, named

Kaddish, had a chorus singing the Aramaic text of the kaddish prayer, which is spoken for the dead. The symphony had an English narration that my father wrote especially for Mummy to recite. The text was a kind of argument with God: If you're up there protecting us, then why is everything so terrible down here? After the assassination, the narration took on an even weightier meaning.

The American premiere of the piece was in Boston, with Charles Munch conducting and Felicia Montealegre as narrator. The composer himself conducted it with the New York Philharmonic a few months later—with Felicia still narrating—and they subsequently recorded the piece. Alexander and I were too young to attend the concerts, but in the fall, when we played the newly released record in Nina's nursery, we were taken aback. The music was dark, often dissonant, even snarly. The chorus was intimidating; sometimes they yelled, or sang in a kind of swirling cacophony. And that narration—it was hard for us to take. Mummy sounded all stagy and melodramatic; it made us squirm. "Tin God! Your bargain is *tin*!" she declaimed in her big scary theater voice, and we shrank into ourselves and covered our faces with our hands. This piece was a long, long way from *West Side Story*. And, as it turned out, the rest of the world had a similar reaction. The text, in particular, elicited scorn; one critic referred to it as "a lava flow of clichés."

We sensed that our mother, too, was uncomfortable with the *Kaddish* Symphony. But of course she was stuck with performing it; her husband had written that overblown narration especially for her. Perhaps she enjoyed the opportunity to perform once again—but even at our young ages, Alexander and I could tell she was ambivalent. This was a new situation: Daddy had composed something that was intensely earnest and impassioned, yet was getting mixed reviews—and even his own wife wasn't entirely comfortable with it. Everything about this symphony was, for us . . . icky.

As if things weren't already bad enough, our parents' beloved friend (and my godfather) Marc Blitzstein was murdered that January by sailors on the island of Martinique. I didn't find out for many years that it was a homosexual hate crime, which must have made the loss even more ghastly for my parents. All I knew at the time was that I'd lost my godfather, that glorious screen villain, tormentor of the pyramid builders in "Call Me Moses." (I subsequently appointed Mike Nichols my surrogate godfather; he graciously accepted the nontask.)

The following summer, our parents invited Mrs. Kennedy, Caroline, and John-John out to Fairfield for the weekend. It had been less than a year since the assassination. Our family felt this visit as both an honor and a burden. Mummy told us we had to be polite, and to play nicely with the two children. We promised

Jamie with Mike Nichols in Fairfield.

to try; we knew Mrs. Kennedy and her children must be very sad. Before the guests arrived, Mummy and Daddy frantically hid all their books on the various assassination conspiracy theories. (Vaughn Meader's *First Family* album had been buried long before.)

The family arrived in several cars, amid a welter of Secret Service agents. The weekend went relatively smoothly. Caroline was about five years younger than I, but we did fine together. I took her to the apple orchard, where we sat in the tree house; I don't remember our conversation, but Caroline seemed cheerful enough. John-John was so little, he couldn't really be a companion for Alexander. But the time passed agreeably, and one afternoon we put on a miniature talent show. When it was her turn, Mrs. Kennedy did a Russian sailor's dance, with her arms crossed, alternately extending one long leg and then the other from a squatting position. That was impressive.

Early Sunday morning, I came down for breakfast and wandered outside, whereupon I discovered that my favorite climbing tree, the big copper beech by the driveway, had acquired a hideous pink gash in its bark, as big as a dinner plate. I gasped in outrage: "*Who* did this? Boy, whoever did this to our beautiful tree is really gonna *pay!*" I soon found out that an hour earlier, John-John had somehow escaped the attention of the half dozen Secret Service guys drinking coffee in the house, and wandered all alone out to the driveway, where he'd opened the door of their station wagon, climbed into the driver's seat, and released the emergency brake, just like the nice Secret Service man had shown him . . . and the car started rolling downhill. Apparently John-John had managed to leap out before the car gained momentum and veered to the right, rolling off the driveway and crashing headlong into the copper beech.

The pink gash eventually healed over, but the scar remained, providing a delicious anecdote with which to regale Fairfield visitors—until 1999, when John-John's plane plunged into the ocean. After that, it was too sad to tell the story anymore.

* * *

After seven years of being the full-time music director of the New York Philharmonic, my father was finally overcome with frustration; he wasn't getting enough composing done. In the fall of 1964, he began a yearlong sabbatical from the Philharmonic to devote his time to composing. He started work on a new show with Betty and Adolph, to be directed by Jerry Robbins, based on the Thornton Wilder play *The Skin of Our Teeth*. Daddy seemed happy to be back with his pals, all of them enveloped in their magic nimbus of cigarette smoke—but for some reason that has never been fully understood, the project didn't go well. They gave it up, and Daddy was bitterly disappointed, and upset that he'd already squandered half of his sabbatical on a stillborn project.

And something wasn't quite right with Mummy. Every now and then, she would have a bizarre physiological explosion: violent vomiting and diarrhea, followed by her blood pressure plummeting nearly to zero. Our parents' doctor, Chuck Solomon, would rush over and arrange for an ambulance to speed our mother to the hospital. It was frightening to see the orderlies hustling her out of the apartment on a stretcher. At the hospital, she'd gradually pull out of it, and a few days later would return home, weak and terribly pale.

She also had developed a sun allergy. To avoid getting the itchy bumps, our mother had to give up her beloved gardening and now spent the better part of our summers in the shade, tackling assorted projects: giving a brass chandelier an antique patina using bathroom cleanser and a toothbrush, magic-markering all the green patches in an Oriental rug to a color she preferred, and executing prodigious feats of needlepoint. She was never still. I noticed that she had developed a nervous tic with her fingers, tapping one, then another lightly and persistently against her thumb in a complex pattern known only to her.

Dr. Solomon, who rescued my mother during her episodes, also wound up saving my father's composing sabbatical. The doctor's friend Walter Hussey, dean of Chichester Cathedral in England, had offered Daddy a commission to compose a short choral piece that, Dean Hussey hoped, would have echoes of *West Side Story* in it. My father had turned down many an offer like this, but maybe because it was Chuck Solomon's friend and the timing was right, he accepted this commission—and that's where a great deal of the *Skin of Our Teeth* material wound up. *Chichester Psalms* emerged quickly. He didn't struggle; it sort of popped out. He'd put so much more toil and travail into his *Kaddish* Symphony, and yet this simple, unambitious work, setting the Hebrew texts of four psalms, was the one everybody loved. *Kaddish* was so thorny, while "Chich," as Daddy called it, was friendly and accessible.

I loved that first movement, with its rollicking 7/4 rhythm, its great joyous bursts of choral singing, and that huge thump of a bass drum at the end. Then the second movement had the boy alto singing "The Lord is my shepherd" (in Hebrew) so purely, so simply; the chord progression was almost like a pop song. Then the men in the chorus interrupted him with their ferocious, bellicose *"Lamah rag'shu"* section—"Why do the nations rage"—thrilling! Daddy told us that the tune was from the original opening number of *West Side Story*: "Mix! Make a mess of 'em, make the sons-of-bitches pay, make a mess of 'em . . ." Those were hard words to spit out in English; it was probably a good idea to cut that opening

On the road with Daddy.

number. (In "Chich," the *"Lamah rag'shu"* words were even harder to sing—but somehow choruses worldwide seem to manage.) The last movement began with a very anguished opening section, but then morphed into a lovely tune in 5/4 for the chorus, serene as a flowing river. And the mystical, hushed chorale at the end was so beautiful, capped off by the chorus singing a hushed "Amen" while a muted solo trumpet floated the five opening notes of the piece, high above them all.

"Chich" had catchy tunes, fun rhythms, and lots of heart. It was accessible, unpretentious, straightforward, and *short*. Everyone loved it. Alexander and I thought it was pure, perfect Daddy music. Why couldn't he compose this way all the time?

For the premiere of "Chich," Alexander and I got to accompany our parents to England, which made us feel very grownup. The performance at the cathedral was underrehearsed but exciting.

Daddy said the cavernous acoustics had hidden a multitude of sins in the orchestra.

We soon left Chichester for London, where the four of us stayed in a magnificent suite at the Savoy, the swellest hotel we had ever seen and ever would see. Our father exhibited an irrepressible, childlike delight in luxurious things, and relished them anew through us, his kids. At the Savoy, he reveled in summoning the liveried headwaiter at the pull of a bell cord, and he couldn't wait to show us how the hotel's fierce water pressure filled the boat-sized bathtub in ninety seconds. But for Alexander and me, nothing could beat the mirrored folding closet doors, in front of which we could create a Rockettes kick line that stretched into infinity.

5

The Beatles Portal

Alexander and Jamie share the Beatles with their dad.

In February of 1964, halfway through my sixth-grade year, the Beatles came to America. By coincidence, Aunt Shirley was returning from a trip to England on the same day the Beatles were landing at the recently renamed John F. Kennedy Airport. When we went to pick Shirley up, the airport was still crawling with dazed teenage girls; the Beatles had landed a mere couple of hours earlier. On the drive back into town, Shirley revealed that she had originally been booked on the same Pan Am jet that the Beatles were on, but at the last minute had changed her flight to TWA because, she explained, they had this great new feature: a projector was set up at the back of the aisle and a screen up front, and they showed a movie. I was aghast: For *this*, Shirley had missed being on the same plane as the Beatles?

A few days later, the Beatles appeared on *The Ape Solomon Show*—an event so seismic that Mummy and Daddy agreed to let us watch it during dinner. Alexander and I wheeled the little TV down the hallway from the library to the Casino Fancy dining room—the same TV on which we'd seen Jack Ruby shoot Oswald just a few months earlier. We fiddled with the antenna until the black-and-white picture lost most of its fuzz, and then watched history in the making once again.

To say I was a Beatlemaniac does not begin to convey the depth of my obsession. The Beatles were my ground of being: like air to a bird, like water to a fish. I wrote poetry about them, kept logs of my dreams about them. (In one dream, George Harrison noticed I was already wearing a bra and kissed me on the cheek. "But real suction!" I wrote.) My girlfriends and I listened over and over to the albums, gazing at the cover art, memorizing the lyrics. Whenever we sang Beatles songs, I always sang the harmony. I *lived* in that harmony.

Daddy loved the Beatles, too, which made me particularly happy. In the swimming pool the following summer, he came up with a third part to "Love Me Do," so that he, Alexander, and I could sing the song together in three-part harmony, right there in the corner of the deep end. On one of his Young People's Concerts, Daddy explained the A-B-A structure of sonata form by singing a Beatles song. Oh, how the girls in the audience squirmed and squealed as he accompanied himself on piano, singing "And I Love Her" in his not-so-McCartneyesque voice! He must have known he was onto something, because he began regularly incorporating the Beatles, and other pop music, in his Young People's Concerts, to illustrate his various points. It kept the kids in the audience interested, just as it had for Alexander and me. (We, and later Nina, were in effect the ongoing guinea pigs for Daddy's Young People's Concert ideas.)

John Lennon was Daddy's favorite Beatle, as he was mine. We were both enchanted by Lennon's book of poetry, *In His Own Write*, and pored over it together. Daddy invented a singing game for Alexander and me to play with him while the three of us lay wedged into the hammock under the big maple tree after dinner. We would invent a round, à la "Row, Row, Row Your Boat," using Lennon's poem "The Moldy Moldy Man." Whoever started the round got to choose what kind of melody it would be: sad, perky, waltz, military. After the first line—"I'm a moldy moldy man . . ."—the second person had to come in, echoing person number one. Then the third person would come in. The fun of the game was, of course, that you couldn't possibly repeat the line you'd just heard while simultaneously listening for the next one. It was deliciously hopeless, and a raucous shambles every time—always punctuated at the end by person number three dolefully singing the last line all alone after the other two had finished: ". . . I'm such a humble Joe."

Eventually, word got back to John Lennon—or to his manager or press agent or somebody—that Leonard Bernstein was thinking about possibly setting some of the *In His Own Write* poems to music. This led to Daddy being invited to meet Lennon backstage during a dress rehearsal for *The Ed Sullivan Show*. It was by now the summer of 1965, and the Beatles were returning to the US to make their highly anticipated second *Ed Sullivan* appearance. Naturally, our father asked if he could bring his two older children with him to the rehearsal.

We were going to meet the Beatles!!!

Daddy drove us into town from Fairfield. I was painfully conscious of the fact that I had braces and still didn't shave my legs. What hope did I have of getting any Beatle to fall in love with me?

Our father was summoned backstage first, while Alexander and I remained, perplexed and frustrated, in the theater seats watching a tedious rehearsal of a comedy duo who thought it was funny for one of them to wear a Beatles wig. Finally an usher came to escort us through the grimy backstage corridors of the theater until we were in front of a door with a star on it. The usher knocked.

No actual event in my life would ever be more exciting than the seconds containing that anticipatory knock, on that particular door, on that particular day.

The door opened and *there they were*: John, Paul, and George. But no Ringo. Why? Because the other three had been eating hamburgers with onions, and any Beatlemaniac worth her salt knew that the two things Ringo hated most were onions and Donald Duck, so of course he'd gone off to a less smelly room.

Alexander and I were introduced, and shown to chairs. I was seated next to Paul, who went to the trouble to be friendly and ask me some polite questions. (I have since heard many similar reports from people who met the Beatles; Paul was a gent.)

Daddy was sharing cigarettes with everyone and chatting away with them as if they were old friends. Maybe we sang them a round of "Moldy Man"? I don't remember. I was in a coma of awe.

The three Beatles had an interesting argument about whether

The Ed Sullivan Show dress rehearsal was very loud.

to put on their signature suits for the rehearsal. John and George didn't want to. Paul said, "Come on, lads, it's a *dress* rehearsal! We ought to be dressed, then!" (Once again, Paul was the one behaving like an adult.)

On our way out, the usher knocked on the adjoining dressing room door. We heard a muffled "Come in," and when the door opened, we saw two feet in red socks on a cot; the head of the bed was obscured by a locker. But when the body wearing the socks sat up, it was a sleepy Ringo; we'd woken him up from a nap. Sorry, Ringo!

The next day, back at my day camp in Connecticut, there was all-out pandemonium when the girls found out where I'd been the day before. Sometimes it was purely great to have Leonard Bernstein for a father.

At that same day camp, a group of us had received little folk guitars, which we were soon to be taught to play. But I couldn't wait. Before the lessons began, I took the instrument home, laid it on the floor, and composed a song with no words. I just hummed my tune while slowly plucking the open strings: E, A, D . . . E, A, D . . . I felt I was expressing all the wonder of life itself through my tiny song.

The camp counselor eventually taught us three chords: E, A, and B^7, of all the less-than-easy choices—oh, how I wrestled with my pinky finger to get it over to that G string—but with those three chords we could play "Easy Rider." When I played it for Daddy, he told me it was a blues song, and explained what a blues progression was, and how the three blues chords were tonic, dominant, and subdominant. Suddenly I felt I had a road map—not just to Beatles songs, but to all the music on the radio.

My father and the Philharmonic recorded on Columbia Records, so the label sent him free records by their pop artists, all of which he passed along to me. I listened to albums by two funny-looking guys called Simon and Garfunkel, and a couple of others by some songwriter with a terrible nasal voice I couldn't stand; I read his name on the album cover as "Bob Dye-lan." His singing sounded so out of tune to my ears compared to the Beatles' celestial harmonies.

I had to give the guitar back when camp ended, but that fall, in a storage closet off our murky back corridor in New York, I found a beautiful classical guitar in a battered case that someone had given Daddy as a present. I figured out how to change the broken strings, then tuned it up, just as I'd been taught at camp—and it sounded beautiful. It was bigger and harder to play than a folk guitar, but I didn't care.

Playing the guitar allowed music to belong to me. It was just for fun—plus, the guitar spoke directly to the music I listened to and cared about. I could pick out the chord progressions of my favorite Beatles songs. I could even correct Daddy when he heard the key wrong on the Supremes' "You Keep Me Hangin' On." He was interpreting the dominant as the tonic, I told him.

The piano lessons, by contrast, were mandated from above, and they were not going well. Our parents insisted upon them, but they couldn't bear, or possibly couldn't be bothered, to nag us to practice. The only practicing we did was in the sickening half hour before the piano teacher showed up for the Tuesday lesson. Everything about piano lessons was lonely and discouraging. After all, I was constantly hearing music all around me being performed in its optimum state. But whenever I sat down at the keyboard, and those little frogs and spiders came squirming out of my fingers, I would think: Oh, who am I kidding. I'll never get there, *never*. Alexander felt the same; he often contracted a stomachache right before the piano lesson. To this very day, he gets depressed on Tuesdays.

As I approached the squirmy years of adolescence, it was the Beatles that provided the happy ground where my father and I most enjoyed each other's company. When a new Beatles album came out, I would run into his studio: "Daddy, it's here, look—I got it!" He'd slap the record right onto his stereo system, crank up the volume, and we'd sit together on his couch to scrutinize the lyrics while the album played. "Hey, that's a sitar!" he exclaimed when he first heard "Norwegian Wood"; then he explained Indian ragas to me. "That's a C trumpet—just like Bach used!" he said when we listened to "Penny Lane." "Wow, can you believe that chord? So *fresh*!" he marveled on the fade-out of "Good Day Sunshine."

My father was genuinely fascinated by rock music. He often declared that it had more energy and inventiveness than the austere contemporary compositions he had to premiere with the Philharmonic. He even made a TV show about rock music, featuring guest musicians including Janis Ian. I was too young to understand her remarkable song "Society's Child," but Daddy completely grasped the power of its music and lyrics.

Another guest on that show was Tandyn Almer, who wrote the ingenious lyrics to "Along Comes Mary," a big hit that year for the band the Association. Whenever the song came on the radio, Daddy would obsess over the torrent of lyrics—but he couldn't quite make them all out. So one day he drove with Alexander and me down the hill to Zera MusicLand in Fairfield to ask for the sheet music to "Along Comes Mary." "Oh, we don't have that just now, Mr. Bernstein," the nerdy store clerk replied. "But we'll order it for you and you can pick it up next week."

The following week, the same clerk brightly presented my father with the lyrics to "Along Comes Mary"—which it turned out the clerk had written out himself. The sheet of paper is long lost, but we still remember one part. Tandyn Almer's actual lyrics to the chorus go:

> *When we met I was sure out to lunch;*
> *Now my empty cup is as sweet as the punch.*
> *Sweet as the punch . . . !*

The nerdy clerk's version went:

> *When we met I was sure out to lunch;*
> *No one in Chicuck is as slee as a bunch.*
> *Slee as a bunch . . . !*

In a footnote, the clerk helpfully explained that "Chicuck" was slang for Chicago.

Daddy was enchanted by the entire episode. He subjected every houseguest that summer to the clerk's rendition of "Along Comes Mary," pounding away on the piano, with Alexander and me joining in on the lyrics. The clerk had neglected to explain what "slee" meant, but to this day, whichever of us siblings is in Chicago always writes to the other two: "Feelin' slee in Chicuck."

6

Summer Games

The family by the Esther Williams swimming pool in Fairfield, Connecticut.

Summer continued to be our family's best time—and now, in Fairfield, the summers stretched out like a long, hazy dream. Lunch was served on the shady back patio. Our dazzling new cook, Anita, made us hollowed-out tomatoes, their innards mixed with sweet corn, fresh-picked basil, and homemade mayonnaise, then reinserted in the tomato shell. Mummy liked offering iced coffee with optional scoops of Häagen-Dazs coffee ice cream, which you could stir in with a tall, reedy, silver spoon that was also a straw. Even outside, every table setting had its own individual ashtray, and both ends of the table had silver cups containing cigarettes. The grownups lit up after the first course, after the main course, and after dessert. They would have smoked while chewing if they could have.

There was always a summer visit from Aaron Copland. Aaron was the closest thing to an official composing teacher that Daddy ever had—but their connection contained so much more. Aaron was mentor, friend, confidant, co-lefty, and devoted pen pal. (If they had ever been lovers, it was the least important aspect of their deep friendship.) I could sense their mutual affection when Aaron shambled in and Daddy enveloped him in a bear hug. Aaron was not the kid-friendliest guy in the world, but his buckteeth, goofy grin, and infectious giggle made him irresistible. His music was part of our family's DNA. Aaron's music had the power to move me as much as Daddy's did; every one of Aaron's notes always seemed to be in just the right place. Daddy told me that Aaron would point to a particular spot in his score and say, "That's the note that *costs*!" Daddy loved this because, he explained, Aaron was such a penny-pincher that it was the perfect expression for Aaron to use in describing the judicious parsimony of his own notes. I also remember Daddy telling me that in the mornings, Aaron was in the habit of flapping open the newspaper with a cheery "Who died?" Daddy sometimes opened the paper that way himself, in Aaron's honor.

We made good use of our tennis court in the summer months. Uncle BB was the strongest player in the family; he had been a high school and college athlete. Daddy had a firm forehand and a nice serve—and of course, he was competitive as hell. Shirley was coordinated but ditzy, and could get addled and silly on the court.

Mummy started out clueless, but took lessons and got much better. She had spirited, laughter-filled games with Shirley, and Uncle BB's wife, Ellen. We all played in our bathing suits so we could walk back up the hill and jump straight into the pool.

Family friends played tennis with us, too. Isaac Stern was portly, but could move with deceptive speed. Our favorite on the court was Adolph Green. He had his own unique way of playing that resembled a cross between Charlie Chaplin and a Mexican jumping bean. When he missed, he would shout spontaneously invented euphemisms, like "shillelagh juice!" His wife, the actress Phyllis Newman, would keep us in stitches with her running commentary on the game.

Alexander and I had tennis lessons a couple of times a week. It was frustrating not to be as good as the grownups, but the tennis lessons were more tolerable than the piano lessons; at least we could go swimming when they were over.

As Alexander improved, he started playing tennis one-on-one with his father. They played at the end of the day—"sunset singles," Daddy called it—and then, as those games became ever more competitive, he began calling them "Oedipal sets," which also gave him the opportunity to tell us all about the Sophocles play. Alexander *hated* losing to his father, and would often stomp back up the hill in tears. That gave Daddy the opportunity to make up yet another expression: ELF'S THREAD, a beautiful anagram of SELF-HATRED.

August was corn time, and Daddy was in his glory. At dinner, he often requested a "monomeal": just a dozen ears of corn, the butter dish close by, and nothing else. "Heaven!" Daddy crowed, the clumps of kernels plopping juicily out of his mouth. He loved any summer food he could eat with his hands: barbecued chicken, or a big steak on the bone (the dogs loved him), or his favorite—

LB tucking into his monomeal.

boiled lobster. That was Daddy in August: sun-burnished, covered in flecks of lobster meat and corn kernels, aglow in joy and butter.

After dinner, we played anagrams. Steve Sondheim whipped up the craze as part of his consuming passion for wordplay. He and Daddy were furiously competitive at the anagrams table—well, they were competitive in everything: crossword puzzles, Christmas presents, symphonic music trivia (to say nothing of composing for musical the-ater). But Steve, to Daddy's annoyance, had the edge in anagrams.

We played "cutthroat" anagrams: that is, it was everyone's turn all the time. True, the players did take polite turns flipping a let-ter tile face-up at the center of the table—but anyone could yell out a word of five letters or more the very second its components were spotted. Once you yelled out your word, you possessed it, and would arrange it proudly face-out in front of you. The game continued as before—but now, in addition to looking for words to make from the center, you also had to protect your own word, because everyone else was staring at it, thinking up ways to steal it from you by scrambling it and adding letters from the center. Which meant you had to think up the changes, too, and shout them out before someone else did, to keep the word in your possession.

As the tile flipping continued, you had to be as poised as a Zen archer, ready to blurt out whichever word changes you were waiting for, the instant your desired letter got flipped up—plus, you had to continue looking for brand-new words in the center. As the players accumulated words in front of them, and the letters piled up in the center, the tension would become nearly unbearable.

Some changes were simply poetry. Steve Sondheim turned BLINDER into INCREDIBLE. Bill Styron caused an uproar when he turned CALIPERS into PHYLACTERIES. My own finest hour came when I changed SUITABLE to INSCRUTABLE. Nina, ever the youngest and scrambling to catch up, eventually skunked us all: she stole CAPARISON from Daddy by turning it into RAPSCALLION. And she took SATURATE from Steve by turning it into . . . MASTURBATE. Nina wins!

Anagrams was not for everyone. Many a houseguest fled in tears—as did Alexander, Nina, and I from time to time. But the day came for each of us when we finally beat our father in anagrams. That was a sweet day—but not for Daddy. He hated losing, and would stalk away from the table, in a drama of gloom about his life being over. He'd wander around outside in the dark just long enough for everyone to start wondering what had happened to him. Then he would reappear, his face haunted by despair, and announce that he was exhausted and had to go to bed. His dejection was so profound, so existential, and put such a pall over the house that it almost wasn't worth the victory.

The annual climax of every summer was my father's birthday,

on August 25. The summer he turned forty-eight, I wrote him another "show"—really just a few pop songs from the radio, with new lyrics. But now, thanks to those lessons at camp, I was accompanying myself on the guitar. I played some Beatles and Rolling Stones songs—with my new Daddy-teasing lyrics—and performed them in the Fairfield living room for the assembled family and friends. I sat on a chair while Alexander sat on my feet, a human music stand holding up my lyrics, which I'd written out on a couple of Daddy's shirt cardboards.

Alexander holds up the lyrics while Jamie sings
the birthday song to Daddy.

Daddy loved my presentation, and I got plenty of stifling, body-squishing hugs. But Daddy's little golden girl was changing.

A few days later, I was upstairs in my bathroom and discovered some brownish splotches in my underpants. I walked out onto the balcony outside my parents' bedroom and called down to my mother, who was on the patio below having drinks with my father and "Uncle" Mikey Mindlin, a family friend.

"Um, Mummy, can you come upstairs for a minute?"

"They all guessed!" Mummy told me after she'd given me a hug. I wished she hadn't told me that, because once she got me all fixed up with the sanitary napkin, I had to face everyone on the patio, knowing that they knew. I came downstairs in a dizzy agony of embarrassment. I was grateful to Uncle Mikey for paying no attention to me. My father, however, silently took my hand and kissed it—a sweet and uncharacteristically restrained gesture, it strikes me now. But at the time, I was mortified. There really wasn't anything Daddy could possibly have done at that moment that I wouldn't have hated, short of ignoring me like Uncle Mikey did. And I probably would have hated that, too.

*   *   *

The following summer, in 1967, our family did something different: we rented a villa in Ansedonia, Italy, on the coast of southern Tuscany. Maybe our parents were feeling restless—even their exciting lives may have become too predictable—or maybe they were feeling pressures we knew nothing about.

Nina was five: precocious and bubbly. Alexander and I played with her and taught her to read. But I was lonely. My friends were all far away, and Alexander's company wasn't quite enough anymore. I was fourteen, in the vise grip of braces and budding libido, the sickening betwixt-and-between.

Mummy's itchy sun allergy kept her to the shade, but she worked hard on her new avocation: painting. She was talented; we loved every still life and portrait. But one day, in a fit of frustration, she threw all her paintings into the sea—well, she thought she had. Actually she'd thrown them over the wall onto the rocks of the house next door. Alexander heroically retrieved them all, and Mummy thanked him, a little embarrassed that she'd subjected us to her own strange episode of elf's thread. The summer resumed its natural rhythms, but I couldn't forget the look on my mother's face as she tossed away her own hard work; this was a side of her I wasn't sure I wanted to know about.

Felicia painting in Ansedonia.

Daddy wasn't in the best of spirits, either. He was trying to compose, but nothing was coming out. He could hardly sleep at all, and when he did, his snoring was so thunderous that our mother had to creep out of bed and sleep on the living room couch, where Dina, the screechy housekeeper, would discover her in the morning— "*Ohhh, mi scuuusi, Signora!*"

But my father always had his diversionary behaviors. That summer, he bought a complete set of scuba diving gear and was attempting to learn how to use it in the swimming pool. (He never quite got the hang of it.) He also bought a rubberized motor boat called a Zodiac so that we could water-ski at a nearby cove. And most manic of all, he bought himself a silver Maserati: an absolute opera diva of a sports car.

Meanwhile, Daddy was giving Hebrew lessons to Alexander in preparation for the latter's bar mitzvah the following summer. They would sit together on a porch swing, where I knew Alexander was gratified to have his father's undivided attention, even as he squirmed with impatience. Now that we were older, we often felt this way when we were alone with him: the push-pull of being the focus of his attention, vaguely thrilling, but with the accompanying tedium of his endlessly teaching, teaching, teaching you things.

Complicating everything in Ansedonia was the constant presence of journalist John Gruen, a family friend who was writing a coffee table book about Daddy called *The Private World of Leonard Bernstein*. It would include photos by Ken Heyman, so Ken was also around a lot, snapping away while we swam or ate lunch or played cards. Gruen interviewed each of us, and spent long hours tape-recording Daddy in a corner of the garden. The tape-recording and photographing rendered us uncomfortably self-conscious as a family—as if we were acting in a TV show about those charming,

Felicia cuts LB's hair in Ansedonia. Jamie was sulky that summer.

carefree Bernsteins, at the very moment when we were becoming a far more complex version of ourselves.

One comforting ingredient of that summer in Ansedonia was Daddy's and my mutual fixation on *Sgt. Pepper*. He knew right away that it was the Beatles' masterpiece, and he played it for everyone who came over to the house, energetically pointing out the highlights: "You hear the sitar in the bass drone in that last verse of 'Getting Better'?" "So deliciously ironic at the end of 'She's Leaving Home' when they sing in that dreary voice: 'She's . . . having . . . *fun* . . .'"

At the end of the record, Daddy wouldn't let anybody talk until that long, long, *long* piano chord had faded into complete silence.

7

A Little Teen in '60s New York

In seventh grade, my best friend, Ann, could do such a persuasive Paul McCartney impression that the rest of us would actually scream while watching her pantomime Paul singing "All My Loving." Ann played guitar, like I did. At Nina's third birthday party, Ann and I repeatedly played the chorus of "Blowin' in the Wind," singing the lyrics in French; we were hoping to impress Mrs. Kennedy, who drifted through the party with her lovely, dazed smile and paid us no attention whatsoever. Meanwhile, Lauren Bacall's hyperkinetic son Sam was downstairs, roasting Nina's doll to an aromatic pulp in her Suzy Homemaker oven.

The '60s were swinging for real by then, and no one could escape the cultural riptide. Over the next few years, Mummy's hemline went way up; her swan's neck rose alluringly from her clinging Pucci dresses. She looked great, I thought—and evidently, so did Robert F. Kennedy, who pressed his thigh against hers at a dinner party. When she told me this, I gasped and asked, "What did you do?" "I pressed back!" she said, laughing.

Meanwhile, Daddy's hair overlapped his collar in the back; his sideburns flirted with his jawline; Otto Perl made Daddy's trousers just a little bit bell-bottomed; and of course Daddy loved the heeled boots of the day, as they gave him an inch or more of extra height. (We were all such hopeless shrimps.)

My girlfriends and I were still a bit too young to be full participants in all the groovy goings-on, while my parents and their friends were just a little too old (I thought) to be dancing the Frug at places like Trude Heller's, the hot Greenwich Village club. But Frug they did.

I got a lucky break over the holidays. Our parents' friend Sybil Burton opened a disco called Arthur. Arthur was *the* spot to go to—just the sort of thing I was still, maddeningly, too young to experience. But in December, Sybil threw a special afternoon holiday party at Arthur for her friends *and her friends' kids*. I wore a short little black velvet dress with white lace trim, and felt kicky as hell. The huge sound system thrilled me. My father and I posed for a photographer who was creating fake antique daguerreotypes. The pictures came out great—especially the one of Daddy with a stovepipe hat and a banjo; he always looked ridiculous in any sort of hat.

It was fun to gad about town with Daddy. He got so much attention—and he liked showing off his cute teenage daughter, too. But somewhere inside I felt a vaguely unclear boundary. Around that time, my friend Ann and I went to see *Gone with the Wind* for the first time, on a giant screen—a wonderful experience. But in the scene where Rhett Butler has taken his little Bonnie to Paris and she wakes up in the night thrashing in her bed and crying, I heard her saying, "Daddy, Daddy, no!" I thought her father was abusing her. Then Rhett runs into the room and turns on the light, and Bonnie repeats, "Daddy, Daddy—dark!" Oh, she was saying "*dark*": she was just afraid of the dark. But to this very day, whenever I see that scene, I still have that quick, sick second of thinking that Rhett is doing something he shouldn't be doing to his daughter. No such thing ever happened to me in real life. But I felt . . . what was it? It was hard not to feel my father's sexuality. I mean, there it was. Everybody felt it. Tricky stuff for a daughter.

And while it was fun to get all the extra attention in public, I could never be sure what Daddy was going to do. On winter break, I went with him and Alexander to the brand-new ski resort in Vail, Colorado. One night, we all went to Casino Vail, a disco. They began playing the theme from *Zorba the Greek*, of all things, and Daddy grabbed me. The next thing I knew, we were dancing full tilt to the bouzouki music, just the two of us, while the crowd made a ring around us, clapping in rhythm and egging us on. Daddy pulled out a handkerchief and was waving it around above his head—then he was down on his knees! I danced in a circle around him; what else could I do? I was trapped: a mortified moon, doomed to eternal orbit around an ecstatic, sweaty, handkerchief-twirling sun.

* * *

Maybe Mummy was getting just a little impatient with . . . everything. She accompanied her husband on tour less and less. She was deeply absorbed in her painting, as well as in working for the American Civil Liberties Union. Maybe it was simply wearing thin to be Mrs. Maestro. In any case, Leonard Bernstein had become the newly anointed musical king of Vienna, complete with rapturous reviews for his concerts with the Vienna Philharmonic and half an hour's worth of curtain calls for his conducting of Verdi's opera *Falstaff* at the State Opera. Neither his wife nor any of his children were present to witness his ascent to the Viennese throne.

I could tell from the way my father talked about it that the level of adulation in Vienna was something unprecedented. Even in Israel they didn't carry on like this—and in Israel, he almost really *was* a king, having been there in 1948 during the war that gave birth to the new Jewish nation. Vienna offered the added frisson of all those former Nazis groveling at the Maestro's feet; that had to feel grimly good.

Daddy would come back from his conducting triumphs in Vienna walking on air—and then everything would pull him back down to earth. The New York Philharmonic's surly union was nothing like the all-embracing Vienna ensemble. And the New York music critics were relentless in their aggrieved sniping. Every Friday morning, Daddy would open the *New York Times* to read Harold Schonberg's latest evisceration of his subscription concert the night before. And then there was his own family, whose sworn duty it was to remind the Maestro that, after all, he was a human being like the rest of us. Shirley and BB teased and interrupted their brother; he hated it and loved it. Alexander, Nina, and I observed and absorbed. We understood that it was okay to make fun of our father: that it was even for a good cause.

Daddy always brought back fun presents from the road, but he came back from a triumphant New York Philharmonic tour to Japan with a truly smashing present for me: a Sony "tummy television," the smallest TV known to man in those days. In the commercial, a fat man balanced it on his stomach—hence the nickname. The TV was so small that I could hide it under the covers, with its single antenna poking out the edge of the sheet, and watch movies all night long without anyone knowing.

Alexander, Nina, and I watched a lot—I mean a *lot*—of television. First it was cartoons. (Our first experience of classical music was not with our father, but with Bugs Bunny.) Then it was sitcoms, Westerns, variety shows—we'd watch just about anything. At age ten, I developed two seething TV crushes: one on Ben Casey—the broody, swarthy brain surgeon—and one on Dr. Kildare, who was soft and blond and girly. And behold, a lifelong template was born: I ping-ponged back and forth for years to come between the dark, Semitic, aggressive boyfriends and the blond, effeminate, gentle (and, it often turned out, gay) ones.

When my friend Ann slept over, we'd sit on my narrow bed, with the little TV on a chair in front of us. This was the position from which we discovered Marlon Brando.

It mattered exactly not at all to me that the score to the film *On the Waterfront* was composed by my father (and is one of his most

Jamie, in her Fillmore East football jersey, with her friend Ann in front of the Fairfield Christmas tree.

thrilling works). Ann and I were too much in love with Brando to care about anything else. We wept over his performance: oh, the way he got beat up at the end! We didn't realize the degree to which my father's music was manipulating our emotions to a fever pitch.

Eventually we saw all Brando's films by combing the newspaper TV listings and planning our sleepovers around the late-night movie broadcasts. He was a blond Nazi in *The Young Lions*, a laconic outlaw in *One-Eyed Jacks*, even a toga-draped Mark Antony in *Julius Caesar*—and of course that almost unbearably sexy motorcycle tough in *The Wild One*.

So it came as fairly big news that Aunt Shirley had a screenwriter friend who'd been married to Marlon Brando's sister—and they had a son, Marty, just my age. And Marty was coming to New York City with his dad for the Christmas holidays! Shirley arranged for me to meet Marlon Brando's nephew, and I could hardly contain my anticipation.

The fact that Marty turned out to be a slightly sweaty fourteen-year-old with braces who bore only the vaguest resemblance to his uncle didn't deter me from developing a crush on him. We went on a couple of dates. While he felt me up at the movies, I became paralyzed as if in an awful dream; it took my last fiber of inner resolve to move Marty's creeping hand away from the front of my blouse, from the hem of my skirt. The unacknowledged tug-of-war continued through most of the movie, with never a word exchanged, the two of us staring resolutely ahead at the screen.

A second lifelong template was forged with Marty, the one in which I bring a boyfriend home: the family thinks he's unworthy, I wrestle with the conflict, and when I finally dump the guy, I'm joyfully welcomed back into the family bosom, where I feel safe and relieved.

Every girl secretly measures her boyfriend against her father. In my case, I soon realized, this was going to be an ongoing problem. After all, what hope did the average teenage boy have in competing with the Maestro? But the situation was made worse by the impossibly high standards of the whole circle of grownups. They could accept no one who was boring, or stiff, or short on wit. They were hard enough on their contemporaries; a fourteen-year-old boy didn't stand a chance.

The next boyfriend was an even bigger challenge for my family. He was into reading French poetry aloud, which my mother could not abide. He was obsessed with Hungarian saber fencing; Steve Sondheim dubbed him "Count Épée." More acute embarrassment. More giddy relief and family celebration when at last I disengaged myself.

*   *   *

During Christmas vacation, Alexander and I found ourselves without much to do, so our father, in his typically generous way, invited us along to his rehearsals for a performance of Verdi's *Requiem* that was to be a benefit for the Philharmonic's pension fund. First we heard the four soloists rehearse with Daddy around the piano in his studio. There was Marilyn Horne; Daddy called her voice "peaches and cream." There was Richard Tucker: old-school and short, but could he ever sing. Justino Diaz was a dashing, up-and-coming bass-baritone. And soprano Galina Vishnevskaya, the cellist Slava Rostropovich's wife, was very Russian and grand, although vocally a little shaky.

Then we went to the Camerata Singers' rehearsal. They piled on the decibels for the "Dies Irae." This was great stuff.

Then we heard the Philharmonic's rehearsal. Daddy put the "*Tuba mirum*" trumpets way up in the balcony; the effect was tremendous. By now we were getting the hang of the piece: so colorful, so varied, so full of tunes. Perfect for kids, actually.

Finally, the big ensemble rehearsal. Alexander and I were riveted by this point. We knew every note; we knew what to look forward to and when to worry. (Galina's pianissimo, supposed-to-be-ethereal high note on "*Requi-eeeem*" in the "Libera Me" section was an ongoing cause for concern.)

At the concert, Alexander and I craned forward in our seats as

if we were at a ball game. It was the greatest fun we'd ever had at
a concert of Daddy's. That night we made the priceless discovery
that the better we knew a piece, the more we'd enjoy the performance.

I was finally developing some interest in attending Daddy's regular subscription concerts—especially if my new friend Linn came
along. We developed instant crushes at the debut of a cute young
pianist named Misha Dichter, and went around for days afterward
singing the big tune from Tchaikovsky's First Piano Concerto.

A few months later at the Philharmonic, Linn and I went to
Mahler's Fifth Symphony, which neither of us had heard before. In
fact, few people in that audience had; this concert was part of Daddy's ongoing education of his public about the neglected wonders
of Gustav Mahler's symphonies. During the Adagietto movement,
the most achingly beautiful music we'd ever heard, Linn fell apart.
I'd never seen her cry over anything before; she was notoriously
flinty. Now here she was, streaming with tears—and that made
me break down, too. She never did explain why that music got to
her the way it did—but that was how we discovered the point of
music like the Adagietto: how it could express the deepest part of
one's inner universe, the part that could never be put into words.
Especially when you're fifteen.

8

School, Family, and the World

In history class that fall, I was assigned to debate my class-mate Nancy, and advocate the position that the US should not be involved in Vietnam. Once home, I went straight to Daddy's studio to get help. I knew next to nothing about Vietnam; these were relatively early times in the conflict, and the national antiwar movement had not yet gained momentum. When my father asked me what I thought about the situation, I groped to sound sensible: "Well, I guess if we're already there, um, we should just finish what we started . . . ?"

He explained the situation to me: the Gulf of Tonkin; the hysteria about the domino theory, where one country after another would ostensibly fall to communism; the proxy war between the US and Red China; even Eisenhower's warning about the military-industrial complex. I walked out of my father's studio feeling thoroughly informed, and convinced that the US should get out of Vietnam immediately. Boy, did I win that debate the next day; Nancy didn't stand a chance.

I was soon swept up, like everyone else, by the tidal wave of events in 1968. First, Martin Luther King was assassinated. Down went the window shades, on went the television; once again the grownups cried and drank. Daddy cried extra; he had strong feelings about civil rights. He'd been immersed in those issues since college; he'd even written his college thesis on "The Absorption of Race Elements into American Music." He'd played me "race records," as the early 78 rpm blues recordings used to be called, introducing me to Lead Belly, and Bessie Smith, and Billie Holiday singing "Strange Fruit"—the most mournful song I'd ever heard. Daddy had been supporting civil rights organizations for years— all of which, we found out much later, was just more grist for the FBI's ever-thickening Leonard Bernstein file.

Mere months after Martin Luther King was killed, Bobby Kennedy was assassinated, mid–presidential campaign. This was almost more than the grownups could bear. My father was asked to conduct the Mahler Fifth Adagietto in St. Patrick's Cathedral at Bobby Kennedy's funeral. That morning, Daddy received some kind of death threat; we had to go to the church with a police escort. The funeral was beautiful and desperately sad. The Adagietto was no longer the special piece I shared with Linn; now I was sharing that music with all the mourners—including Bobby's eldest son, Joe Kennedy, with whom I had a staring match during the music. Afterward, Daddy drove Alexander and me to Fairfield in his new convertible, with the top down. As we drove past the buildings on Third Avenue, Alexander was having a nervous breakdown in the back seat, convinced that there was a sniper on every roof, ready to mow our father down. A bit later, as we drove along the highway, Daddy and I were chatting up front, oblivious to Alexander's back-seat trembling, when I noticed that the car ahead of us at the mouth of the approaching tunnel wasn't moving. "Daddy, that car isn't moving . . . Daddy, watch out for that car . . . *DADDY, WATCH OUT!!!*" He slammed on the brakes, and the car screeched and skittered across several lanes, ending up on the side of the road facing backward, the engine purring quietly as if nothing of any consequence had happened. And, in fact, nothing had. We resumed our trip, but now I was the one who was shaking.

We arrived in Fairfield unscathed—as a result of which Alexander was able to travel to Boston the following month for his bar mitzvah.

This was an important family event. The whole clan gathered at Temple Mishkan Tefila in Newton, Massachusetts, where our grandparents were congregants. Grandpa, the family patriarch, was frail but in his glory. Daddy, after a lifetime of conflicts with his own father, was probably feeling like a pretty good son himself that day: presenting his own young son to the Torah and stitching together the generations of Bernstein males. Grandma glowed with pride, having her whole family assembled there. This was the first time Alexander and I had ever seen all our Bernstein relatives collected in one place—including many distant cousins we'd never met before. Suddenly we understood the roots of Rybernian: the old-world accents and the nasal shouting were all emanating from this motley bunch.

Whenever we had visited Sam and Jennie Bernstein in the past, our mother could barely disguise her displeasure at her in-laws' tacky, plastic-on-the-living-room-furniture, middle-class, margarine-y Jewish ways, and she'd bristled when they Yiddishized my name to "Jamela." It was not Mummy's world, and now that I was older, I couldn't help seeing everything in Brookline through her eyes. Daddy had more patience; it was, after all, his own background, his own *mishpoche*, and they adored him beyond all measure. But I had the sense that Mummy was holding her breath the whole time we were up there. She tried to be a "good egg," as she would say, but she clearly loathed it. So a part of me loathed it, too, and that was confusing.

In addition, I was picking up on my father's own conflicted feelings about Grandma and Grandpa. Daddy had gone to considerable lengths to prepare his son for the bar mitzvah, which seemed to indicate filial respect—but it was also true that Daddy and his siblings made constant, wicked fun of their parents, particularly their way of speaking. Grandpa, whose thick old-world accent never abated, was the king of malapropisms: "I canceled the trip to Miami; I got cold shoulders." "They song-and-danced me." Grandma, who acquired a nice broad Boston accent, made immortal remarks, as well. In his book *Family Matters*, Uncle BB recalled their maid with a beautiful singing voice whom Grandma called "a regular Florence Nightingale." All these sayings were lovingly collected and recounted—but I sensed a subtext from the three Ivy-educated siblings who had made their own hard-won assimilative leap, while their parents still had one metaphorical foot in the old country. In making the distinction between the generations crystal clear, the three grown children seemed to be conveying just a whisper of . . . disdain.

Alexander, the bar mitzvah boy, was terribly nervous, and not particularly motivated by any spiritual matters; he just knew he had to get through the whole thing to please his father and his grandfather—and he succeeded, nicely.

I got away with not having a bat mitzvah; nobody pressured me, and I certainly didn't request it. It was the one time in my life I was glad that my gender had relegated me to the status of second-class citizen. But I was impressed by the money Alexander received; he walked off with about $800. That came in handy the following year, when he started buying pot.

As soon as the bar mitzvah was behind us, we returned to obsessing over the presidential election. In the absence of Bobby Kennedy, our parents had gravitated to another Democratic candidate, Senator Eugene McCarthy. McCarthy was vociferously against the Vietnam War, and my father provided the campaign with a touching antiwar song written with Betty and Adolph, called "So Pretty," which Barbra Streisand sang as part of a Broadway for Peace concert at Philharmonic Hall. He wrote a second song, this time for a campaign event at Madison Square Garden, that had a more boppy feel: "Are we for Gene McCarthy? *Yeah!*" The refrain was: "Aaaaay-*MEN*." Alexander and I were right there, below the raised stage platform—in the veritable trenches of the antiwar movement.

Eugene McCarthy was the first political candidate I'd ever gotten excited about. That summer, I was a campaign volunteer, doing whatever one did in those messy, switchboard-beeping, typewriter-clattering, paper-choked days. We were convinced we

On tour in Europe in '68, but always campaigning for Eugene McCarthy.

were changing the world, over at the campaign headquarters in Columbus Circle.

Now that I was older, summers in Fairfield were less appealing. I wanted to stay in the city with my friends, but my mother wasn't comfortable leaving me all alone in our apartment. Then a wonderful solution presented itself: Shirley gave me an open invitation to stay with her in her cozy apartment on West 55th Street. At the time, Shirley was working in a theatrical agency, and had become quite the dashing career woman, constantly reading scripts and talking deals over the phone.

That summer, while we devoured triple-decker sandwiches delivered from the Sixth Avenue Delicatessen, I would regale Shirley with stories about my girlfriends and my boy troubles. She always had plentiful advice for every situation. "I minored in psychology at Mount Holyoke, you know," she would remind me.

I never stopped to think too carefully about why, if Shirley was so full of wisdom about my love life, she never seemed to have one of her own. She told me she'd once been engaged to someone, but then she noticed that his bare leg was visible between his trouser cuff and his sock—and concluded upon the instant that she had to break off the engagement. That sure sounded like she was looking for any excuse to flee.

And who could blame her, really? Where was the man out there who could provide a fraction of the warmth, the hilarity, the sheer comfort of her own brother?—to say nothing of the talent and the brilliance. And the good looks.

For Shirley, never getting married had its distinct benefits. She was an embedded member of her older brother's family, reveling in all the goodies—the dinners, the holidays, the country house, the children—while bearing none of the responsibilities. She had, somewhat by accident, found a legitimate way to remain a subadult for the duration of her adult life. At the time, however, what I saw was a clever career woman with cool clothes, a sweet apartment, and her devoted, malodorous basset hound, Daisy. I couldn't see what was wrong with any of that.

*   *   *

The year 1968 was a big one for my father: not only was he turning fifty, but he was changing his position at the New York Philharmonic from full-time music director to something the orchestra management invented to make sure he'd come back on a regular basis, called conductor laureate. This new relationship was going to give him more time to compose, which was what he said he wanted to do more than anything. But the transition wouldn't be official until the following spring. First up was a tour through Europe and Israel with the Philharmonic, beginning right on his fiftieth birthday. So before he left, Mummy threw him a big party in Fairfield, with a tent set up behind the house. For the occasion, I outdid myself in the birthday-show department. This time, I composed most of the songs myself. I tortured poor Alexander, forcing him to sing the tunes against my harmonies. "One of us is flat," I would say tactfully during our rehearsals.

Looking back on this birthday party, I'm astonished by my chutzpah in getting up in front of all my parents' friends—those illustrious friends—to regale them with my Daddy-roasting sketches and songs. One song, called "Fastest Beast in the East," was about that silver Maserati he had acquired in Italy the summer before, which turned out to be a lemon and was nothing but trouble:

> *The morning sun shines on my face,*
> *I'm getting looks from everyplace:*

"Hey—there's Leonard Bernstein the movie star,
And man oh man, look at his car."
Ho-hum, I say, an average day
In my Masera-ti, my Masera-ti, my Masera-ti . . .

Alexander's big number in the show was "Haf Torah Will Travel," in which he recited, verbatim, Daddy's explanation of the project he'd been working on all that year with Jerry Robbins: an ambitious musical based on a play by Bertolt Brecht. Every dinner guest of the last several months had been subjected to this long description—which was how Alexander and I had learned it by heart. Our gimmick for the birthday show: Alexander chanted Daddy's description to the cantillation from his bar mitzvah the month before. That brought the house down.

But Daddy was depressed about turning fifty. It spooked him. He'd given notice at the Philharmonic, and now he was going to compose like mad. But there was trouble already with the Brecht musical; it wasn't coming together. His turmoil over that show was intertwined with his despair about the country. He supported Eugene McCarthy, but the senator wouldn't take a hard line on gun control—even after the two ghastly assassinations that year. Daddy couldn't sleep, couldn't compose, and he talked openly and incessantly about it. A few months later, the Brecht show was abandoned altogether—yet another stillbirth, like the one my father had experienced with *Skin of Our Teeth* four years earlier.

*   *   *

In November, Election Day arrived at last. Eugene McCarthy was long gone. Weakly, we rooted for Hubert Humphrey, but it was hard to be enthusiastic for someone we viewed as a glad-handing party hack—and anyway, he lost: to Richard Nixon. Once again, the grownups were drinking and crying.

That same November, my father made a special arrangement with Columbia Records and his longtime record producer, John McClure, for me to record those songs I'd written for the fiftieth birthday. I found myself in a real, professional recording studio, playing the guitar I'd found in the closet five years earlier, singing into a fancy microphone, getting McClure's instructions over the loudspeaker while he and my father sat in the control room behind the glass panel. Was this actually happening?

Our parents arranged for the pressing of a couple hundred copies of *Daddy's 50th Birthday*, and gave the record to all their friends for Christmas. It had a black-and-white Columbia Records label on it, and the cover showed Alexander, Nina, and me seated at the mirrored table in the Casino Fancy dining room, so that our images were reflected in the table, upside down. At school, this record got me almost more attention than I could handle, leaving me with a sickening combination of emotions: immense excitement, along with a creeping discomfort about inviting comparisons with the more illustrious musician in my house.

My various teenage preoccupations left me with little remaining bandwidth to process the next big family event: that spring, Grandpa died. Back we went to Boston, with a funeral instead of a bar mitzvah at Temple Mishkan Tefila, a graveside ceremony, and yet another gathering of the motley relatives in my grandparents' parlor. I suspected my father was feeling, above all, relief that his complex relationship with *his* father had drawn to an acceptable conclusion.

They'd had a rough ride. There were the boyhood tussles over the piano lessons; the pressure on young Lenny to take over the family business; the intensity of Sam's Talmudic fervor combined with his cold, punishing ways with Jennie; the constant bitter squabbling over money. On the other hand, he'd taken his eldest son to synagogue on Friday nights, where Lenny experienced his first thrill of live musical performance. It's no accident that the notes of the shofar, the ram's horn blown on high holy days, appear in several Bernstein works—including the three notes that provide the key to the entire score of *West Side Story*. The cantillation of the rabbis provided my father with rich material, as well; those ancient melodies show up in his Symphony no. 1, *Jeremiah*, which he'd pointedly dedicated to his father. It was through his music, really, that Daddy found the most success in working out his complex father issues—all confusingly interwoven with his equally complicated feelings about God.

After Sam's death, Grandma went on to have a rich extra chapter in her own life, unencumbered by a bleak marriage: just hanging out with her two remaining sisters, Bertha and Dorothy—"the Three Fates," Daddy and his siblings called the trio. They went everywhere together—even, one day, to the White House.

Right on the heels of Grandpa's funeral came another conclusory event: my father's last official concert as music director of the New York Philharmonic. The incoming new conductor was to be Pierre Boulez, a Frenchman who composed notoriously difficult atonal music and whom Daddy considered a bit grand, a bit arrogant and chilly. The Philharmonic could not possibly have found a sharper contrast to Leonard Bernstein.

The whole family and all the close friends showed up at Philharmonic Hall for the emotional evening. The last movement of Mahler's Third Symphony seemed to linger beyond time itself, as if the musicians and their conductor were lovers who couldn't bear to part. The president of the Philharmonic presented my father with a set of keys to a high-speed motorboat, christened the *Laureate*: their thank-you gift to him. They certainly knew their maestro.

After the performance, we were all crammed into Daddy's dressing room, waiting as usual for him to be ready to leave. Finally he was showered and dressed, and the group started walking up the corridor. The last one out of the dressing room was Uncle Mikey Mindlin, who came bustling toward us, his arms loaded with toilet paper rolls and piles of hand towels from the dispenser in the bathroom. "We leave Boulez *nothing*!" he proclaimed.

9

Stone Teen

Felicia vamping in Jamie's bedroom on Park Avenue.

By now I was about as tall (short) as my mother, and she was generous about letting me borrow her beautiful clothes. But I couldn't shake the feeling that I was a hopeless clod: that I would never be elegant or graceful or have a clever aesthetic eye like my mother. In a lifelong recurring dream, I'm pawing through my clothes, trying to find something appropriate to wear to my father's concert. When at last I put on an outfit, Mummy looks at me and says, as she so often did in my youth: "You're not going out in _that_."

It was easier to identify with my father, who was more spontaneous, less critical.

One trait of his I'd hoped to inherit was his confidence. My mother may have had an unerring visual sense, but she had those fears. The stage fright. The self-consciousness about playing the piano in front of my father. The fear of heights, and airplanes. All of this, combined with her inevitable role as family policeman and Lenny stabilizer, made her less fun to be around—and I didn't aspire to becoming such a person. Daddy, by contrast, was a daredevil: he loved roller coasters, fast boats, vertiginous ski slopes. He shared vaudeville jokes and radio jingles and recited Lewis Carroll. Who wouldn't prefer to be like *him*?

When I was in eleventh grade, Mike Nichols invited my mother, whom he adored, to replace the actress Margaret Leighton in his Broadway revival of Lillian Hellman's play *The Little Foxes* when it went on tour. She played the fragile character Birdie, who was fond of her elderberry wine. My mother was wonderful in this role, and we were thrilled that she was acting again. Despite her return to the stage, I wrote an English class essay that year asserting that I'd inherited all my artistic tendencies from my father. I got a good grade on the paper, and proudly showed it to my parents. Afterward, Mummy confronted me. We were standing in Daddy's studio, ironically enough, when she told me how stung she'd been by what I'd written. Was *she* not a creative artist: a pianist, a painter, a working actress? Her tone was so plaintive; I was sick at heart over what I'd done—not just because I'd hurt her feelings, but also because I'd been caught in an unconscious, unseemly act of favoritism.

But it was hard not to buy into the Bernstein family's own mythos: hard to resist the dynamism of its larger-than-life chief representative. I liked thinking of myself as a true Bernstein— even if I didn't have all the characteristics. For example, I lacked

After school, still in Brearley uniform, seeking advice in LB's studio.

the "Bernstein chest"—chronic respiratory problems like asthma and bronchitis, which Alexander had—and the Hebraically prominent "Bernstein nose," visible principally in the men. But when it came to the "Bernstein stomach"—that perennially gaseous, noise-generating mechanism—I was blessed with that one.

All the Bernstein self-mythologizing must have been exhausting for my mother. I don't recall her attributing any shared characteristics to herself and her two sisters. She loved them, but the three women didn't have that obsessive closeness that my father had with his brother and sister. Mummy was able to leave her sisters behind in Chile, and move all the way north to New York—whereas my father and his siblings never put more than a handful of miles between one another.

It was my mother's fate to be repeatedly cast in the thankless role of the lone grownup supervising a sandbox full of quasi-adults. It was the Bernstein siblings' childlike exuberance that made them so irresistible, but it also made them exhausting to be around so much of the time. Maybe Mummy was starting to weary of it.

When I wrote in that essay that I was like my father, perhaps what I might have better clarified was that I was, above all, *obnoxious* like my father. I was so bossy, so excitable and loud. Still, I had my fans. Steve Sondheim was, incredibly, one of them. We obsessed together over the genius of singer-songwriter Laura Nyro. I learned so much about songwriting by listening to Steve describing what made Nyro's songs so terrific: how she'd tweak a phrase so it was different the second time it came around; or how, in the closing section, just when you thought nothing new was going to happen, she'd suddenly shift to a new melody in a new key, and make you gasp as if you'd opened the door onto a bright, windy day.

Steve introduced me to a photographer friend of his, Simon: twenty-six, handsome, a dead ringer for the actor Tony Perkins. Steve knew I'd be excited that Simon was photographing Laura Nyro for her upcoming album, *New York Tendaberry*. It was arranged for me to accompany Simon to one of Laura's nighttime recording sessions. This was heady stuff. Simon the photographer picked me up in a cab, and then picked up someone else, and then we went to where Laura lived. We were instructed to wait in the cab while Simon fetched her. He was gone for a long, long . . . long time. It was uncomfortable, sitting in the cab with a person I didn't know, making forced small talk and waiting for Simon to come back out with Laura Nyro. When they finally appeared, I was beyond shy. I was grateful, in a way, that Laura barely addressed me.

The recording session focused on a small slice of the song "Mercy on Broadway." It was the usual recording studio mixture of fascinating and excruciatingly tedious. These were the halcyon days of Columbia Records, when pop artists got all the time and money and session players they could ever want—and Laura Nyro made the most of it. There was a story going around about the ten trumpet players she'd demanded to play the single note at the end of "Save the Country." But at the time of the session I attended, apparently what was mainly going on for Laura Nyro was a lot of heroin—which may have accounted in some way for her delay in coming down to the cab.

That evening seemed all of a piece with a new thing that was happening to me. I'd finally quit my piano lessons the year before, and now I was creeping back to the piano on my own and writing songs—very Laura Nyro–esque songs, in fact, full of passion and wailing. I wrote a stormy song called "Dear God" that ended this way:

> *Dear God, I wish you were everywhere.*
> *There must be someone that I can turn to*
> *Instead of you . . .*
> *But who?*

I would play my new songs for my friends at school—craving their compliments, even as I dreaded their contempt for my showing off.

But playing my songs for Daddy was toughest of all. I would stumble on the piano keys, mangle chords on the guitar, forget my lyrics. When he gave me his suffocating hug at the end, I could hardly bear it: Did I deserve the praise, or was he just being an indulgent dad? And if he had any advice or criticism at all, I would crumble in disappointment. He probably knew how vulnerable I felt—but my discomfort was built-in, unavoidable.

Being a high school senior provided some escape; my busy life and thick welter of friends were a perfect distraction from my private fears. Collectively we seniors felt, finally, like we owned the city.

Those were the glory days of the Fillmore East. I saw Crosby, Stills & Nash there, and Steve Miller, and Jethro Tull. I still felt just a little young for it all; it was like hanging on for dear life on a very fast ride. One night an unknown English guy was opening for Leon Russell. I was electrified by this performer: his songs were brilliant, and he played the piano and sang with a galvanic energy that had me screaming with excitement. Afterward, I raised my forefinger in the air and solemnly predicted to my friends: "This guy is gonna be as big as the Beatles." And little Elton John didn't do badly for himself, at that.

When we went to the Fillmore to see Blood, Sweat & Tears, Daddy came along. It was pretty loud for him, but he loved the excitement of the music, the kids, the huge old vaudeville theater reeking of pot. "Because Daddy was Daddy," as I used to put it, we got to go backstage, and even took turns working the psychedelic gels in the famous Joshua Light Show.

My friends and I were obsessed with the Who's rock opera *Tommy*. When we went to see the Who perform it at the Fillmore, I brought my father along yet again; he was a big *Tommy* fan. Like me, he was thrilled by the sheer ambition of it: the long form, the grandiosity. And they even used French horns. I was proud to share my music with my father; he was so interested, so responsive. While my parents' friends mostly turned up their noses at their kids' music, my dad was actively embracing it. Sometimes he was even ahead of me; he liked the Rolling Stones far better than I did in the beginning, because he understood the context of their rough edges: their blues roots. Back then, I just thought they sounded messy.

No one else among my friends was bringing their parents with them to the Fillmore. But then, neither were any of those parents composing an orchestral piece with rock music in it. My father by this point was already working on his theater piece *Mass*, which would inaugurate the opening of the Kennedy Center in Washington two years later. So when he went to the Fillmore, he was taking notes, in a sense—although I didn't realize it at the time.

After the Fillmore concerts, our friend Willie from Hong Kong often took us over to Chinatown, where we'd have delicious three a.m. meals that he'd order for us in Cantonese. Although there were no cell phones back then, it would not have been that hard to find a pay phone to call home and say I'd be out late with my friends—but I hated doing it. One night I got home at five a.m., and my mother was waiting for me, wild-eyed and spectral in her bathrobe, beside herself with that toxic parental brew of worry and fury. "*I was about to call the police!*" Both Alexander and I pulled this stunt several times. We were terrible.

Alexander had started smoking things not long after I did—in fact, my friend Linn and I turned my brother on to pot, just as Linn's younger brother Richard had turned us on. Richard heard somewhere that waving a magnet in front of a color TV would ruin the color, so of course he had to try it on the big, hulking color TV in his parents' bedroom. Linn and I would watch *Star Trek* sitting on her parents' bed, stoned as could be and never sure if the peculiar colors were in our heads or the result of Richard's magnet. (It was the magnet.)

The pot was so friendly, so connecting. The ritual of it, the sharing. It was always best with my girlfriends. The mad giggles, the late-night munchies, the secret knowledge in public places. And best of all, listening to music: being transported by sound. The year before I started smoking pot, I sat at my father's desk in his studio one night with the Doors' "Light My Fire" cranked up on his powerful stereo, imagining what a pot party would be like. During the song's long, spacey instrumental break, I wrote a poem about losing myself in the rhythm and trance of that music. I was getting myself high by imagining being high before I'd even gotten high.

And then there were the cigarettes. I started smoking them because Linn smoked, and I wanted to do everything Linn did. But the bigger picture was that *everybody* smoked cigarettes—starting with my parents, but also Shirley, and Uncle BB, and Mike Nichols and Steve Sondheim and Betty and Adolph (although in a form of quitting, Adolph chewed unlit cigarettes for years). A perennial sight in every household was the spreading brown-orange stain of a discarded cigarette in the toilet. We smoked Marlboros and Kools, Winstons and Camels. Daddy smoked L&Ms; Mummy smoked Chesterfields (filterless, for crying out loud). Smoking made me feel elegant, urbane, graceful: adult. Plus, it gave you something to do with your hands. It woke you up, stirred your bowels, bonded you with your friends. What *didn't* cigarettes do? The answer: much for your health. But who thinks about such things at the age of fifteen? Our parents scolded us for smoking—but they knew how hypocritical they sounded.

Pot, cigarettes, and sex. At the school lunch table, sex was all anybody talked about. All my girlfriends seemed to be losing their virginity, but I hadn't. I felt that if I didn't hurry up and sleep with someone, my friends were going to start thinking I was what we termed a Stupid Idiot—something I secretly feared I was.

One Friday night that senior year, I was alone in the New York apartment while the rest of the family was up in Fairfield. (Now that I was a high school senior, my mother deemed it safe to leave me in the city on my own.) I was playing Daddy's piano in his studio downstairs, feeling a little spooked, writing that "Dear God" song and putting myself in a dangerous frame of mind. The phone rang and it was Simon the photographer, asking if I wanted to drop by his place a few blocks away. It was already ten p.m., so I called my parents in Fairfield, told them I was going to bed, and wished them good night. Then I left the house.

That night I lost my virginity. It was awkward, painful, and conducted in pitch-blackness. There wasn't a shred of comfort or emotional connection, or even the slightest acknowledgment of what was going on. All I kept saying to myself in that darkness was: Wait'll I tell Ann. Wait'll I tell Ann.

Things never progressed beyond that one encounter with Simon, but more action was just around the corner. My all-girl school, Brearley, and Alexander's all-boy school, Collegiate, collaborated on a coed senior drama production of *Guys & Dolls*. Since so many of our pals were Collegiate boys, a few of us girls decided to meet them at the auditions, "just for a goof." To our astonishment, we all got cast. Ann got a role in the chorus, and my friend Debbie and I walked off with the two leading female roles.

The *Guys & Dolls* production became our social hub. After Saturday rehearsals, we all went back to my place (my whole family being reliably up in Fairfield) and partied for hours. I was in the habit of making bourbon sours in the Waring blender, batch after batch. Neither my mother nor Julia ever made close inquiries about my weekend activities—and they either never checked on or didn't care about the dwindling levels in the Old Grand-Dad bottles.

As Christmas vacation began, our whole extended bunch of friends was celebrating at our hangout, Malachy's, on 75th and Lexington, where the proprietor could not have cared less that we were underage high school students. The boys were singing into ketchup bottles Mick Jagger—style as the Stones played on the jukebox. I walked back up to 79th Street between two handsome Collegiate guys, Andy on one side and Nick on the other. We went upstairs to my empty apartment, and I think I was on the rug, making out with both of them by turns. Which one would I end up with?

Andy finally bowed out, and Nick spent the night. And so began my first really big—and thoroughly disastrous—love affair.

Nick was tall and slim, with aviator glasses and bushy hair. I thought he was dreamy, in a pleasingly New York Jewish way. He told me he was a famous author's nephew, but this proved to be a lie.

Our mad love sucked the oxygen out of every room we occupied. Nick would make out with me everywhere we went; it made me uncomfortable, but I was powerless to speak up. "Well, we've cleared another room!" he would joke. I felt a twinge of sadness when my own friends moved away from us, but I was spellbound, paralyzed.

My parents didn't think much of Nick. Ordinarily that would have bothered me, but I was past caring. Julia soon figured out that Nick and I were sleeping together. She was appalled. "How you can give yourself to *that man*?" she would say to me. The only grownup I confided in was Shirley, who loved being the repository of my secrets; I sensed that it gave her some kind of power in the family dynamic. But I couldn't think about that too much, either. I couldn't think . . . at all.

Nick wasn't in *Guys & Dolls*, and it galled him no end. All his friends had gone to that audition, but he hadn't bothered, thinking it would be lame. Now Nick was the odd man out, and jealous of all the fun we were having without him.

He liked it better when I tagged along to watch him play the drums at a school dance. I would stand to the side, admiring his cool-ness, but also feeling a little bored, or jealous, or something. Why wasn't I feeling fulfilled? Didn't I want to be just like my mother and cheer on my brilliant man? Wasn't that how a loving, worshipful girlfriend ought to act? Nick certainly seemed to think so.

As my romance blossomed in January, both my parents were busy. My father was preparing two operas at once: *Cavalleria Rusticana* at the Met, and a concert performance of *Fidelio* at the Philharmonic. He'd rehearse one opera in the morning, then walk around the Lincoln Center fountain and rehearse the other opera in the afternoon. Meanwhile, my mother's longtime involvement in human rights issues had reached a new level. Through her work with the American Civil Liberties Union and the Committee for Public Justice, she'd agreed to organize and host a fund-raising event to assist the families of twenty-one men in the Black Panther Party who were in jail, with unfairly inflated bail amounts, await-ing trial for what turned out to be trumped-up accusations involv-ing absurd bomb plots around New York City. My mother's dual purpose was to raise money for a legal defense fund and to help the men's families stay fed and sheltered until the trial came around. (And when the trial finally did come around, the judge threw the whole case out for being unsubstantiated and patently ridiculous.)

To most white Americans at the time, the Black Panthers were scary. They were socialist, they advocated Black empowerment "by any means necessary," and they were anti-Zionist, which had considerable negative resonance in New York City. So it was auda-cious of my mother to advocate on their behalf. But she understood better than most how politicians exploited the image of a group like the Panthers to pander to white voters, and how the news me-dia turned the volume up on fear to boost readership and ratings. What my mother didn't know at the time—none of us did, until much later—was how intensively the FBI was inflaming the entire situation for their own purposes.

My mother pointedly did not invite any press to the fund-raiser, but the society writer for the *New York Times*, Charlotte Curtis, managed to sneak in, as did a rascally young journalist named Tom Wolfe.

I myself had absolutely no interest in the Panthers or in my mother's efforts on their behalf. On that day, I was hiding downstairs, and so only later learned that after an hour of snacks and drinks, my mother had introduced the Panther representatives and invited them to speak about their situation and solicit support from the assembled guests. At some point in the proceedings, my father arrived from his *Fidelio* rehearsal and joined the gathering. He wound up having an exchange with Panther representative Donald Cox, during which he asked questions and Cox explained the Panther philosophy further. In the corner, Tom Wolfe was silently ingesting all of it, like a python gradually swallowing a rabbit whole.

Afterward, I found my parents together in my father's studio downstairs. They were pleased at how things had gone; my mother had raised nearly $10,000, a terrific take in those days. She sat in Daddy's lap, something she almost never did. They both looked tired but happy. I saw them as they saw themselves in that moment: Lenny working hard, making music, spreading beauty in a tough world—and Felicia, with her passion for social justice, representing their joint commitment to a nation that protected all of its citizens. I could feel how they felt right then: united, aligned, purposeful, loving.

They probably never felt quite that good together again.

The next morning, Charlotte Curtis's story appeared in the society section of the *Times*. It was filled with scorn for the Manhattan socialite wife of the Maestro, hobnobbing with Black Panthers:

Felicia, LB, and Black Panther Field Marshal Donald Cox.

Leonard Bernstein and a Black Panther leader argued the merits of the Black Panther Party's philosophy before nearly 90 guests at a cocktail party last night in the Bernsteins' elegant Park Avenue duplex. The conductor . . . did most of the questioning. Donald Cox, the Panther field-marshal . . . did most of the answering, and there were even moments when both men were not talking at the same time.

Even worse, the article quoted the Maestro out of context. As my father explained it later, he'd asked Donald Cox some question about Panther philosophy, and Cox ended his answer with the phrase "You dig?" Daddy, in his typical way, picked up the word and tossed it back at Cox, saying, "I dig, absolutely, but . . ." and then went on to refine his question. Charlotte Curtis merely quoted Leonard Bernstein saying, "I dig absolutely," which made him sound like a pathetic, middle-aged guy trying to act groovy. Everything about this article was loathsome, and my parents were both aghast.

But that was just the beginning.

The day after that, the *Times* followed up the Charlotte Curtis piece with an editorial.

Emergence of the Black Panthers as the romanticized darlings of the politico-cultural jet set is an affront to the majority of . . . those blacks and whites seriously working for complete equality and social justice. It mocked the memory of Martin Luther King Jr. . . . .

The word "shitstorm" had not yet been coined, but that is what the situation now became. Lenny and Felicia's own friends were criticizing them for what they had done. Uncle BB was furious at Mummy; he felt she'd taken a foolish stance against the Jews and Israel and didn't speak to her for months. My classmate Kathie, who was both black and Jewish, strode up to me during recess and hotly announced that she would never come over to my house again; her Jewish side was apparently the more outraged. I was surprised Kathie didn't join the noisy Jewish Defense League picketers outside the entrance to 895 Park Avenue; I had to thread my way through them to get back into the building after school. (Not until the 1980s did we learn that most of those picketers were FBI plants. What was more, the hate mail piling up on my father's desk had also been churned out by the FBI.)

My mother wrote a furious letter to the *Times*:

As a civil libertarian, I asked a number of people to my house on Jan. 14 in order to hear the lawyer and others involved with the Panther 21 discuss the problem of civil liberties as applicable to the men now awaiting trial, and to help raise funds for their legal expenses . . . It was for this deeply serious purpose that our meeting was called. The frivolous way in which it was reported as a "fashionable" event is unworthy of *The Times*, and offensive to all people who are committed to humanitarian principles of justice.

She delivered her letter to the *Times* by hand on the same day the editorial ran, but they didn't print it until five days later. By then, it was too late for her message to make any impact.

My parents were the butt of ridicule, all over New York City and beyond. Mummy was very pale and quiet over her morning coffee. Daddy buried himself in his pair of operas. I buried myself into my boyfriend Nick. And still it wasn't over.

The following month, when our final *Guys & Dolls* rehearsals went into overdrive, my parents were in Europe, where my father was conducting the Verdi *Requiem* in London and *Fidelio* in Rome. They were going to miss my pair of performances as Sarah Brown, the mission doll.

Our show was a smash. After the Friday night performance, there was a cast party at Debbie's town house on East 85th Street. We were feeling like veritable teenage gods walking the earth. When Steve, my Sky Masterson, walked into the party, I yelled out, Mick Jagger–style, *"Well, ALL RIGHT!!"* Everyone cheered and whooped—everyone except Nick, who grabbed me by the hand and said, "Come with me." He took me to the top floor of the town house, sat me down on Debbie's bed, and earnestly explained to me that I was "loud and obnoxious," nobody liked it, and I would have to change my ways. "Oh Nick, oh Nick, I'm sorry," I wept. He took me in his arms and told me he loved me and would help me improve my conduct. I dried off my face as best I could and went back downstairs, but I was too shaken to enjoy the party anymore.

The second and final performance the following night was even more spectacular than the first. This time the cast party was at my place—chaperoned by Shirley and her best friend, Ofra. The two ladies stayed downstairs watching TV in my parents' room while "the kids" reveled upstairs.

Finally, around two a.m., the last guests were straggling out. As my pal Dick (Nathan Detroit) was saying good-bye at the front door, he spontaneously swept me up and gave me a big wet kiss on the mouth. We were just fooling around: we were actors! And pretty drunk besides. But as Dick got in the elevator, I turned around to behold Nick, pale as death, his eyes black pools of fury. He grabbed me by the wrist and marched me into the library, closing the double doors behind us. "How could you do that to me? What are you, some kind of *whore*?" And he slapped my face, again and again, as I sank lower and lower into a chair. He was raging, howling at me, and I was sobbing, "Oh Nick, oh Nick." The library doors burst open and Ann came running in with Steve, who was a football player, an enormous guy, and he hauled Nick away from me. Then Shirley and Ofra came running in. Steve dragged Nick, still roaring like a bull, out of the house. Shirley made a late-night transatlantic call to Europe. All I could think was: Oh no, Nick is mad at me.

Mummy dashed home from Europe to deal with the crisis. Nick was banned from the house, but Mummy knew I'd see him elsewhere. She said to me, "I can't prevent you from seeing Nick, but at least I can keep you from getting pregnant." And she took me to a doctor to get me on birth control pills.

Despite her loathing of Nick, Mummy arranged for him to meet a physician she knew who was helping young men secure the coveted 4-F draft status that would relieve them of serving in Vietnam. The draft was a terrifying specter hanging over every teenage boy's head in those days. (Girls didn't get drafted.) My mother's coming to Nick's aid was a particularly poignant manifestation of her seriousness of purpose; she didn't believe in that war, and she wasn't going to stand by and watch young men be shipped off to their deaths if she could help it. Even if one of those young men happened to be someone she couldn't abide.

Meanwhile, I was applying to college. It was the last thing on my mind. I had no interest in changing my life: leaving Brearley, New York, my friends, or my family. Or Nick. Neither of my parents took me on campus visits; of the four colleges I applied to, I visited only Radcliffe, on my own. At the time, Radcliffe was somewhat uncomfortably merging with Harvard—so going to Radcliffe would mean, in effect, that I'd be going to my father's beloved alma mater. That was certainly his wish, and his expectation.

I didn't see much of Daddy that year, but when he was home, our best moments were late at night, running into each other in the kitchen. We'd have long just-us-awake-in-the-world conversations while I made tea and toast, and Daddy spooned baby food straight out of the jar, or he would make a hole at both ends of a raw egg and suck out the innards.

Often, in the morning, I would find a piece of paper slipped under my door with a British-style crossword puzzle clue that Daddy had made up in the night:

This conductor toils madly! (5)

(Answer: SOLTI—the renowned conductor—an anagram of TOILS.)

When my graduation rolled around in early June, Daddy was away again, triumphantly conducting *Fidelio* in Vienna. His career seemed centered in Europe now; he was away more than he was home. It was starting to bug me in earnest that he kept missing my important events.

The very week of my Brearley graduation, Tom Wolfe's infamous "Radical Chic" article appeared in *New York* magazine, with the title "That Party at Lenny's." My mother's very serious fundraiser had become her celebrity husband's "party." When Wolfe's article came out soon afterward in book form with the title *Radical Chic*, the misinterpretation and mockery were set in stone.

It's likely that to this day, Tom Wolfe may not understand the degree to which his snide little piece of neo-journalism rendered him a veritable stooge for the FBI. J. Edgar Hoover himself may well have shed a tear of gratitude that this callow journalist had done so much of the bureau's work by discrediting left-wing New York Jewish liberals while simultaneously pitting them against the black activist movement—thereby disempowering both groups in a single deft stroke.

Nor may Wolfe truly comprehend the depth of the damage he wreaked on my family. Maybe not so much on my father, who suffered embarrassment but could immerse himself in his various musical activities, most of which weren't even in the United States. No, it was my mother who bore the brunt of the humiliation, anchored as she was in New York, with no illustrious career of her own to cushion the blow. *Little Foxes* had come and gone; she'd gone back to being Mrs. Maestro—and now, this was her reward.

After that year, Mummy grew increasingly dejected and discouraged. The lines on the sides of her mouth pulled ever downward. She would stare into space in a way that made my stomach turn over, and I would have to look away. Four years later, Mummy was diagnosed with cancer and underwent a mastectomy—still a primitive act of surgical butchery at the time. Four years after that, she was dead of the disease, at fifty-six. Even now, my rage and disgust can rise up in me like an old fever—and in those nearly deranged moments, it doesn't seem like such a stretch to lay Mummy's precipitous decline, and even demise, at the feet of Mr. Wolfe.

One Toe Out of the Nest

Sledding in Central Park during Harvard winter break.

I did get accepted into Radcliffe/Harvard—but by then, I'd cooked up the great idea to attend NYU, which would keep me in New York City near my family, but above all near Nick, who'd been accepted into Columbia. "What are you talking about?" Daddy said when I told him. "You're going to Harvard—best school in the world!" End of discussion. It was one of the few times I can remember my father acting like a traditional, assertive parent.

Sometime that spring, I'd received a remarkable invitation: to act (and sing!) in a film Milos Forman was directing called _Taking Off_—in which a group of young singer-songwriters participate in an audition. Maybe I got the offer through the playwright John Guare, who was writing the screenplay; he'd worked with my father and Jerry Robbins on the stillborn Brecht musical project a couple of years earlier, and had probably heard me sing at Daddy's fiftieth birthday. Anyway, the contract lay on my desk for several weeks while I pondered whether to sign on the dotted line or take a summer job as a "guide" at Tanglewood, the Boston Symphony Orchestra's summer home in the Berkshire Hills of western Massachusetts. My father, who had participated in Tanglewood since its founding in the 1940s, was able to pull some strings and get Nick a job there, too. If I went to Tanglewood, Nick and I would be together. If I did the movie, we'd be separated—plus, crucially, I'd be getting a lot of attention, and Nick would not. I knew that wouldn't go well for us. He was already bitter that my college was grander than his.

I turned down the movie and went to Tanglewood to be with Nick: to be with his doe eyes and hippie cool, his wounded rage and slim-hipped New York intensity. I knew no one could stand him but me. I was grateful that my family seemed to have resigned themselves to his presence.

The decision felt like a safer one in another way, as well. When Nick informed me that no one liked my being "loud and obnoxious," he may not have known that his criticism echoed my deepest fears. There was a palpable vertigo that came along with all the attention I'd received in school for my record, for *Guys & Dolls*, for writing the senior show. What if my friends thought I was conceited? What if they stopped liking me?

At home, Mummy shushed and scolded us if we got too loud or acted too self-important. The unspoken message was that there was only one person in the family who got to be an annoying show-off, and that person got away with it because He Was a Genius. Nick was unwittingly echoing my mother's subliminal message that too much showing off was, for the rest of us mortals, unacceptable behavior.

So yes, there was some comfort and safety in shunning the spotlight. Life was changing fast, and maybe I just needed to hunker down for the summer with my job and my boyfriend. As for that outgoing part of me, the part that really did like to jump around and draw attention to myself—well, I was just going to put that troublesome creature in a little box and seal it up. Tight.

The Berkshires were beautiful, but the Tanglewood job was exhausting. Guides did everything from giving tours of the grounds, to standing guard backstage, to giving directions at the front and back gates. Nick and I had frequent fights. One particularly tearful episode ensued when he caught me deliberately spoiling my winning hand of gin rummy so as not to beat him yet again. I devoured buckets of Colonel Sanders fried chicken, and felt my body thickening.

I took it upon myself to do Nick's laundry along with mine. Ironing his shirts made me feel very wifely. But I discovered it was quite boring to iron all those shirts. Wasn't I supposed to like it? What was the matter with me?

Tanglewood tried a new thing that year: they invited the Fillmore East to present three rock concerts in the big open-air Shed with its copious surrounding lawn. The day of each concert, a convoy of yellow Ryder trucks would roll into the backstage area and its occupants set up enormous quantities of equipment, including stacks of Marshall speakers capable of blowing the hair off the hippies at the farthest reaches of the lawn. I was assigned to backstage duty on the night of the Who concert. The crowd was enormous, and the music so deafening it was an out-of-body experience—especially where I was, crouched between two towers of speakers, directly behind bass player John Entwistle. Midconcert, a shiny black june bug crawled in front of me along the stage floor. I was fixated on this large insect, lumbering obliviously into the middle of that titanic human event. Then, just as obliviously, Entwistle took a step backward, and the heel of his mighty black boot came down squarely on the june bug. So cosmic, man!

The grounds were so torn up after the Fillmore concerts that Tanglewood ended that experiment permanently. But after the Who concert, I made off with a great prize: Roger Daltrey's sweat-drenched snakeskin-pattern fringed polyester shirt, which he'd ripped in two midway through the show, and which I worshipfully fished out of the wastebasket in his dressing room.

Alexander was also at Tanglewood that summer, working as a gofer to run back and forth across the campus with messages and documents. He was fifteen, had cascades of curly brown hair, and was stoned nearly all the time, shuffling around the Tanglewood grounds with his torn jeans and his one and only ornament: a graying shoelace permanently tied around his neck. Alexander was sweet and cute and everyone loved him—particularly the slightly older women. Everyone at Tanglewood did not love Nick. I alone loved Nick—fiercely, toxically, relentlessly.

Tanglewood and Leonard Bernstein had entwined histories. He was in the summer festival's first conducting class there in 1940. Thirty years later, Daddy was still devoted to Tanglewood, and most summers he was up there at some point, teaching "the Kids," as he called the student orchestra, and conducting. The summer I worked there, I observed how Daddy's arrival turned the place into an adulation machine. Oh, how they carried on over him! His Sunday afternoon concert with the Boston Symphony attracted a huge mob; the lawn was packed with picnickers. It never rained on Daddy's big concert days; the Tanglewood staff called it "Lenny weather." Daddy's magic was on extra-bright display at Tangle-wood, and I was seeing it up close in a way I never had before. He was a *superstar* up there. I found it a little disconcerting.

Composer and conductor Lukas Foss was at Tanglewood that summer, as well; he and my father had been friends since they'd attended the Curtis Institute together, decades earlier. Lukas was a dashing flirt, and my fellow guides whispered about his late-night carryings-on with the female students in the Curtis Hotel swimming pool.

The guides also seemed to know a lot of stories about Leonard Bernstein's wild youth at Tanglewood—including his amorous escapades with other men. This brought me up quite short; you weren't supposed to hear such things about your own father. There were tales of moonlit naked swims in the lake, scurryings between practice cabins.

They talked about it quite casually in front of me, so I pretended I knew all about it—but I didn't. I mentally reviewed past experiences; had I sensed, or observed, anything to indicate that my father was homosexual? He was extravagantly affectionate with everyone: young and old, male and female. How could I possibly tell what any behavior meant? And anyway, weren't homosexuals supposed to be girly? There were plenty of attractively effeminate men among my parents' friends, and often I'd develop crushes on them. When I'd tell my mother, she would say, "But, Jamie—he's queer as a coot!" Yet there was nothing I could detect that was particularly effeminate about my father. How exactly did he fit into this category? I was bewildered and upset. I couldn't understand any of it—but in any case, my own existence seemed living proof that the story was not a simple one.

The guides' stories, combined with my hurt feelings over Daddy's missing my recent big events—and all of it doused in the kerosene of teenage agita—detonated a righteous indignation that I expressed to Daddy in a long letter, which I mailed to him in Fairfield. I also mentioned the rumors I'd heard about his past.

It was Mummy who wrote me back. She suggested I come down to Fairfield on my day off. The following weekend, I drove the two hours down to Fairfield in my Band-Aid-colored Buick Skylark, my graduation present from my parents. After a relatively normal, chatty dinner, Daddy invited me for a walk. We didn't go far: just up the driveway to his studio. We sat outside together on the glider on his little deck, the cicadas chirping and buzzing away in the humid darkness. Then Daddy got up and started pacing in front of me. Over the course of the next hour, he told me about the various people in his life who'd been envious of him, and who'd made up wicked stories about him to jeopardize his career . . . In short, he denied the rumors.

All these years later, I find myself wondering whether my mother put him up to it. My father would certainly have had his reasons to obfuscate the truth—but that really wasn't his style. More likely it was my mother who had begged her husband to make the denial, to preserve her own dignity.

At that point, they'd been married for nineteen years. Alexander, Nina, and I learned later from our parents' letters that they'd entered into marriage with a clear-eyed acknowledgment of Daddy's sexual complexities. "You are a homosexual and may never change," she wrote to him the year of their wedding; "I am willing to accept you as you are, without being a martyr and sacrificing myself on the L.B. altar." Felicia had assured Lenny that she could handle it—and because they genuinely loved each other, both felt they could take on the challenge. (But they were very, very nervous on that honeymoon in Cuernavaca.)

During the early years of raising their children, while Lenny conducted the Philharmonic and Felicia performed her Mrs. Maestro duties, there was no behavior that would raise the eyebrow of any family member or close friend. But who knows what happened when he was on the road and his wife stayed home. As I look back, I surmise that if they'd struck any kind of deal, it was that Lenny should keep his extramarital activities elsewhere, and not speak of them. It must have been very upsetting for my mother to crash into that long-suppressed issue through a communication from her own daughter.

When I got back to Tanglewood, I searched out my brother in his "office" in the attic of the main house, where he rolled around on an ancient wheelchair that had reportedly belonged to our father's conducting mentor, Serge Koussevitzky. While we smoked a joint together, I told him about the rumors. He'd heard them, too,

Confab by the tennis court.

he said. I told him what Daddy had said to me over the weekend. Alexander and I stared helplessly at each other and were silent. But at least we had aired the subject. From that moment on, it was something we could talk about together—and that was going to matter more and more.

I never spoke to either of my parents again about my conversation with Daddy on the glider. At the time, it was perhaps more upheaval than I could process. I flung myself with renewed fervor into the clinging arms of Nick, feeling not entirely reassured—about anything.

*   *   *

The station wagon was filled to the brim with my belongings. I stood on the Fairfield driveway with my parents on a bright September morning. They were about to drive me to college. I felt like I was being marched to the scaffold.

For thirteen years, I had never been to any school but Brearley. Now I had to confront a brand-new school, in a hugely complex environment, crammed with people and things unknown. I had never really left home before, and now I was being (literally) driven out of the nest. And worst of all, naturally, was the impending separation from Nick.

At least I had my own room, in a dorm up on the Radcliffe campus. My mother fixed it up ingeniously to be as cozy and comfortable as a college dorm room could be. She'd brought along a white wicker rocking chair, and she unrolled a cheerful Mexican carpet that had been in the family for years, tattooed with the pee trails of many a Bernstein dog. She also let me have the framed cover art from Daddy's recording of Mahler's Fourth: a collage of hazy mountains with Victorian paper-cutout angels hovering above. I was glad for those angels; I needed them.

Jamie in her dorm at Harvard. The cover art to LB's recording of Mahler Symphony no. 4 is hanging on the rear wall.

The three of us went to dinner at a Harvard Square restaurant called the Wursthaus, which Daddy remembered with fondness from his own undergraduate days. He was so excited to be up there, and I was so miserable—all the more so for ruining my father's good spirits. Mummy smoked and tried to remain chipper; it wasn't really a comfortable environment for her, either.

When they left me alone in my dorm room that night, the

hammer of despair slammed down on the anvil of my sorry little soul. And the marathon phone calls with Nick began (until
Mummy cut off my long-distance service, one month and $300
later).

My disarray was clearly visible, and my parents made a few
arrangements to help me out. After several unfortunate highway
scrapes in the Band-Aid-colored Buick, they supplied me with an
Eastern Air Lines Charge-a-Trip card. Back then, there was youth
fare; I could take the air shuttle—or, as Grandpa had called it,
"the Shuffle"—from Logan Airport to LaGuardia for $18. And I
Shuffled often.

Also, my parents got me a shrink: none other than Robert Coles,
whose *Children of Crisis* books—about disenfranchised groups
such as migrants, Eskimos, and Native Americans—were already
gaining attention. Dr. Coles eventually won the Pulitzer and many
other prizes, but in 1970 he was still a practicing psychiatrist in the
Harvard Health Services.

I dread to imagine what he made of me. Some years later, I found
out he wrote a subsequent *Children of Crisis* volume called *The
Privileged Ones: The Well-Off and the Rich in America*. My heart
sank as I pictured Dr. Coles listening to me sniveling on and on
about my illustrious family, my troubles with Nick-oh-Nick, and
my Eastern Air Lines Charge-a-Trip card. (In a freshman year's
worth of sessions, I don't think I ever brought up the revelations
about my father from the summer before.)

Every night in the dining hall, I would eat alone, my back to the
room. My intention to be solitary was bright as neon, but occasionally some guy (always a guy) would attempt to sit with me. They
got nowhere. I was so determined to remain faithful to Nick that I
wouldn't so much as speak to a person of the opposite sex. At last,
I'd become as quiet and meek as Nick had always wanted me to be.

All I needed was to be abysmally depressed, and bingo—loud and obnoxious was gone.

I decided to take a psychology course in life histories. I scooped up an A on a paper entitled "The Cases of Shirley Bernstein and Burton Bernstein: A Study of the Influence of an Older Sibling on Two Younger Ones." In my concluding paragraph of the Shirley section, I wrote:

> *My problems related to my father are similar to the ones Shirley had; the "right man," for me, too, must live up to my standards which are based on my father's qualities. I have had the unusual good fortune of already finding such a person; Shirley has not been so lucky.*

For a smarty-pants, I sure could be a Stupid Idiot.

* * *

I had no friends and spoke with virtually no one, but my dorm-building-mate Benazir "Pinky" Bhutto was inexplicably kind to me. We studied for the History of Islam exam together. Only afterward did I find out that Pinky's father was president and later prime minister of Pakistan. I never guessed that Pinky, too, would one day be Pakistan's prime minister, and that she, like her father before her, would be assassinated. Back then, we were just two maladjusted schoolgirls, giggling as we tried to absorb the difference between Sunni and Shiite. Surely she knew all that stuff already! Nevertheless, there we were, cramming for the exam, and she appeared to be just as insecure about the material as I was.

By the end of that grisly freshman year, I'd finally made a couple of friends, and even had fun from time to time. That summer, Nick's mother sent him to England to live with a family and work at some job. In his absence, I gradually noticed that I was in a much better mood; that my close friends did not, in fact, mind when I was loud and obnoxious; they even seemed to like me that way. The faintest glimmer of a notion formed in my mind that maybe life was possible—and maybe, just maybe, even preferable—without Nick.

All that summer, Daddy was hard at work finishing the most challenging piece he'd ever written: *Mass*. A couple of years earlier, Mrs. Onassis had called her old friend Lenny to ask him if he would be the artistic director of the soon-to-be-constructed John F. Kennedy Center for the Performing Arts in Washington, DC. My father accepted the honor, hung up, and was in despair. "How could I say no to Jackie?" he moaned to his wife. "But I don't *want* to be the artistic director of the Kennedy Center! I'll hate it, and I'll be *terrible* at it!" And it was true: Leonard Bernstein was not put on this world to be an administrator.

Felicia saved the day by calling Jackie back to say how honored Lenny was, but really, might it not be better if he were to, perhaps, compose a piece for the inaugural? And that, according to my parents, was how Leonard Bernstein came to write *Mass: A Theatre Piece for Singers, Players, and Dancers*.

Mass was the piece in which my father's fascination with rock music was finally going to express itself through a composition of his own. He really believed that the pop music of the day contained more creative energy than the so-called "serious" music coming from the new generation of conservatory-trained composers—ironically the very composers whom, as the conductor of the Philharmonic, he was passionately committed to presenting. It was his lot, in the mid-twentieth century, to introduce one thorny, cerebral piece after another to his recalcitrant subscription audiences. Those pieces usually employed the academically approved twelve-tone system: that meant they had no melody and were in no key. My father would twist himself into a veritable pretzel of explanation in his preconcert talks, trying to put that music into some sort of graspable context for his listeners. Sometimes his talk went on longer than the piece itself.

So with *Mass*, Daddy was giving himself the freedom to compose using unapologetically tonal elements—and not just rock, either. In addition to the rock band, *Mass* would include a blues band, a marching band, a kids' chorus, a grownups' chorus, twelve Broadway-style soloists, the lead Celebrant, a dance corps, and a full symphony orchestra. Two hundred people were going to fill the stage and pit of the Kennedy Center Opera House on its inaugural evening, September 8, 1971—which would also be my nineteenth birthday.

Aunt Shirley, who had started her own theatrical agency, had a young composer-lyricist client by the name of Stephen Schwartz. She took my father to see the off-Broadway production of *Godspell*, for which Steve had written the score and lyrics. Daddy liked what he heard well enough to invite Steve to cowrite the lyrics of *Mass* with him. Steve could write more inner rhymes than we thought humanly possible. Sometimes it felt a little over the top. For *Mass* he wrote: "There are local vocal yokels / Who we *know col*-lect a crowd . . ." (Today, thanks to his megahit *Wicked*, Stephen Schwartz is one of Broadway's most successful and beloved composer-lyricists.)

Most evenings in Fairfield that summer, Daddy would arrive from his studio before dinner, carrying a piece of manuscript paper with music scrawled on it. "Listen to this!" he would say, and we'd follow him to the piano, where he'd slap the paper against the rack, then accompany himself croaking out whatever he'd written that afternoon. Alexander and I were a little uneasy with the rock music stuff. Even the truly beautiful "A Simple Song" featured a moment where the accompaniment devolved into a decidedly hokey *boom . . . chick, boom-boom . . . chick* that left Alexander and me squirming.

Any self-respecting teenager feels uncomfortable when a parent seems to try too hard to be in-with-the-kids. But this was the tricky part: we were pretty sure Daddy wasn't composing *Mass* to be with-it; he *meant* every note he wrote. This music, and everything it was trying to say, came from the composer's heart in a way that no other piece of his ever had before. And precisely because this was true, we knew he felt more vulnerable than he ever had before. That's why, when he planted that fresh sketch on the piano rack and sang for us, our response always needed to be "Wow, that's great!" And we'd leave it politely at that.

During the dress rehearsal in Washington, carpenters were feverishly banging away, trying to finish the building before the opening the following night. My high school pal Steve and I found an empty room backstage, where we ceremoniously lit up what was surely the first joint ever to be smoked in the Kennedy Center.

Like the carpenters, Daddy and his collaborators were also hammering away right up to the last minute. In his spacious suite at the Watergate, Daddy would sit around the dining table with his creative team, all of whom were desperately trying to convince Daddy to make cuts in his music. The show was intermissionless, and long. Could he at least cut one of the three instrumental Meditations? He could not.

Mass was the first piece Daddy wrote during which Alexander and I fully experienced his process. (Nina was nine and still a little young.) And it did seem as if he were aiming the piece so much at us—not just with the rock music but also with the antiwar theme. The scruffy members of the "Street Chorus" were supposed to be a bit like hippies: questioning authority, challenging their elders' assumptions, searching for fresh meanings. Meanwhile, the be-robed chorus, representing dogma—or the Establishment, as the rule makers were referred to back then—would sing the Latin liturgical text in robotic, unmelodic twelve-tone phrases. We knew this was Daddy's sly dig at the rigidity of the musical Establishment, who decreed that all "serious" music had to be composed using the twelve-tone system.

Unlike the robot chorus, everyone else in the cast of *Mass* would be singing tunes in a multiplicity of tonal genres. The message was clear: twelve-tone was rigid and soulless, while melody was organic, authentic, diverse, human. Daddy had been wrestling with these issues for quite a while. Tunes were fiercely fighting twelve-tone back in his *Kaddish* Symphony. Daddy once told me about some academic types who'd attended a *Kaddish* rehearsal. They were nodding contentedly through the spiky twelve-tone passages—but then, when the grand, sweeping, thoroughly tonal main tune kicked in, the visitors rolled their eyes in disgust and left. Oh, that pesky Bernstein: he'd let them down again.

So now, by putting tonal music—and even electrified rock—front and center in *Mass*, Daddy must have known he would be taking himself off the Serious Composer list for good. It bugged him, it really bugged him, not to be on that list. But he took his stand with *Mass*.

While it was exciting that our father was speaking straight to us and our contemporaries through *Mass*, it also gave Alexander and me that old queasy combo of pride and embarrassment. Particularly embarrassing for me was the clear resemblance of the main character, the Celebrant, to Daddy himself. The Celebrant is the charismatic leader, the one the young people love, the one the congregation joyfully turns to. He begins as a humble guy in blue jeans, strumming his guitar and singing, "Sing God a simple song." The little choirboys give him a robe. His congregants have questions, worries. As their demands and questions increase, they give the Celebrant ever grander and heavier vestments. He struggles with his own doubts; can he come through for his flock? Does he even believe in what he's doing? The piece had become, among other things, a meditation on the cumulative effects of adulation, the trappings of success, the mounting pressure of the public's ever-increasing expectations.

It becomes too much for the Celebrant. He finally cracks up . . . and has the composer's proxy nervous breakdown.

That mad scene scared me. My father named it the Fraction, referring to the Latin word for breaking something; the Celebrant smashes the monstrance and chalice, destroying the symbols of his faith. But the Fraction was also a kind of fragmentation of my father's musical self. The tune that begins the Fraction was borrowed, Daddy explained to me, from the last movement of Beethoven's Ninth—and what's more, it was a twelve-tone row! All the tunes that appeared earlier in the piece come back in an ingeniously interconnected, demented jumble. The Celebrant finally crumples into himself; his notes dwindle and sputter, and with one last keening burst—"Ohhhhh, how easily things . . . get . . . broken . . ."—he gives up. He just sort of slinks off, and maybe dies. It's not clear.

The mad scene was huge, extravagant, way too long. (Of course Daddy refused to cut a note of it.) After such a cataclysmic disintegration, I felt a little uneasy about how everything gets patched up so quickly. But it does—by a small choirboy. "Sing God a secret song, *lauda laude*," he sings into the dark with his bright, tiny voice. All the players who'd swooned to the floor of the stage when the Celebrant broke the monstrance and chalice, and had lain there motionless for the entire eighteen minutes of the Fraction, now stir to life as they each receive the magic Touch of Peace from the little choirboy. They rise, one by one, until everyone is singing "*Lauda laude*" together, followed by a truly gorgeous chorale, "Almighty Father," during which the audience itself is asked to pass along the Touch of Peace (Daddy had wanted it to be a kiss!) and then the Celebrant sort of limps back on stage and says, "The Mass is ended; go in peace." The end.

It was a lot to absorb, a lot to accept—but against all odds, the performance at the Kennedy Center inauguration was immensely moving. Much of the audience was in tears. *Mass*, with its thrashings over faith and its audacity to ask some of humankind's toughest questions, reached people at their core. It was in essence the same fist-shaking at the heavens that Mummy had done in her narration of the *Kaddish* Symphony: If you're up there taking care of us, why do you let these terrible things happen to us down here, and why do you let us do these terrible things to one another? In a time of war, as we were back then, these questions had tremendous resonance. And the John F. Kennedy Center for the Performing Arts was the perfect place in which to pose such questions.

The Kennedy Center opening was splashy and exciting, but there were a few notable no-shows. One of them was Mrs. Onassis. (She saw it later, and told my father she loved it.) The other big no-show was President Nixon. He had been warned by the FBI to stay away from the event because there was a "secret message," disguised in Latin, hidden in the piece for the express purpose of embarrassing him. The secret message? "*Dona nobis pacem*," give us peace, a line in the standard liturgical text of the Catholic Mass. Typical Nixon administration hyperventilating. But I guess they couldn't be blamed for squirming; the piece did convey a pretty pointed antiwar sentiment. In the process, about a hundred pages were added onto Leonard Bernstein's FBI dossier.

It took a delicate mental balancing act for me to appreciate *Mass*. I loved so much of it, even as parts of it made me uncomfortable. I'm sure my mother was on that same tightrope—and she had far less affinity for the rock music and the hippie sensibility than Alexander and I did. But so much of *Mass* was actually *for* our mother. Daddy was drawn to that text in the first place as an acknowledgment of Mummy's Catholic background in Chile. She'd even gone to a convent school—although she did almost get thrown out by the nuns, she told me, for passing out communist literature there.

What with *Mass*'s references to liturgy from both the Old and New Testaments; the rock, blues, and symphonic elements; the adult and children's choruses and the Broadway-style singers; and the intense toggling between the universal and the deeply personal, my father had managed to weave together virtually all the threads of his life into one big expression of himself. *Mass*, with all its flaws, its grandiosity, its daring, and its tremendous, broken heart—it simply *was* Daddy.

So when the reviews came in, he was deeply hurt. Some critics loved it: "The greatest music Bernstein has ever written," wrote Paul Hume in the *Washington Post*. But Harold Schonberg, my father's old nemesis at the *New York Times*, called it "pseudo-serious . . . a showbiz Mass," adding the very observation I thought wasn't true: "The work of a composer who desperately wants to be with-it."

Many critics at the time were dismayed by the mixing together of rock and orchestral music in *Mass*; this is such a common occurrence by now that it's astonishing to recall how shocked people were in 1971. The Catholic Church had problems with the piece, as well. They blew hot and cold; some nuns and priests swooned over the piece, while over at the neighboring diocese, a planned local production of *Mass* would be forced to close down.

In the new millennium, the world has caught up to *Mass*. It was, in many ways, ahead of its time. The mixtures of styles, the unapologetic tonality, the urgent questioning of authority, the openhearted political outrage—all these elements freshly resonate today. And those passages Alexander and I found hokey? What once sounded dated now sounds . . . vintage.

11

Shifting Grounds

Jamie about to graduate from Harvard, and not too sure about much of anything.

My pleasant, Nick-free summer had cleared my head. Once the spell broke, I couldn't believe I'd been under it. What had I been thinking? Well, that was just it: I hadn't been able to think at all, for nearly two years. I managed to break up with Nick before heading back to Cambridge for my sophomore year; it felt like the single most assertive act of my life. My family was overjoyed; their relief and love poured over me like a balm, as had become the traditional, post-boyfriend ritual.

I moved into my new dorm at Adams House, euphorically unencumbered, and in gleeful possession of a hefty brick of hashish that would last my roommates and me right up to Thanksgiving.

At the beginning of the school year, every student received a free calendar booklet from the Harvard Cooperative Society ("the Coop"), where we bought our textbooks. My roommate Jane and I used our Coop calendars to keep track of our carousing: an *x* meant getting high, an *o* meant getting drunk, and an asterisk meant having sex. There was the occasional infinity symbol, for tripping on psychedelics.

While I was having fun, Alexander was having a rough year. Collegiate School had finally informed his parents that their son was not really, uh, participating, and it was decided that he would go to a boarding school in upstate New York that embraced the Shaker philosophy "Hands to work, hearts to God"—which translated into extracting free groundskeeping from the students. It was essentially an expensive combination of reform school and labor camp, and Alexander was miserable. He would come down to Cambridge on a few precious weekends and sleep on the couch in my dorm suite, grateful for the brief escape.

Nina, meanwhile, was so much younger that it was as if she were growing up in a different family. She liked horses—not the way I had at age ten, when I drew pictures and read books about them; Nina had an actual live horse. Mike Nichols, in his classically generous fashion, had given Nina a sweet little horse named Dixie. On the weekends in Fairfield, Nina would ride Dixie in shows, and take care of the grooming and currying and all the rest (although it was usually our mother who wound up mucking out the stables).

Unlike her siblings, Nina was industrious at her piano lessons. She practiced; she improved. For several years her teacher was none other than our father's own early piano teacher and lifelong secretary, Helen Coates. Nina derived little joy from her piano lessons with Nanny Helen, but she stuck with it longer than Alexander or I did. She was altogether more obedient than we had ever been—but she was not having fun, at all.

Now that both her older siblings were away at school, Nina felt isolated, contending alone with our mother, who was tending more and more toward melancholia, and with Julia, who was relentlessly cantankerous and bossy. Nina would later compare her early youth to that of an only child in a Victorian novel—complete with wicked nanny. Also, Nina was struggling with her weight. I knew how much she was suffering over her changed appearance since her younger days as a sprightly preschooler.

By the spring, Jane and I had tabulated quite a few adventures in our little black Harvard Coop books. A few months' worth of my asterisks had been with Chris, a Greek-American from East Saint Louis who was at Harvard on a soccer scholarship, and had thighs so enormous he needed special jeans. Chris stopped by Fairfield once, and Mummy got to meet him. Afterward, as we stood together on the driveway watching him roar off in his Datsun 240Z, Mummy said, "I liked him. He's got . . . a motor. I like a man with a motor."

*　　*　　*

Meanwhile, Felicia's own man with a motor was making some changes in his professional life. Harry Kraut, who had been my fearsome boss during the summer I worked at Tanglewood, was now Leonard Bernstein's new personal manager, running his company, Amberson. (The German word for amber is "Bernstein.") Harry had taken over for Schuyler Chapin, my father's trusted friend and colleague of many years, who was now running the Metropolitan Opera. It was immediately clear that Harry was going to do things differently from the charming, gentlemanly Schuyler. Harry Kraut was an aggressive businessman, always a couple of moves ahead of everyone else. Like my father, he was a Harvard alumnus; Daddy admired Harry's musical knowledge, as well as his ability to solve word puzzles. Harry's chin strap of a beard, combined with bald pate, yellow-tinted aviator glasses, and an increasingly prominent paunch, gave him the aura of a slightly dissipated Mephistopheles. He perpetually wreathed himself in cigarette smoke, which contributed to the general sulfurous effect.

LB's Minders. *From left to right:* Harry Kraut, Margaret Carson, and Helen Coates with LB.

Also, unlike Schuyler, Harry was gay, openly so. He loved talking about sex; that was how he chose to break the ice at meetings and dinners—although perhaps it didn't so much break the ice as it did disconcert, which Harry could use to his advantage.

The summer after my sophomore year, Harry invited me to work at Amberson, thereby becoming my fearsome boss yet again. But I wasn't a guide anymore, stationed all over many acres; now I would be right across the hallway from Harry in the Amberson offices on West 58th Street. Everyone who worked at Amberson lived in fear of Harry. It was no fun when he turned his yellow aviator glasses on you to point out that you'd done something wrong. But I learned to type letters correctly, and to work the ungainly keys on the telex machine.

I had a summer romance with my office mate, Peter Lieberson, who was a composer (and would one day become a celebrated one). Peter was helping with the research on my father's next big project, the Charles Eliot Norton Lectures, to be delivered at Harvard later that year.

Peter's father, Goddard Lieberson, was president of Columbia Records and a brilliant, dashing presence. Goddard and his wife, Brigitta (the former ballet and film star Vera Zorina), were dear family friends and had two sons, Peter and Jonathan. In Peter, the blending of his parents' good looks was so devastating that Peter, as if to reject his own beauty, wore little wire-rimmed spectacles, grew a wispy beard, and shuffled around with a pronounced slouch. Jonathan, his younger brother, could not have been more different: he was a philosopher, dazzlingly articulate, a bit clownish, and flamboyantly gay, back when flamboyance took courage. (In a matter of years, Jonathan would be one of the earliest AIDS victims. Daddy was anguished to lose someone so young and promising—a brand of grief that would become all too familiar.)

Since the Liebersons were so close to our family, it was "cute" that Peter and I were an item. But it didn't last long. By summer's end, we'd parted ways, and I went back to college, on the loose as ever.

My junior year at Harvard had a brand-new feature: Leonard Bernstein was there, too. I'd known, of course, that he was preparing the Norton Lectures, but I hadn't really thought about what it would mean to have my father on campus with me. Whatever slim momentum I'd built toward becoming an autonomous person since going off to Harvard, whatever hopes I'd had of figuring out who I might be, independent of my last name—all such aspirations were now effectively frozen in their tracks for the rest of my college days.

That fall, my father resided in a suite in Eliot House, the very building he'd lived in as an undergraduate. He was having the time of his life—not just preparing his lectures, but also giving seminars and master classes, constantly surrounded by college students who had the stamina to stay up all night with him, yakking and drinking and playing music.

Daddy *loved* being a professor. Everything he did, after all, was a form of teaching, and now he was engaging daily with the smartest cookies in the country. He immersed himself in his grand intellectual adventure: connecting Noam Chomsky's theories of transformational grammar with the organic elements of tonality. My father was in way over his head and relishing every second of it.

Also, he had an assistant on the project: Tommy Cothran, a ruddy-cheeked, elfin young man who was brilliant, deeply musical, well-read, and amusingly zany. Daddy loved him. No, really: Daddy was in love with Tommy Cothran.

Alexander and I didn't quite get it at first. Sometime that fall, our father had brought Tommy along to Fairfield, where we were given the impression that this young assistant was becoming a fun new family friend. But on the Harvard campus, we heard the gossip. Slowly Alexander and I grasped what was going on, but we almost never talked to each other about it. It was so much easier, when we were together, to smoke pot, watch TV, listen to music— all our usual ways of drowning out any uncomfortable realities. In particular, I was suppressing the evident fact that my father had lied to me that night on the glider outside his Fairfield studio. I couldn't begin to figure out, or even dare to wonder, how I myself felt about any of it.

At home, nothing was being acknowledged at all. The daily routines continued: the tennis, the dogs, the before-dinner drinks, the anagrams—as if everything were the same as always. And in fact, everything was—almost—the same as always.

Mummy must have known the truth of the situation, but if she did, she never let on. Maybe she was just as glad to have Daddy out of the house for the better part of that year. She hunkered down with Nina, shuttling between New York and Fairfield, clinging to her close friends, drinking a lot of vodka, and smoking endless cigarettes through her elegant white Aqua Filter, a device that was supposed to remove all the carcinogens.

My most reliable source of distraction was, as usual, my own love life. My junior-year boyfriend, Peter, was a clever, wiry, ambitious whippersnapper from South Orange, New Jersey. He was the managing editor of the *Harvard Crimson*, and seemed like the kind of guy who might run for office someday. (He did.) People either loved him or hated him. My family loved him. It helped that he was perfectly fearless around my father. He was the first boyfriend I'd ever had who seemed . . . plausible. That in itself made me nervous.

It took Leonard Bernstein the full duration of my junior year to prepare his lectures—and still they weren't ready. So now he was scheduled to come back to Harvard to deliver the lectures in my *senior* year. There was simply no getting rid of the guy; I just had to accept it.

Harry Kraut invited me once again to work at Amberson that summer, this time to put together a "feasibility report" (new term for me) about starting a top-tier classical music festival in the Canary Islands. My assignment was to visit the island of Gran Canaria, learn about its infrastructure, scout around for possible locations and venues for concerts, take a lot of notes, and write the whole thing up.

The Canary Island business began with a wealthy German friend of Harry's who had a house on Gran Canaria, perched at the top of a volcanic ravine. Across that ravine was a new house just built by two German pianists: Christoph Eschenbach and Justus Frantz. In Europe, Harry and his German friend introduced my father to the two young pianists; an invitation to stay at their house in the Canaries soon followed. Daddy fell in love with everything there: the rough rock and searing sun; the airy house full of music, wine, and laughter; the talent and charm of Christoph and Justus. He was especially enchanted with Justus. "Oh, Jamie, you're going to *love* him!" he crowed at the dinner table when he got back to New York, tanned as the devil and radiating good health.

By proposing a classical music festival in the Canaries, Harry was essentially cooking up an elaborate excuse for Daddy to go on a regular basis to his new favorite place. This initiative was an early iteration of what we came to call a Harry Kraut Special: an elaborate scheme that would grow and diversify the Amberson company or build the Bernstein "brand."

The Canaries were indeed lovely—although strangely marred by a local law that said residents need not pay taxes on their houses until construction was complete. So of course no one ever finished their houses, and the roads were lined with ugly cinder block semi-structures. The more I delved into the matter, the less enthusiastic I was at the prospect of further disrupting the Canary Islands' fragile ecosystem with yet more human gunk. My grand recommendation at the conclusion of my feasibility report was: don't build the festival.

While I was there, I met Christoph and Justus. Christoph had a lovely, whimsical way about him, and he was a deeply gifted musician. Justus had dazzling good looks and the more outgoing personality. Christoph was clearly gay; it was not clear what Justus was, but the two pianists lived together—in Hamburg, as well as in the Canaries—so what was one to think? In any case, just as Daddy had instructed the winter before, I fell right in love with Justus, who was so blond and tawny, so charming and musical and full of laughter. We began a delicious romance.

All the more delicious for being ill-advised. First of all, wasn't he, um, Daddy's friend . . . ? An explanation of their own relationship wasn't offered and I didn't ask for one. I was drawn to the vague aura of transgression, but I was reluctant to discuss it, or give it a name.

And what about my boyfriend Peter back home? When I returned from the Canaries, Peter sensed that I'd been up to something. I denied it, but he kept pressing. My side of the conversation went something like this:

"No, I didn't."

"No, really, I didn't."

"I swear, I didn't."

"I didn't, I didn't."

"Okay, I did."

I was the world's most pathetic liar.

At the end of that summer, there was another visit to the Canaries. This time my parents, Nina, and I were all there together, spending time with my father's new best friends, Justus and Christoph. I'm not sure at what point I let my father know that Justus and I were having a romance. But I do recall all of us being at the pianists' house on my twenty-first birthday, an evening with much wine, four-hands piano playing, and raucous conviviality. I found myself at one point manipulating a sock to explain to the assembled guests the difference between a circumcised and an uncircumcised penis—a distinction I'd ever so recently come to understand.

*   *   *

My father began delivering the Norton Lectures in the fall of my senior year. The first lecture was disrupted by a bomb scare; everyone had to be evacuated from the Harvard Square Theater. When the full audience didn't return after the all clear, Daddy took it hard. He was all set to shake the very earth with his pronouncements about linguistics and tonality.

That was the only one of the six lectures that Alexander attended. Now a Harvard freshman, he was keeping his father at a distance. If it had been tough for me to have Daddy on campus in my junior year, it was even tougher now for Alexander—plus, there was that eternal question mark hovering over the very fact of our enrollment. I had crippling doubts as to whether I would have gotten into Harvard had my father been less of an illustrious alumnus—and I'd been a pretty good student at Brearley. Alexander, with his checkered academic record, had even more misgivings about how he might have landed in that freshman dorm in Harvard Yard. So the only way for him to get through his college experience was, as he would say, to "goof on it": to take none of it seriously. It was all a silly cosmic joke. But maintaining that level of Zen humor about the situation required a lot of pot.

In one of the Norton Lectures, my father referred several times to "my blond inquisitor." That was me; I had evidently asked him some provocative question that he'd then used as a structure for that lecture's material. I must say, though, I wasn't exceptionally inquisitive (or blond). I couldn't maintain focus on those lectures. It was all just too much: the intensity of the material, the surrounding hoopla, the distraction from my attempts to have my own life. It was hard enough to figure out who I was and what I was doing on that convoluted Cambridge planet without the additional solar glare of the Maestro and his grand theories. So I smoked a lot of pot, too, just like Alexander.

On campus, the Lenny Show never stopped. He was a major Harvard celebrity for everyone to fuss over. The *Crimson* ran a joke article: "Cretin Found in Bernstein's Eliot House Closet." Was this a veiled gay reference? I find myself wondering now— although no one alluded to it at the time, not even the gay male students who were making that era's first cautious attempts at coming out. I felt comfortable around that bunch; they were witty, antic, quick on the trigger—like my parents and their New York friends. It was such a puzzle that one's boyfriends could never be like that.

The Norton Lectures were a complex operation. Not only was my father lecturing; he was also providing musical examples at the piano, as he used to do on his Young People's Concerts. In addition, there were orchestral performances, prerecorded with the Boston Symphony and projected on a screen as part of each lecture. All of which meant that the lectures were . . . long. But he had so much to say! I knew how excited Daddy was about his major academic inquiry. He was constructing an elaborate apologia for tonality: really sticking it to the twelve-tone academic cartel by "proving" that tonality was organic, instinctive, essential. In their own way, the Norton Lectures were as deeply personal a statement as *Mass* had been.

A day or two after each lecture, my father would go to WGBH-TV studios and videotape the whole thing. They were later shown on television and released as books, and after that, they came out on video. Another Harry Kraut Special.

Harry was ratcheting everything up: booking big, ambitious concerts that were also complex coproductions; arranging for the concerts to be recorded, filmed, released on LP, and also televised. Everything had become so *mega*. Harry had a vision for the Bernstein legacy, and he was a brilliant businessman. But Alexander, Nina, and I didn't care about such things back then. It annoyed us to see our father being so aggressively marketed. Yet we weren't sure we could put the whole blame on Harry; after all, Daddy was okaying Harry's suggestions, wasn't he? And that was the problem: we felt that maybe our father was buying into Harry's aggrandized vision of Leonard Bernstein, and we didn't much like what that implied about our father's personality. So it was easier, *safer*, to blame Harry than it was to put the onus on Daddy himself.

Equally tough to process was the way Harry seemed to be enabling Daddy's slow creep toward overt gayness. Harry threw parties where our father could meet interesting, attractive young men. On the road, Harry brought young men over to my father's hotel suite. And whenever Tommy Cothran went along, Harry arranged for him to get special status in the entourage—either as personal secretary, or assistant editor, or whatever the situation accommodated. When Alexander and I tagged along on a tour, everything was as exciting as ever, yet vaguely sickening. We were getting all the familiar perks: the adventures, the concerts, the parties. But now, our very presence rendered us complicit in a betrayal we couldn't quite express—and so we traveled wrapped in a gossamer-thin but unremovable membrane woven of elf's thread.

Still, we couldn't help softening on Harry when, midway through a European junket, he would pull out his wallet and say to us, "You need any money?" When you're college age, "No, thanks" is not in your inventory of responses to that question.

Mummy, to no one's surprise, simply loathed Harry. But she strove to keep things normal, maybe most of all for Nina's benefit. Had our mother declared overt war on Harry, Alexander and I might have felt moved to take her side, even give voice to our anger at our father's infidelity. I sensed that Alexander, in particular, was harboring some deep resentment, and would have been glad for a way to express it. But both our parents were dyed-in-the-wool confrontation avoiders; they loathed and feared melodrama. We offspring grew up avoiding confrontation, as well. So, as long as our mother pretended all was normal, that gave the rest of us permission to play along.

When Alexander and I returned to Harvard in the fall, we discovered that Harry had arranged for Daddy and Tommy to have a spacious suite all to themselves at the top of Quincy House. At home in New York, our family appeared as an inviolable unit; our parents were a well-established couple; our friends and extended family wouldn't have seen any change in our routine. But up in Cambridge, Massachusetts, Leonard Bernstein, Charles Eliot Norton Professor of Poetry, was test-driving a new life for himself.

* * *

Over the holidays, I visited Justus in the Canaries. Christoph was there, too. So, were the two pianists lovers? I couldn't figure it out. Justus certainly seemed to like girls, but what about him and

Daddy: Had something gone on there? Justus had told me no. It was hard to know what to believe. I wanted to know, but also I didn't want to know. I rather enjoyed living wrapped in my damp, erotic fog.

Justus had some recitals in Switzerland, and I tagged along. Each performance was followed by a reception, where I had to be polite and charming with assorted dull but important patrons. It occurred to me that I was playing my mother's role. So this was what it was like to be Mrs. Maestro, eh? Christ, it was *awful*! If this was what my future with Justus held in store, I was not at all sure I wanted to sign up for it. No wonder Mummy had been accompanying Daddy on the road less and less over the years. I was beginning to get an inkling of how complicated life might actually be for Felicia Montealegre Bernstein.

I thought for the first time about how a successful performing artist is constantly replenished through performance and audience adulation, while the artist's companion gets slowly but inexorably depleted. Now I understood the darker implications of my mother's frequent joke that she would title her memoirs *Waiting for Maestro*. Yes, her life had its distinct compensations: three children, two houses; brilliant, fun friends; music, theater, and travel; everything gracious and beautiful. My parents' affection for each other was warm and genuine; we all felt it. But I wondered about the cost to Mummy. Might she have blossomed as an actress had she married someone less involved with his own career? Might she have had a more fulfilling union with a husband who had fewer complications of his own? Some essential part of my mother was not being nourished, and it was starting to show.

My separations from Justus were painful. Transatlantic phone calls were expensive and maddening, with their fuzzy sound and second-and-a-half delay. We wrote letters, but there were never enough of them. As part of my campaign to be nearer-my-Justus-to-thee, I'd been taking German A at Harvard, an intensive yearlong course that met five days a week. In January, a new guy, Sam, showed up in the class. We would study together sometimes, drilling each other on verbs and vocabulary. With his shaggy blond hair and pink glasses, his skinny faded corduroys, his clogs, and his single earring, Sam was cute. And smart as hell. And a poet. Okay, Sam was amazing. I was head over heels in love with Sam. Good-bye, Justus—over the fuzzy transatlantic phone!

I was so preoccupied with my busy life that I barely registered the premiere of Daddy's latest piece: the score to a ballet called *Dybbuk*, choreographed by his longtime complicated pal Jerry Robbins. They'd been toiling over this ballet for months, but I'd been oblivious. I remember nothing from the premiere, except that Alexander, Nina, and I could not warm up to this piece, with

The family, with LB and Jamie as the Harvard "goal posts."

its heavily Jewish thematic material; its kabbalah-inspired nu-
merological intricacies; and the overall sound of the score, which
was very—to use Nina's word—pointy. Ironically, after my father's grand defense of tonality in the Norton Lectures, he was
now presenting the most aggressively twelve-tone piece he'd
ever written.

When my parents came up to Cambridge for my graduation,
they seemed strangely distracted and irritable—although they
were excited that the Russian cellist Mstislav Rostropovich, who
had just defected from Soviet Russia, was receiving an honorary
degree at the Harvard commencement ceremonies that morning.
There was much hugging of their beloved friend Slava—so much
hugging, in fact, that they wound up missing my own diploma ceremony at Adams House.

It wasn't until we were all back in Fairfield the next day that I
discovered why my parents had been acting so oddly at commencement. That afternoon Mummy asked me, uncharacteristically, to
take a walk with her. When we got to the frog pond, she sat down
on the little stone bench and patted the empty space next to her
for me to sit there. Some kind of confrontation was coming, and
I was almost unable to breathe, so acute was my discomfort. She
turned to me with the most distraught expression I'd ever seen on
her face. Sitting there in the pleasant shade of the big Norwegian
maple, my mother told me in a shaking voice that they'd found
a cancerous mass in her left breast, and that she was going in for
a mastectomy in a couple of days. She hadn't wanted to ruin my
graduation by telling me the day before.

My first reaction was to be angry that she'd hidden this enormous piece of news from me, and then had proceeded to act so
jittery and distracted at my graduation events. It was far easier to
be angry than . . . panicked.

After hugging my mother and saying whatever words I could summon up that were encouraging, I went up to my room, and cried myself to a husk. After that, I didn't cry about it again for a very long time. We all had a new job now: to get through everything that would happen next.

12

Not Really Grownup

Just because something cataclysmic happens in a family's life doesn't mean that the rest of life stops happening.

Yes, Mummy had her mastectomy, but also she was moving us out of our Park Avenue apartment. The East Side wasn't a perfect fit for us: too WASPy and wealthy and everyone the same. We'd all grown weary of the area, our beautiful penthouse views notwithstanding. The West Side felt more real. And so, the family was moving back across the park, to live in the fabled, gabled Dakota—a building delightfully stuffed, in those days, with writers, artists, and theater folk.

Earlier in the year, my mother had taken me over to see our future apartment. The ceilings in the 1880 building were stratospheric: sixteen feet high. The views out the second-floor windows didn't compare with what we'd had across town, but looking at the tops of the trees across Central Park West conveyed the pleasant illusion that the park was our very own backyard. (We didn't find out until the following November what was *really* amazing about that view.)

Mummy showed me excitedly through apartment 23. "And this is the dining room . . . and here's the morning room: a lovely place for breakfast, we'll sit right by the window . . . and here's Nina's room . . . and this is Lenny's bedroom . . ."—which was connected to my mother's bedroom by a Gothic-shaped ecclesiastical oaken door she'd found in some antique store.

Oh: they had separate bedrooms now.

Mummy said how thrilled she was not to have to dress in

darkness every morning during those hours when her husband was finally fast asleep—and not to listen to his stentorian snoring anymore. But it was hard not to read a deeper meaning into it. Was this a new phase in their marriage—and were they both okay with it? Alexander and I may have exchanged a sardonic sentence or two about the implications of our parents' new sleeping situation, but as usual, it felt safer to act like we didn't care. And we couldn't bring ourselves to discuss it with Nina; she was only twelve. Nina was not being informed about anything. Mummy hadn't even been able to tell her about the mastectomy until after it was over. She called Nina from the hospital and said, "The doctor was going to take a little bump off my nose, but guess what? It wasn't about my nose after all . . . He took off something else."

". . . and this is Nina's room . . . and here's the dining room, and the kitchen, and behind it is Julia's room . . . So, what do you think?"

Oh: I didn't have a bedroom in this house. Neither did Alexander.

Well, yes: I was graduating from college, and it was time to be a grownup and find my own place to live. But it stung all the same. To add insult to injury, Mummy had engineered the move without consulting either Alexander or me about our belongings. In her brisk let's-get-this-done manner, she'd thrown out, among other things, Alexander's priceless baseball card collection and my precious Tanglewood memento: Roger Daltrey's ripped-in-two fringed polyester snakeskin shirt. But you can't get mad at your mother when she's recovering from major surgery.

The other big change at the Dakota was that my father's studio was now a separate apartment: two rooms on the ninth floor, tucked under the gables. Apartment 92 was, in its way, even more wonderful than the big apartment downstairs. Its ceilings were lower, which made it cozy—and the windows had cushioned seats where you could sit and look out over all, all, ALL of Central Park.

Back on Park Avenue, Daddy had often complained about the noise and interruptions resulting from the central location of his studio. So now it was as if his wife were saying: Oh, you want privacy? I'll give you privacy! But of course, there was so much more subtext in the kicking of my father upstairs to apartment 92. Maybe, in some way, our mother was tacitly giving him a private space in which to do whatever he needed to do to feel like a complete person, while allowing him to remain connected to his family downstairs. Yet at the same time, she had installed a charming but very small Murphy bed up there, the kind that pulled down from the wall; who even knew they still made such things? The bed was adorable but, perhaps pointedly, there was no way two people could squeeze themselves onto that bed. (I know; I tried.)

Apartment 23 wasn't ready yet when we vacated the Park Avenue apartment in June. After Mummy came out of the hospital, there were a few weeks when we were camped out, two floors up from our new place, in Lauren Bacall's Dakota apartment, while she was off making a movie somewhere. We had never seen a home so crammed with objects in all our lives. We thought our mother was a mad collector, but she was austere as a monk compared to Betty Bacall. Not a square millimeter of those tall walls was left uncovered, and every horizontal surface was covered with tchotchkes from her world travels. It was charming, but exhausting—not unlike Betty herself. When she was in the mood, Betty could seduce a stone, but she was also notoriously imperious and cruel. Waiters shrank from her; maids quit; doormen held their breath as she strode past them with her coddled King Charles spaniel, Blenheim.

Yet Betty was unfailingly warm to our family—and she had made a truly generous gesture in offering us her place at such a

The two LBs at Sardi's.

difficult moment. Betty and my father had a soft spot for each other. It wasn't simply an erotic attraction; it was more like a mutual recognition of their shared magical quality: the mysterious and powerful charisma that made both of those LBs the stars that they were.

Another of the Dakota's denizens was the actor Michael "Mendy" Wager. Mendy was already a close family friend, but now that he lived three floors above us, he would become a crucial thread in the family fabric. A son of one of the founding fathers of Israel, Mendy (né Emanuel Weisgal) had read all of Proust several times over, and was by turns encyclopedic and maniacal about opera. Mendy was my first opera queen, and he was the real deal. (The lead character of Terrence McNally's play *The Lisbon Traviata* was based on Mendy, and even named after him.) Mendy was bisexual, with children from two different marriages. And he was madly hyper; today he would be quickly labeled with ADHD. He self-medicated, as everyone did back then, and eventually became a bona fide amphetamine addict.

Mendy's walls were covered in framed photos and posters from the many theatrical productions he'd acted in over the years. He'd been dusky-eyed and handsome in his youth, and he still cut a fine figure in his beige turtlenecks and velvety corduroy suits. But by the time we moved to the Dakota, Mendy's primary source of dramatic activity (and considerable income) had become TV voice-overs. At the first rehearsal with the Harvard Glee Club for a concert of Stravinsky's *Oedipus Rex*, my father introduced Mendy, who was performing the work's narration, by saying: "I give you Michael Wager—the voice of Drano." Mendy took the teasing in remarkably good spirits; he loved any kind of attention.

Mendy knew so much about music and literature that Daddy found him amusing company, in measured doses, but it was our mother who had the truly deep friendship with Mendy. They were almost in love, and would spend enormous amounts of time together, often trolling the antique stores along Route 7 in Connecticut (the activity we'd found so unbearable as kids)—because, in addition to all of Mendy's other gifts, he had a sterling decorator's eye. His apartment in the Dakota was splendidly beautiful, with its William Morris wallpapers, Pierre Deux fabrics, and antique brass bed. He mostly lived in that bed, floating in a sea of books, newspapers, and literary magazines.

Some people in this world have a special gift: they remember jokes. Daddy himself was an accomplished joke archivist, but Mendy was the master—especially of the Jewish ones—and the Bernstein family was his most appreciative audience.

All the jokes and their punch lines became so deeply woven into our family fabric that we still refer to them today. "Vat is doing de dogs?" "Schmuck—buy a ticket!" "*My* maid said *hot* water."

"Whatsamatter, you don't like the *other* tie?" We call them Life Jokes: treasured family heirlooms that together comprise a collection of human wisdom more precious than gold.

Mendy bought a little white farmhouse in Roxbury, Connecticut, which he promptly rented out, and then converted the old red barn down the hill into a heavenly country hideaway for himself. We all loved it there at "Menderly," as he called it. In the living room, behind the piano, if you pushed the bookcase in a certain spot, it sprang open to reveal a bathroom with a spiral staircase that took you up into the silo, where Mendy had his bedroom.

From up in the silo, you could see the surrounding hills and meadows, a gorgeous eyeful in every season. And across from the

Mendy and Felicia sharing a moment at Mendy's wedding.

bed was a raised platform covered in Oriental rugs and many pillows: Mendy's "harem." There was no sweeter spot on earth in which to smoke pot, and Mendy was very generous about letting "the kids" have fun in the harem. He often joined us, in fact; Mendy was barely an adult himself, so he fit right in. Sometimes Daddy came up there, too. He would take a puff off the joint and explode into coughing. "This must have hash in it!" he always said, gasping after those pot-induced coughing fits. He'd decided at some point that he was allergic to hashish.

For my mother in those years, Mendy would fill much of the emotional space that my father used to occupy. Mendy could be friend, brother, offspring, almost husband. Maybe even wife. They amused each other endlessly. Sometimes they'd rearrange all the furniture in a room, just for the fun of it. And sometimes they squabbled. "I'd like to hit you right now, but you'd *like* it too much!" Mummy would fume, and Mendy would cackle with glee.

Mendy also gave Mummy a crucial escape valve for her deepening ambivalence about the world of gay men, a world that had become such a direct threat to her. Harry's parade of handsome young fellows was on constant display: at parties, dinners, and concerts. Their tendency to sport the same fashions and grooming led Mummy to refer to them as "Chinese waiters." Yes, we groan now at the awful reference, but this is how people spoke back then—and yes, the men all looked alike to her; she did not hide her contempt. But at Mendy's apartment, as well as in Roxbury, she would spend many evenings with highly accomplished gay men—writers, directors, actors, painters—who showered her with attention and love, as did Mendy himself. For my mother, Mendy was a nontoxic iteration of her own husband—almost like a vaccine that would keep her from being sickened by the full-strength pathogen.

Mummy recovered well from her surgery, and within weeks was installed in Fairfield for the summer, with the rest of us by her side as much as possible. For Alexander's birthday in July, Mummy fixed up the ground floor of the caretaker's cottage at the end of the driveway so that Alexander and his friends would have their own "pad." It was the perfect solution: all that summer, Alexander could go off to smoke pot, drink beer, and watch sports to his heart's content—yet he was always close by.

Nina was a little shaky that summer. It was a tough combination: being on the cusp of adolescence, dealing with her mother's illness, and still being younger than everyone else. She flatly refused to go to any kind of summer camp, so she rode her pony Dixie and watched plenty of TV.

Well, we all did. In our family, as in so many others, television was a potent ally in our daily avoidance of topics that caused distress. Alexander was glued to his Yankees games. Nina knew every episode of *The Odd Couple* by heart. And there was the group ritual of the evening news before dinner. That summer there was a lot of news: we'd been glued all year to the Watergate hearings, and now impeachment was in the air. Sometimes Daddy would get so furious at our government's dirty doings that he would slam his fist on the dinner table and the flowers would jump in their vase. (We even felt personally involved as a family; President Nixon's infernal "enemies list"—in which he'd aggregated everyone he hated in politics, the media, the arts, and beyond—had eventually, inevitably, included Leonard Bernstein. Yet the Christmas before, our parents had also received a generic holiday card from the White House. Mummy framed the card together with the enemies list—and for extra effect, Daddy wrote in felt-tip pen at the bottom of the Christmas card: "With special love and esteem from Pat and Dick.")

Many nights that summer, Daddy and I—always the ones who stayed up latest—would find ourselves watching old movies together on the TV in the living room. It was the perfect way to enjoy each other's company without ever venturing into difficult conversational territory. One night we came upon one of his favorites: *All About Eve*. "It's the movie-est movie of them all!" he said; he adored Bette Davis. His spirited running commentary filled the annoying commercial breaks, and he recited all the famous lines along with the characters: "Fasten your seat belts; it's going to be a bumpy night." "I'm not to be had for the price of a cocktail, like a salted peanut." "I'm Addison DeWitt—I am nobody's fool, least of all yours." That was the night I learned the word "oleaginous"—my father's perfect description of the actor George Sanders as Addison.

Another night we caught *The Treasure of the Sierra Madre*. Daddy pointed out how Max Steiner's march theme morphed along with the story: when the prospectors started out on their journey, the tune was jaunty and purposeful; later, when the men were down on their luck, slogging miserably through the mountains, the march slowed down to a doleful minor dirge. He reveled in the performances of Walter Huston and Humphrey Bogart, who was at his meanest and snarliest in that movie. Of course we knew from Betty Bacall that in real life, her husband Bogie had been the sweetest man on earth.

Watching those movies, we could temporarily bury every discomfort and concern. But it must have been hard for my father that summer, dealing with the aftermath of his wife's surgery. They still shared a bedroom in Fairfield, but Daddy worked so late into the night in his studio that he might as well have stayed up there—and sometimes he did. They certainly had their own set of problems already, but in addition, what husband wouldn't shudder over his wife's losing a breast? Back then, there was no reconstructive surgery; Felicia Montealegre, that delicately beautiful creature, was disfigured.

Also, just possibly, it was a little tough for Daddy to find himself not at the center of family attention for once. This was a feeling he couldn't express openly, but it sometimes came out in other ways. So maybe he was feeling a bit underattended to on the night in July when he got it into his head that the lobsters weren't still alive when they'd been dropped into the boiling water. (He believed that if they weren't alive right up to that moment, you'd be poisoned.) Sure enough, after dinner, he started feeling awful. He was sweaty

LB, back from Bridgeport Hospital, jumped in
the pool wearing the doctor's outfit.

and fearful, and was making such a scene—was he having a heart attack?—that finally an ambulance was called, and Daddy was taken to Bridgeport Hospital. They kept him there for two days of tests. He was fine. When he returned to the house, he arrived dressed head to toe in doctor's whites, with a stethoscope around his neck. He made a grand entrance, then jumped, fully doctor-clothed, into the pool.

Later that month, while Daddy was on tour somewhere, Dick Avedon came out to Fairfield to recover from a heart ailment. Mummy and Dick bonded in a new way through their mutual convalescence. He, too, was "a man with a motor"; also, he was sunny and goofy and full of fun. He took wonderful pictures of

Dick and Felicia in the play that Beckett never wrote.

us all while he was there—though we were amused to see that his helpers had affixed labels all over his little camera, because he didn't know how to operate it by himself. He was enamored, as well, of Shirley's Polaroid camera. His best shot of the week, he announced, was the Polaroid of himself and Mummy, their heads floating surreally in the swimming pool. "Beckett never wrote his greatest play because he didn't see this picture!" he crowed. Shirley pointed out to Dick that he couldn't possibly have taken the photo because he was *in* the photo; in fact, Shirley had taken it herself. It was a much-needed laugh—and Dick laughed the hardest over his logic-defying mental lapse.

Those same helpers later assisted Dick in assembling his best shots into a beautiful little spiral-bound book, which he gave to us the following Christmas. Daddy wasn't in the book, and somehow that absence was part of the story those pictures were telling.

My father was also not there in August, when at last Nixon resigned. While the rest of the family gathered around the living room TV in Fairfield, champagne glasses in hand, Daddy was up at Tanglewood, conducting for his adoring crowds.

*   *   *

Sam and I decided to move in together. For my birthday in early September, everyone gave me stuff for our apartment in Cambridge. Harry gave me a set of Le Creuset pots and pans, a terrific present. (I use them to this day.) But Mummy was dismayed. She ran upstairs and came down with a pair of her earrings. "Here! I just can't bear that it's so much like a kitchen shower," she muttered, pressing the earrings into my hand.

Off I went to live with Sam in our little apartment on Harvard Street. I drove back to Fairfield regularly with Alexander, now a Harvard sophomore. In a family game of musical cars, my Band-

Aid-colored, radioless Buick now belonged to Uncle BB's wife, Ellen; I was driving Daddy's blue Oldsmobile Cutlass Supreme convertible—FM stereo, air-conditioning, and all. Meanwhile, Daddy had gotten himself a cute little red Fiat Spider two-seater, just like the ones we'd rented on the Canary Islands the year before.

In November, we discovered the feature of the new Dakota apartment that erased every shadow: the Macy's Thanksgiving Day Parade came streaming down Central Park West, right below our second-floor windows. The signature giant balloons floated just above us; from our pair of tiny balconies, we could almost touch Snoopy and Superman and the Cat in the Hat. Sometimes in a strong wind they listed precariously close to our heads, while below us, the mad mosaic of hats, scarves, and kids writhed and oohed in excited alarm.

It became, for Alexander, Nina, and me, our favorite morning of the year. Julia, however, did not love the parade. Thanksgiving was a purgatory of toil for her, and she made sure we understood how burdened she felt. After our feast, it made my heart sink to find Julia in the kitchen all alone, eating the turkey neck and staring balefully into space over her big cup of oversteeped Lipton tea. The older I got, the more it bothered me. The world was changing around us, and Mummy's traditional South American domestic model was getting harder and harder for us to accept. Years later, we would beg Julia to eat with us at the Thanksgiving table, but she categorically refused; Mummy's old model was Julia's model, too.

* * *

Justus had his New York debut in a concert with my father and the Philharmonic. I took the Shuffle down from Boston for the occasion. Justus was basking in the attentions of one and all, and

Daddy seemed to enjoy presenting this handsome, gifted young musician to his hometown. If a tongue or two wagged, he evidently didn't care. For my part, I was vaguely titillated, knowing I'd had my own recent romance with the blond German pianist.

The other half of the program was the US premiere of an orchestral suite my father had created from his *Dybbuk* ballet the year before. It sounded pretty good—albeit "pointy" as ever. But the bleak, airless Jewishness of the piece was hard for Alexander, Nina, and me. The S. Ansky story of a young girl being possessed by her dead lover was intriguingly spooky, but the three of us were actually more spooked by the whole notion of Jewish Orthodoxy. The kabbalah rites evoked in the *Dybbuk* ballet—the numerical chanting, the knockings on the floor a certain number of times— struck us as disturbingly compulsive, while in real life, the rocking and muttering of Orthodox Jews seemed to us almost like a neurological disorder handed down through the generations.

Our way of being Jewish was nebulous. We loved our raucous Passover seder—closely followed by Mummy's ingeniously devised Easter egg hunt. In December, we lit the Hanukkah candles for a few nights—but our attentions were soon diverted to decorating the Christmas tree.

On Yom Kippur, Daddy and Alexander would go "shul-hopping" together, catching various cantors in assorted synagogues around Manhattan. One time, I was invited along on the shul-hopping. When we arrived at an Orthodox synagogue, the usher informed me that I had to go upstairs and sit with the other women. *What?* But—but I was with my father and my brother! Sorry: rules were rules. As I trudged up to the balcony, I thought to myself: That's it. Count me out.

Culturally, however, we were very Jewish: the Yiddish expressions, the music, the literature, the theater people—and the Life

Jokes. That was the part of being Jewish that spoke to us; the religion part spoke to us less and less.

My father's way of being religious was quite personal. He seemed mainly to explore it through his reading and his music, so maybe his own kids' indifference didn't bother him too much (we hoped). After all, he'd married our mother, who was raised a Catholic. True, she took "the vows of Rachel" when she and my father were married, but that seemed to be mainly for the benefit of Sam and Jennie. I always imagined that Mummy might have had her fingers fibbing-crossed behind her wedding dress, for her mother, Chita, to see. It had certainly been important to our father for Alexander to have his bar mitzvah—but once Grandpa died the following year, my brother was off the hook.

The morning after Justus's concert, I went upstairs to Mendy's apartment, where Justus was staying. We wound up in bed together. I thought nothing of it; it was, as I told my friend Ann, "like dancing with an old friend."

I was still living with Sam. Back then, the thinnest of walls separated the notion of fidelity from the possibility of the next amorous adventure. There was as yet no fear of disease; we young women were all on the Pill and felt no particular pressure to settle down with one person, get married, have kids. In fact, we felt we were expressing ourselves as liberated women by postponing wedlock and motherhood, pursuing our careers, and making the most of our unfettered youth.

That was certainly my outlook, and so I felt increasingly uncomfortable to observe my mother's slow descent into a mute, existential despair. As I saw it, she'd given up her theatrical career to be Mrs. Maestro, and it struck my twenty-two-year-old mind as an old-fashioned, limiting choice for a woman to make. Back then, I could not begin to imagine my mother's calculations as she'd leaped into that marriage. Only much later, when I read her letters, did I come to understand what a complex but clear-eyed decision it had been for her. She knew the challenges; she knew she was marrying a tsunami—and a gay one at that. She believed she could handle it all, that she wouldn't sacrifice herself "on the L.B. altar." And she did handle it, for a long time. But then there was Tommy Cothran. And a mastectomy. And loneliness.

My father was conducting in Tanglewood on July Fourth, and we all went up for the holiday. We were given rooms in a grand old Berkshire pile called Wheatleigh, where Daddy had his own marvelously idiosyncratic quarters in a renovated aviary. (The Baldwin Piano Company had a hell of a time getting the Maestro's requisite piano up the spiral staircase.)

A bunch of us were sunning down by the pool when my mother arrived. She immediately walked over to the shadows and sat down. We knew it was because of the sun allergy, but still, Mummy's cold unhappiness chilled us like a damp cloud.

During the Haydn symphony that night, I saw her shoulders shaking. Was she crying? Later that night, she told me her beloved childhood nanny had died. I wondered if losing her *Mamita* had opened a rare floodgate for all the other grief my mother usually forbade herself from expressing.

Everyone seemed out of sorts that summer. A few weeks later, at dinner in Fairfield, Mummy remarked that my father had agreed to write a commissioned piece for Eugene Ormandy, the music director of the Philadelphia Orchestra, "out of vanity." It was a Mummy barb like any other, but Daddy bristled. "*Vanity?*" he yelled, rising out of his chair. "*Vanity??*"

He went outside and stalked around by himself for a while.

Later that night, he came up to Alexander and me and asked us, a bit sheepishly, what it was exactly that had made him leave the table. We weren't even sure ourselves, but we tried to reconstruct the conversation. "Hmm," Daddy said, "I guess I must be getting a little paranoid in my old age."

In a letter to Ann the following day I wrote: "It's as if the whole family's going through adolescence this summer. Everybody's so TOUCHY."

In August we all convened in Salzburg for the summer music festival—along with Mendy, whom Mummy was fond of introducing as her "retarded stepdaughter." (Mendy loved that.) My

The family in Salzburg, summer of 1975.

father spent the week rehearsing Mahler's Eighth Symphony with the Vienna Philharmonic: a huge and historic undertaking. After decades of resisting Mahler's music, the orchestra was finally coming around, largely due to my father's advocacy. We went to the rehearsals and reveled in the magnificent music-making. We had to pinch ourselves sometimes: remind ourselves to stay amazed at our good fortune as we witnessed Daddy driving forward those earth-shattering Mahler symphonies. It was our task—our life's work, really—not to take these experiences for granted.

That week, we had a strange, stiff lunch with the Austrian conductor Herbert von Karajan and his wife, Eliette, a French former fashion model, at their house outside of Salzburg. The decades-long rivalry between the two maestros was legendary, so we all felt self-conscious. I was braced for encountering a rigid, authoritarian presence; he was a former Nazi, after all—a fact that had very much exacerbated the Bernstein-Karajan rivalry. So I was taken aback to witness Mme von Karajan flirting, it seemed to me, almost maliciously with Daddy, while making jab after jab at her frail, tense, socially awkward husband. From that lunch, I would never have guessed he was a titan on the podium. My father had certainly infuriated Mummy many a time, but I never saw her belittle her husband in front of others the way Mme von Karajan did to her own husband that day. I left that lunch with a lump in my throat I couldn't explain.

*   *   *

Sam and I drifted apart; he returned to live with his parents in New Jersey, and I moved into room 126 on the ninth floor of the Dakota—a "servant's quarters" that had come with the downstairs apartment. Mummy installed a bathroom so I wouldn't have to use the old communal bathroom down the narrow, spooky hallway.

Room 126 was an ideal transition between living at home and being independent: I could come and go and entertain visitors however I wished—but a hot meal and laundry opportunities were always just down the back stairs.

In the midst of those complicated times, I was persuaded to take the Erhard Seminars Training, known as est. Many of my parents' friends thought est's founder, Werner Erhard, was the most enlightened man in the world. His repackaging of Zen Buddhist principles for Western consumption put us in touch with our true emotions, the reality of our relationships, and what an "asshole" we could be a lot of the time. Many people emerged from the est training feeling a little bit smarter than everyone else around them—in other words, more of an asshole than ever. I was no exception, even though I thought I was, which made it even worse.

Jamie in front of the Dakota.

When my solipsistic twenty-three-year-old self collided with
the human potential movement of the 1970s, a little monster was
spawned. I tortured my family with my new revelations about
our interpersonal dynamics. I wrote both of my parents letters of
deep, frightening, est-worthy truth. I can't remember if I handed
them over; I hope I didn't. But est seemed like a promising tool for
helping my family communicate honestly with itself; our ongoing
inability to articulate our feelings to one another was making me
nearly frantic.

I joined the grownups who had done est in trying to persuade
my parents to take the training themselves, but we never could
convince them. Daddy was too busy, and Mummy was put off by
est's tacky jargon. (I wasn't too fond of it myself: "You are your
own reality!" "Create your own space!") Above all, my mother
loathed est's essential idea of "telling it like it is." The very thought
of articulating one's feelings in front of others was abhorrent to
her. She could barely tolerate visiting her new psychiatrist, whom
she delicately referred to as "my doctor." It was someone's dirty
trick to plant Felicia Montealegre into the middle of the blabber-
mouthy 1970s.

I decided to take graduate writing courses at Columbia—not
for the degree, but for the experience and the training. I liked being back in school in this unburdened, part-time way. Writing had
always come easily to me, and my courses provided a pleasantly
legitimate means of postponing any serious career decisions. The
truth was, I had no idea at all what to make of my life. But I had
to admit one thing: writing was so much less fraught than making
music. I'd definitively moved on from my fledgling attempts at being a singer-songwriter. What a ridiculous idea that had been.

But maybe it wasn't quite that simple. One night at the Dakota, Alexander and I were watching TV in the library with some

friends when we discovered that Leonard Bernstein was on PBS, conducting my old favorite, Mahler's Fourth Symphony. The sleigh bells! I danced around the library to the familiar music. Then, when the soft, aching third movement began, I slipped into the adjoining living room and settled cross-legged into the big upholstered rocking chair. The back of the chair was so tall that no one in the library could see me as I listened to the slow movement with my eyes closed, tears streaming down my face.

The next day I wrote in my journal:

I was crying because I can't be a musician. I was crying because I can't be a musician. I was crying because I can't be a musician.

13

Here Come the Terrors

My father was finally gaining some momentum in his new musical with Alan Jay Lerner. He'd been working on it off and on for a couple of years now, squeezing in the composing between all his conducting and traveling. But now the crunch was on; he and Alan Jay were determined to get it done in time for 1976, the Bicentennial year, mere months away. During the summer, I was often conscripted to pick Alan Jay up at the marina in Norwalk, Connecticut, where he would arrive in his seaplane. He had his very own island in Long Island Sound; I surmised that if you'd written the book and lyrics to *My Fair Lady* and *Camelot*, you could afford to buy an island and a seaplane.

Alan Jay was a most peculiar man: always hidden behind tinted glasses, full of nervous tics, perpetually smoking—as well as pulling on and peeling off a pair of beige linen gloves that either protected some skin condition he had or helped him not bite his nails, or maybe he just needed always to be picking and pulling at something.

Once again, we found ourselves gathering around the piano at the drinks hour as Daddy played us the latest number he'd written—just as we'd done when he was writing *Mass*. But our family was different now, four years later. We were older, stuff had happened—and the anger that lodged in our collective craw like an indigestible piece of gristle only made it harder for us to summon up the enthusiastic encouragement we knew our father craved.

He told me that when he started writing for Broadway in the

1940s, he was convinced that musicals were the genre of the future, that they would develop into a rich and sophisticated art, like opera. He was bitterly disappointed, he said, that somewhere along the line, musicals had stopped evolving in some crucial way. The great exception, of course, was his kid collaborator on *West Side Story*, Steve Sondheim, whose shows were steadily transforming what was possible in Broadway theater.

But apart from Steve, my father said, Broadway remained mostly silly, safe, and essentially mass entertainment. The money came from the box office, so you had to please the crowd, he explained. But maybe now, he said, with corporations footing the bill the way Coca-Cola was doing for his new show, things could open up a little.

It was indeed true that the Coca-Cola Company had sunk *one million dollars* into the Bernstein-Lerner show: a corporate first. However, the show wasn't going well at all.

Not only was *1600 Pennsylvania Avenue* a story of the White House, with its presidents and their wives upstairs, and successive generations of a black servant family downstairs; not only was the White House the metaphor for the nation's ongoing struggle to preserve its democracy; not only was the show about our nation's original sin of slavery, and how racial injustice remained at the core of our national discourse; but in addition, all of this was supposed to be played out through the relationships of the actors themselves, who were in a *rehearsal* of the show, you see—because our country is in constant "rehearsal" for attaining true democracy—and the actors in the mixed-race cast would occasionally step out of character and argue among themselves about the meaning of the work they were rehearsing, and their fraught relationships with one another.

Like the Brecht musical my father had worked on seven years earlier, this show had *levels*—the collaborators' favorite word.

Alexander could have recited a hell of a Haf Torah cantillation for this one. Hearing Daddy repeatedly describe the show's intricacies gave us a bone-deep exhaustion. We had the uneasy sense that this project meant more to him than anything that had come before it.

Nixon, Vietnam, and Watergate had shaken up thoughtful lefties like Alan Jay Lerner and Leonard Bernstein. Now the two collaborators wanted to make a major statement about the meaning of democracy: to remind their country of its true purpose. It was all terribly earnest and ambitious. I think they really believed that if the show was good enough, they could bring a troubled, divided nation to its senses.

But maybe Daddy had another, more personal agenda. Maybe he was doubling down on the very commitment to civil rights and social justice that had got him—and his wife—into so much trouble six years earlier with the Black Panthers incident. Maybe he felt he could avenge all the heartache and humiliation our mother had gone through. Maybe he felt that with this one show, he could fix . . . everything.

As the *1600* rehearsals progressed, all the reports were terrible. The director was fired. The choreographer was fired. The expectations were enormous, and Coca-Cola, our Bicentennial Beverage, probably had the highest hopes of all. After all, with those two Broadway giants at the helm, how could they lose?

While the show was still out of town, the authors, with their new director and choreographer, made a radical, last-minute decision. They cut the whole "surround" story: the part about the rehearsal and the black and white actors coming out of character to talk with one another about the meaning of the show. Alexander and I had thought the in-rehearsal device was somewhat clunky, but at least it turned the actors themselves into characters that developed, that you could possibly even root for. Without that element, the show was reduced to a lengthy pageant. We imagined the Philadelphia audience members, after president number five or so, feeling doomed in their seats—trapped until the end of the parade.

There were other strange decisions, too. Act 1 ended with the conclusion of the Civil War, but we never actually met Lincoln; we saw only his top-hatted shadow. In Act 2, in the part depicting the corrupt Grover Cleveland administration, there was a "minstrel show." It was supposed to be riotously funny and a bit outrageous. But Alexander, Nina, and I cowered in our seats when the black actor sang "I got those red, white, and blues" in falsetto—and in drag.

The all-too-brief marquee for *1600 Pennsylvania Avenue*.

And yet, and yet: So much of Daddy's music was beautiful. Wipe-your-eyes beautiful, stuck-in-your-head-for-days beautiful. But his huge score had been stuffed into a vehicle that could not carry it.

A few days before the New York opening, we went to the "gypsy run-through" of the show, a Broadway tradition in which friends and family comprise the majority of the preview audience. That night may have been the show's single oasis of optimism. After the performance, the front rooms of the Dakota apartment rang with the babble of voices sharing their collective conviction that the authors had a hit on their hands. "You know," my father said happily after several scotches, "I think this is going to be a really *important* work."

I thought: Oy vey.

I remember only two things about the opening night of *1600 Pennsylvania Avenue*: my blinding headache, and the way Daddy, who was sitting to my left, would grip my knee each time he wanted the audience to be particularly ravished by the beauty and emotion of his music—as if he were *willing* the show to be good through my patella.

Clive Barnes's review in the *New York Times* the next morning was a death knell. Harry Kraut called the Dakota apartment to report that the show would close on Saturday, after seven performances. Coca-Cola would lose all its money.

My father and Alan Jay were so shattered, they couldn't even face making a cast album. And so all that work, all that music—it was simply gone.

As Steve Sondheim liked to say: "At least when Lenny falls off the ladder, he falls off the highest rung."

Lenny may actually have believed that if he just wrote the right combination of notes, he could unlock the secret to saving the

Jamie, Felicia, Alexander, and LB on the opening night
of *1600 Pennsylvania Avenue*.

planet. *1600 Pennsylvania Avenue* was his most earnest attempt
yet to heal wounds and open hearts through the power of his own
music. He had always tried, as hard as he knew how, to make
the world a better place through his outspoken advocacy for the
things that mattered: civil rights, human rights, world peace.
He'd often gotten in trouble for saying what he felt, or composing
as he chose. But we, his kids, understood from his example that
you stood up, you spoke out, for the things you believed in—and
you took your lumps.

Leonard Bernstein had certainly taken his share of lumps. But
it hadn't been difficult for us to cling to our vision of him as an

essentially successful human being. Those Grammys and Emmys that ran the length of his studio shelves displayed a shiny parade of achievement. His concert audiences went into paroxysms of adulation, all over the world. He'd written the score of *West Side Story*, for God's sake! But *1600* was a Failure with such a great big capital *F* that the scales felt like they were tipping vertiginously toward some other definition of who he was, and therefore who we all were.

There's a line that can be traced through so many Bernstein pieces, showing one iteration after another of his crisis of faith: his lifelong battle with his spiritual Creator. Alexander, Nina, and I now found ourselves in a similar crisis over our biological creator—and *1600* was its inflection point. When we were little, our father had been unassailably magnificent to us—just as he had been to the world. Now he seemed complex, flawed, mortal. Squaring the early Daddy with the later one would be our challenge from now on.

* * *

Finally, in July, arrived the endlessly hyped Bicentennial. On the Fourth, Daddy was conducting the Philharmonic in Central Park. Alexander and I chose not to go, which made me feel guilty, but I felt better when Nina announced she didn't want to go, either. With Nina now fourteen, Alexander and I were expanding into a trio, far more capable of resisting the Lenny juggernaut. Anyway, we were *pretty* sure our father would forget all about us not being there at the concert.

A few days later, for Alexander's big twenty-first birthday party up in Fairfield, Daddy had arranged for a small plane to fly over the house trailing a banner that said "Happy Birthday Alexander!" But when the plane made its appearance overhead, Alexander was indoors smoking pot with some friends; he missed the flyover. Daddy flew into an uncharacteristic rage.

Mummy didn't join the party until late in the day. She emerged at five p.m. with big sunglasses on; that meant she'd been crying.

Later, we pieced it all together. Julia reported that she'd heard the two of them arguing the night before and that La Señora was using her big, scary theater voice. Alexander found Daddy's watch in the guest room the next morning. It emerged that our father had decided not to go up to Martha's Vineyard with the rest of the family the following month. It further emerged that he was planning instead to spend the month in Northern California with Tommy Cothran. And Mummy had apparently told him that if he did that, he would not be welcome to come back to the Dakota in the fall. And Daddy had said okay.

Alexander said, "He's coming out of the closet ass-first."

For the next several weeks, Mummy was alternately furious or bleakly exhausted. Alexander couldn't bear to discuss the situation at all, beyond the occasional sarcastic remark. I couldn't tell if Julia knew what was happening. Nina was being kept in the dark, as usual, but she couldn't escape noticing that everyone was deeply out of sorts—her mother most of all. The entire family seemed to be in some kind of paralysis, where no one could speak honestly to anyone else. It was a rough month on Martha's Vineyard—all the rougher because our mother's idea of renting a house there in the first place had been a quixotic attempt to recapture the family bliss of all those years ago, on the figure-of-speech lagoon. How could the rambunctious, close-knit family that had resided there be the same one that was now in such sorry tatters?

I went back and forth between the Vineyard and New York; I could take the atmosphere on the island for only a few days at a time. But Alexander was truly devoting himself to looking after Mummy; he'd decided not to go back to Harvard in the fall so he could be near her. Well, maybe that was his rationale—he wasn't enjoying his college experience much—but it was a compelling one. I wondered: Was I not being supportive enough of my mother during this most awful time for her? Alexander seemed to be "taking sides," while I was trying so hard to be equitable. I wanted my father to find his true self and be happy with who he was—that was my est graduate's thinking—but I couldn't help being ambivalent over how gracelessly he was going about it, and how much pain he was inflicting on our mother. It was bad enough that he was leaving her, but leaving her for a man, and leaving her to deal with the social repercussions in New York while he gallivanted with impunity on the West Coast—well, it was galling as hell. Sometimes I wondered if I *should* have been taking sides.

At the same time, though, I knew my father was suffering over the debacle of *1600*. Maybe that was part of what had hurled him into his new life with Tommy: a fresh, healing life of love and poetry and composing. Later that month, I read something that reminded me of why the business of composing was more fraught than ever for him. It was an article in the *Atlantic* magazine about twentieth-century American composers, with a family-tree arrangement of the names spread across several pages. I started reading the names: a catalog of American musico-academic orthodoxy. Leonard Bernstein's name was nowhere to be found. His diverse, tonal compositions had effectively wiped him off that tree. I never discussed the article with him, but I guessed that, while he couldn't have been too surprised, he was probably stung all the same.

I talked with my father's lawyer and friend, Paul Epstein, about what we could do to help find new composing projects for LB, as everyone had taken to calling him. (I myself felt the initials injected a welcome millimeter of distance between my father and me.) Paul came up with the idea that I should collaborate with LB on a project: write him a set of lyrics, or a libretto, or *something*. It was a tempting fantasy: the joint project, the rehabilitative element. But hadn't I been striving all these years to attempt to define myself *apart* from LB? Did I really want to hitch myself to his blinding star before I'd made anything bright out of myself?

"It's a terrible idea," my shrink declared. He then told me about Anna Freud, and how she'd wound up devoting her life to her father's work at the expense of any gratifying personal life of her own. Beware of turning into Anna Freud, he said. (That warning haunts me still.)

My father came back from California sporting, of all things, a beard. I told Alexander I thought Daddy looked "like a Hasidic koala bear." He moved into a suite in the Hotel Navarro on Central Park South, and Tommy Cothran was there with him much of the time. LB was madly in love, starting a new life—so he was cheerful, acting exuberantly gay and calling everyone "darling." He'd even adopted my mother's elegant white Aqua Filters, which elongated his every gesture into campy extravagance.

It was Mummy who was suffering. What a godsend that she got cast in an interesting play, *Poor Murderer*, by Czech playwright Pavel Kohout, directed by her old friend and drama teacher, Herbert Berghof. It was the ideal distraction; she was busy day and night with rehearsals and performances. The play got a good review, and all Mummy's friends came to see her. Her old stage fright seemed to take a back seat to her pleasure in having this intense work to focus on. In one scene, while dressed in a skimpy corset, Mummy leaned over the actor Laurence Luckinbill from behind. From the audience, I could see down her cleavage into the empty space on her left—or was I just dreading that I could see the empty space?

While our mother stayed at the theater for her two performances on Thanksgiving Day, the rest of us had turkey at the Dakota—LB included. It was all primarily for the benefit of Nina and Julia, neither of whom had been told exactly what was going on. Nina was always being "protected" from bad tidings. She'd found out that her parents' separation was public knowledge by reading the gossip column in the *New York Post* over someone's shoulder as she rode the bus to school: "West Side Story '76: Bernstein and Wife Split." And, incredibly, no one—either in our family or anyone close to us—ever thought to take a moment to sit down with Nina and attempt to explain her father's complexities: that he was gay, or bisexual; that he still adored his children; that adults were complicated. Or whatever one might say to reassure a child at such a time. Maybe, in the mid-1970s, adults didn't have the words yet for this situation. In any case, Nina felt painfully isolated, and would have a great deal of unraveling to do later on, when she began visiting a psychotherapist.

Julia, meanwhile, had heard rumors that there was "another woman." Everyone felt Julia would have a nervous breakdown if she found out it was another man. Yes, Julia was Catholic and old-fashioned, but I felt it would honor her more as a human being, and as a member of the family, to tell her what was actually going on. So I sat down with her at the little round table in the Dakota kitchen, and over our cups of Lipton tea, I told her about El Caballero's relationship with Tommy. She didn't act exceptionally stricken; maybe she'd guessed after all. Afterward I felt grateful to have had at least one genuine exchange with a family member.

A few nights later, Mummy asked me to walk with her to her bedroom; she had something to say to me. The dread clenched my

Bearded LB with Tommy Cothran in Carmel, 1976.

solar plexus; the last time this happened, she'd revealed her up-coming mastectomy to me on the little stone bench by the frog pond. What would it be this time?

In her bedroom, she didn't invite me to sit. We stood awkwardly near the little Gothic wooden door that connected her bedroom to her husband's. Looking intensely at me, she asked me a very special favor: to please refrain from socializing with Daddy and Tommy together while they were in New York. She told me Alexander had agreed to her request.

This was everything I'd hoped to avoid: a demand to "take sides," which my est-enlightened self was trying so hard not to do, combined with the sinking feeling that maybe Alexander was being a better offspring than I was. But what if there was one of those typically large postconcert dinners that just happened to include Tommy among the guests? I didn't feel I should be compelled to bow out of such a gathering, and I told my mother so. The anguished look on her face made my insides crumple; I knew how hard—humiliating, even—it must have been for her to beg this favor, and how badly I was wounding her by turning down her request. I also knew that she needed, at this most vulnerable of moments, to feel that everyone, *everyone* was in her corner . . . but I just couldn't do it. I stood there in front of her in her bedroom, feeling as stiff and inhuman as the oak on the ecclesiastical door frame.

In those uneasy times, with all the guilt and pain in the air, it was difficult not to resent Harry Kraut. Sometimes it seemed as if everything had started going rotten when he came on the scene. It was confusing for me: I had so many beloved friends who were gay men, but Harry, who was gay, was so repellent. He had encouraged LB to embrace his new gay life, and I certainly wanted my father to be happy, but I couldn't help feeling that Harry's machinations were causing our family untold grief.

Harry went out of his way to be kind, but it often backfired. He cooked up the idea that after Christmas, I should take Nina on a week's vacation in Puerto Rico; it would be a nice way to get her out of the oppressive home atmosphere. He set the whole trip up for us, and off we went. We arrived in San Juan to discover that he'd installed us in a seedy motel many blocks away from the beach—where, in any case, there were signs posted saying no swimming because the water was polluted. At midnight on New Year's Eve, Nina and I found ourselves hugging each other in a bus shelter. But from that trip forward, we were more than older and younger sister: we were unshakable allies.

Soon after Nina and I returned from San Juan, LB took off on his next big adventure, a very gratifying one: he was invited to perform at Jimmy Carter's Inaugural Concert. It was the first really good piece of political news in a long time; at last, the final remnants of Nixon had been swept away. We all (minus Mummy, the hardworking actress) went down to Washington, a big noisy mess of us, for a weekend of celebrations. At the Inaugural Concert, LB conducted an excerpt from his new work, *Songfest*: settings of American poetry spanning three hundred years. He and Tommy had spent many hours together researching and choosing the texts; this piece was their "baby." The text of the excerpted song, "To My Dear and Loving Husband," was by seventeenth-century Puritan poet Anne Bradstreet. Daddy said he was dedicating it to President Carter's wife, Rosalynn. In the song, a trio of women's voices wove a rich harmonic tapestry expressing the depth of a woman's love for her spouse. Hmm.

If ever wife was happy in a man,
Compare with me, ye women, if you can . . .

Why did Daddy always have to make everything so *squirm-worthy*?

But after spending several months in Palm Springs with Tommy Cothran that winter, LB apparently concluded that he couldn't make a life with him after all. They squabbled constantly; they had completely different living habits. They remained affectionately in touch, but they parted ways. I suspected that my father wasn't quite ready to adapt to life as an openly gay man. He was still considerably tethered to his middle-class immigrant upbringing, which prized assimilation above all; being openly gay sure didn't figure into that time-honored trajectory. Aunt Shirley was trying to be supportive; maybe she even found it vaguely preferable not to be competing against another woman for her brother's attentions. But Uncle BB wasn't enjoying any of it. And my father, as well, could not have been too happy about this new element of discomfort with his beloved siblings—even though he'd generated it himself.

Above all, it was no small thing that Jennie Bernstein was still very much alive. Her son had not explained his new situation to her. Mothers are good guessers about such things—but if Jennie guessed, she preferred not to acknowledge. LB was very careful about his dealings with his mother. He called her every Friday, no matter where in the world he was. She adored him above all else— she called him "my prince of peace"—and he tried not to upset her. But he was tiptoeing around his mother more than ever.

And finally, maybe my father just couldn't live with his guilt over abandoning his wife. He knew how badly she was suffering. So there were considerable forces at work to make him want to come back.

It happened gradually.

When LB conducted William Walton's charming piece *Façade* at the brand-new Alice Tully Hall, Mummy and Mendy were the droll co-narrators. All of that went pretty well. As usual, Mendy served as the emulsifier: cracking jokes, singing aria snippets, and feigning melodramatic outrage over nothing at all.

Soon after that, my parents started going out to the occasional dinner, just the two of them. Sometimes, my father even came to the Dakota for dinner. That was very confusing. We felt the tide was turning—but turning into what, exactly, we weren't sure. Alexander was at one of those dinners; Mendy was there, too, of course, and maybe a few others. At one point, the conversation turned dark over something. Mummy pointed her finger across the table at her estranged husband and, with her biggest, scariest actress voice, laid her curse on him: "*You're going to die a lonely, bitter old queen.*"

Maybe it was partly a campy joke—but not a very funny one. Daddy never mentioned the incident again to any of us, but we had

Mendy the emulsifier.

the sense he never forgot what she said that night. It may well have accounted for how hard he worked in later years to keep the curse from coming true.

*   *   *

And then, one day, things were sort of back to normal. The beard was gone, and our parents were a couple again. There was tentative relief all around. Mummy sure was coughing a lot, though.

At first, Felicia's prerequisite for her husband's return was that he unload Harry. But the next thing we heard, she was planning to spend the month of August in a schloss in Austria, while LB conducted a festival of his own music over there. That sounded like she'd be jumping squarely back into the middle of all the difficulties—Mrs. Maestro, Harry Kraut, and all.

LB went to Europe first. Meanwhile, in New York, it was 104 degrees on July 21 when I arrived at the Dakota with friends, and Alexander asked me to "help him in the kitchen." We got as far as the dining room when he slumped into the big mustard-colored chair. "Mummy's fucked," he said. She had a tumor in her lung. Her breast cancer had metastasized.

The doctor subsequently told us that the tumor was in a lymph node and not in the lung itself, which meant it could be successfully treated. Everyone was euphoric. Our mother was released from the hospital and we all went out to Mendy's house in Roxbury for a raucous dinner where Mummy played the castanets. The next

Felicia, after the diagnosis, July 1977.

day in Fairfield, Mike Nichols came over with his wife, Annabel, and their two kids: Max "the Mouse" and Jenny "the Peach." Dick Avedon came out, too, and a few other close friends. My mother looked somehow more beautiful than she ever had. The heat had subsided, and there was plenty of tennis and swimming, eating and drinking. All the usual elements, framed in an unspoken panic.

Some family friends asked me to help persuade my mother to take laetrile—a countercultural anticancer remedy made from apricot pits that was getting a lot of attention at the time. My shrink, who had actually testified in court on the subject, told me that laetrile was a lot of hooey. I felt caught in the middle—but in any case Mummy didn't want to discuss it: any of it, with anyone, at all, ever.

LB rushed home from Austria, and there we all were at the dinner table: Mummy, Daddy, Alexander, me—and Harry Kraut. (Nina was at her summer job at Tanglewood.) With the new health crisis, any discussion of ejecting Harry had been set aside. He was, after all, a manager—and the new circumstances certainly cried out for management.

Up at Tanglewood, Nina was being told nothing, as usual. I began filling her in through an exchange of letters. I think our parents were clinging to the illusion that as long as they didn't tell their littlest child what was going on, none of it was really happening.

All summer, I cringed to hear Mummy's cough: a long, slow, tearing sound, over and over, as she tried to get to the bottom of the congestion. My father's lavish attentions on Mummy were also hard to take. He would stretch himself out alongside her on the bed; the nicotine stink of his breath made her nearly retch, she confessed to me. But the most she could ever bring herself to say was, "Lenny, you've been smoking a lot today." He never took the hint, and she never kicked him off her bed.

My mother had the lymph node removed, but the new reports were that maybe the disease wasn't just in the lymph node after all. At the hospital, LB befriended Dr. Lewis Thomas, whose best-selling book, *The Lives of a Cell*, had turned the author into everyone's literary hero. LB described the situation to Dr. Thomas, hoping for a better interpretation from the brilliant physician. "I'm afraid it's going to be pretty grim," Dr. Thomas said. That turned out to be an accurate diagnosis.

LB had brought his wife a present from Austria: a little plaster angel from a country church, painted pink, green, and gold. She placed it on a stand to the left of her bed so that it perched over her shoulder. All I could think of, looking at that angel, was what Daddy had said to Alexander and me the day before, as we stood in the murky corridor, keeping our voices low: "We simply have to accept that every day of Mummy's life from now on is going to be about death."

Alexander, Daddy, and I accompanied Mummy to her radiation therapy. We sat in the waiting room with all the cancer patients. After twenty minutes, my father and brother got up. Daddy turned to me and said, "We're going to do the unspeakable for a moment. We'll be right back." Cigarettes.

LB returned to Europe, and Mike Nichols invited the rest of us to his house in Bridgewater, Connecticut, for the weekend. It was heaven to be out of the steaming city, to be taken care of. Mike was gentle, funny, welcoming. At dinner, he sliced and served the meat, passing plates around, so graceful and completely without airs—and there were suddenly tears in my eyes.

As far as I could recall, my father had never carved a roast in his life. Suddenly that felt like the most grievous possible omission in my upbringing.

In the fall, the author Susan Sontag began coming over to the

Dakota to spend time with my mother. Daddy had organized these visits, because Susan herself had recently gone through breast cancer. She was brimming with knowledge and advice, and was writing a fascinating book, *Illness as Metaphor*, about diseases and their relationship to the culture in which they occur. Susan Sontag was handsomely beautiful, an intense and brilliant woman who had handled her own illness by immersing herself into every aspect of its science and history. The dining room walls reverberated with the authority in her voice.

But the last thing on earth my mother wanted to do was to talk about her condition with others. The bouts of chemo-induced sickness were so awful that when they were over, she just wanted to flush away the entire experience, pretend it hadn't happened: that was her own way of coping. So it was a hardship for her to put up with Susan Sontag.

Alexander continued to be close at hand, in his fugue state, relying heavily on the many substances in constant supply all around us. Well, we both relied on them. Not only were we smoking pot all the time, but there was an inexhaustible supply of liquor at home, as well. Plus, there was our father's toiletry case.

It was a hefty black leather valise, with upper tiers that lifted out sideways, like wings. Each winged tier had a little round box with a tortoiseshell screw lid. One box had the blue Valiums and red Seconals; the box on the other wing had the green Dexamyls and orange Dexedrines. Downers on the left, uppers on the right. Alexander and I visited that toiletry case often, but Daddy never remarked upon the attrition rate of the pills, nor did any of his assistants; maybe they, too, were availing themselves of the contents.

I resorted to my various diversionary behaviors to distract myself from the fearsome troubles. Swanning around New York with my father was a reliable source of distraction, and Mummy often let me borrow her clothes for these excursions. One evening, I wore her beautiful gray silk Halston pajamas to accompany my father to some gala event, which was followed by a party at Studio 54. The next day, as I walked past the lobby newsstand in the office building where I had a part-time job, I did the double-take of a lifetime: there, on the front page of the afternoon edition of the *New York Post*, was a picture of me in the Halston pajamas, dancing with Daddy at Studio 54! Was it the coolest thing or the silliest thing that had ever happened to me? Maybe both.

On the front page of the *New York Post*!

Like a homing pigeon, I sought refuge in old boyfriends. I even made a date with my old nemesis, Nick-oh-Nick. "Get off my bed!" Mummy shouted when I told her. "Don't do it!" Alexander said. But it was as if I had some old, grisly, dangling string to tie up; I slept with Nick that night, and was consumed with a deranged glee.

One iteration of my diversionary behavior was to develop obsessive crushes on celebrities—comedians mostly, for some reason. One was with Chevy Chase, then the absolute king of the new hit TV show *Saturday Night Live*. I would walk dreamily through Central Park, certain that I would run into Chevy at any moment, whereupon our lives would be forever united. Then it was Lily Tomlin. She was the only person I ever waited for at a stage door to get an autograph.

And then it was Steve Martin, whose comedy made me feel fizzy to my very bones. Alexander, Nina, and I doted on his routines and catch phrases—and I also loved his unaffected, accomplished banjo playing.

I arranged for a whole bunch of us to see a late-night Steve Martin performance at Avery Fisher Hall. I even insisted that my father come along; what could be a better distraction from our family troubles than the zany hilarity of Steve? As I think back now to that evening, I wonder if Daddy had consumed an orange pill; his disconcertingly flirtatious manner of tormenting me was in high gear that night. I described the events in a letter to Ann:

I arrived at the Dakota. Oohs and aahs over my very red dress. Mummy said I looked swell. But LB had a problem. He wanted me to tie up the strings that hang from the collar. "But they're supposed to hang loose like that," I explained. "That's impossible," he said. "Come on, tie them up." "No, really, it's okay, Daddy." "Tie them up! You look like a slut!"

he roared. He was half playing with me, making a fuss for the fun of fussing with me. "Ask Mummy," I said. "Go ahead, ask her!" Mummy said that just the other night she'd seen some chic woman wearing her shirt that way. LB was undaunted. He started in with me all over again.

Fortunately, Betty Bacall arrived, and LB's attention was diverted for a while. Then he started in AGAIN about my shirt. He started coming after me to tie up my dress. Half laughing, I kept backing off and he kept advancing, all the way from the bar to the living room. "Jamie, Jamie . . . why do you hate me so much?" *What* was going on??

LB laughed and laughed at the Steve Martin show. He was completely won over. After all the comedy gags and hilarious insincerity and bouncing around, Steve played his banjo. The incredible serenity that was suddenly washing over the audience from that stage!

Afterwards, the backstage manager escorted us to the good old green room. Steve Martin made fun of himself for being ignorant of LB's field, yet there he was occupying the Maestro's very own dressing room. At one point LB, inspired by Steve Martin's antic energy, attempted to scramble on top of the grand piano in the green room. I wanted to die.

As we were leaving, we ran into Madeline Kahn. She said she was too shy to go in to meet Steve Martin, so LB said he'd take her in. The rest of us stood in the corridor, exhausted, hot, standing around, Waiting for Maestro. Finally I volunteered to go back in and get him out of there. Bravely I strode in and put my arm around LB and cleared my throat. And then, he did the unbelievable:

"Steve, will you please tell my daughter to tie the strings on her shirt?"

*   *   *

I tried to hew to my writing and my various jobs, and yet I couldn't quite set aside my guitar; songs kept leaking out. There was a little piece of me that craved musical connections, hungered for performance—but I had such a terror of performing. The odious comparisons frayed my nerves, and I could never get through a song without making error after maddening error. While I practiced a tough passage, my stomach would writhe in distress as I fought down an overwhelming urge to flee. I realized one day that it was the identical feeling I used to have in that sickening half hour before the piano teacher arrived.

One drunken night at the grownups' favorite hangout, Elaine's, Alexander and I were sitting at a long table with family friends when it emerged that there was a new place across the street called Erik's, and somehow I was persuaded by the owner, Erik, to perform my songs there *that very evening*—on the condition that I bring over all my pals from Elaine's. It took courage and cocaine to pull it off, but I did in fact wind up later that same night performing three or four of my songs on the little stage of Erik's restaurant, in front of the likes of Bill and Rose Styron, Nora Ephron and Carl Bernstein, Jann Wenner, and a few others. I was in an agony of excitement and uncertainty. I made mistakes; I sang off-key. I felt sick from the vertigo of my possible humiliation. To this day I'm not sure whether I did all right or made a colossal fool of myself. One thing was for certain: cagey Erik took advantage of Leonard Bernstein's clueless twenty-four-year-old daughter to stack his new restaurant with luminaries.

It was a tough break, in a way, to have to debut in front of such a glittering little crowd. But that was my world, and I wanted so badly to make a splash in it—even as I feared that my very ambition meant I was a bad person. In my family universe, LB's ambition and grandiosity were tolerated. In the rest of us, such behavior was unacceptable—or at least that was the unspoken policy emanating from our mother. This perfect muddle of mixed signals was the conundrum I lived with. I couldn't imagine how to be an assertive performer without courting the risk of becoming a vain, obnoxious monster whom no one would love.

In spite of all my ambivalence, I pushed forward. I found a voice teacher, and I bought a guitar—a newfangled hybrid called an Ovation that could be plugged into an amp. In my ignorance, I thought it would sound all rock-'n'-roll-y, like an electric guitar, and was disappointed when it merely sounded like an amplified acoustic guitar, which is exactly what it was.

I even took some sight-reading lessons from my Harvard friend Jonathan. Reading music was painfully difficult for me. I had a good ear, so in my piano lessons I'd always memorized quickly, to get away from the printed page. How did my father *do* it? How did he read entire orchestral scores, forward and vertically at the same time? It was such a mystery to me. When I saw a chord, I had to spell it out to myself, one note at a time, until finally I would realize: Oh, it's D-flat major—just as people with dyslexia have to spell out a word letter by letter until they realize: Oh, it spells "table."

I arrived chronically late to my music lessons with Jonathan; they were a visceral torment for me. When it came to making music, I felt as if I were driving a car with one foot flooring the accelerator while the other foot was slamming on the brake.

*   *   *

LB had an endlessly revolving series of personal assistants. Once Harry came on the scene, the assistants tended to be attractive young gay men. None of them ever worked out for long. LB would subject his assistants to everything from scary word games to even scarier, shrinky discussions of their personal lives; he was eerily good, almost psychic, at locating a young person's most vulnerable inner bruise. Meanwhile, Harry would make excruciating logistical and scheduling demands. That winter, the assistant was a sweet young guy named Jeff. He was looking for a place to live. I'd just moved into a funky railroad apartment on Madison and 93rd. The even funkier apartment underneath my own became available, and I'd added it to my monthly rent, thinking it might come in handy for playing music. It was an eccentric floor-through space: not for everyone, but Jeff was a drummer, and he'd be able to play music down there without bothering people. (Downstairs was a store and upstairs was me, and I didn't care.) I thought it would be perfect to have a friendly, tidy, gay musician subletting the downstairs apartment.

He was tidy, all right—but it turned out that Jeff wasn't so gay. And what was more, we fell head over heels in love.

Harry inadvertently discovered the situation by calling Jeff from the airport. Jeff's visiting friend Phyllis answered the phone. When Harry asked for Jeff, she said, "He can't come to the phone right now, he's sleeping upstairs. Can I take a message?" Phyllis reported much spluttering at the other end of the line.

So Harry went off to Japan, and Jeff and I had skated out of a confrontation. But soon enough, Harry returned, and Jeff was fired. Whether or not Jeff had been good at his job, it was not okay for the personal assistant to be sleeping with his boss's daughter.

Meanwhile, Mummy rode the pitiless waves of chemotherapy, and had more hospital crises. Twice, the Dakota employees carried her downstairs in a wicker chair to a waiting ambulance. (One of

those times, she'd gone into fibrillation after becoming rhapsodi-
cally overexcited earlier in the evening at an extraordinary Vladi-
mir Horowitz recital at Carnegie Hall.)

I went to see her at the ICU in Mount Sinai. Her eyes were wide
with fear, dark around the edges. Her skin was flaky and discol-
ored. My father told me later that under "Religious Affiliation" on
her admission form, she'd written "CATH."

Once she was out of the ICU, my mother's hospital room was
regularly overrun with visitors, everyone very garrulous and
"on." I would see her body tensing when my father gave her one
of his long, adhesive kisses, full of meaning and depth of emotion.
I couldn't help thinking that the preponderant emotion might be
guilt.

My mother had to have her pericardium removed. My father
asked her oncologist, Dr. Holland, if he was sure they had to do
this; weren't they being a little hasty? Dr. Holland said, "We can't
be hasty enough."

Writing in a notebook in the waiting room at Mount Sinai, I
gnawed at the situation like an animal trying to chew its paw out
of a trap:

She is scared. I am scared. LB is scared. He tells Mummy
he's not scared. They struck a bargain that if he's not scared,
she won't be scared. But, Mummy said, what if I'm not scared
and you are scared? Then I will be scared. LB says he hasn't
been really scared until now. Now, he says, he's really scared.
But he was scared before; he just doesn't remember that he was
already scared.

When she came home from the hospital, Mummy began wearing a frilly white cotton mobcap threaded with an apricot-colored

satin ribbon; it was a present from her hair salon, Kenneth, where she'd had her hair done every week for the past twenty years. She looked like a sweet, ethereal old lady in a fairy tale. One afternoon, while I was lying at the foot of her bed, my mother asked me: "Why don't you apply to law school?" I couldn't have been more shocked if she'd flown to the ceiling. *Law school?* Hadn't our entire family's existence been based on the assumption that the arts were where the really interesting people were? All our friends were writers, musicians, painters, actors. But lawyers, accountants, businessmen—they were all drudges, weren't they? I was so confused by this bizarre piece of advice coming from my own pianist-actress-painter mother. But maybe she was suddenly feeling fed up with artists.

Because there was not already enough medical drama in the house, Daddy went and got himself a face-lift: just the eyelids and under the chin. He enjoyed the grandly appointed town house on East 78th Street where the surgery took place, and told us how he'd charmed the nurses and patients, and how his surgeon invited him to watch other people's operations. All the attention did him good. But he looked strange to us afterward—a bit like a panda startled out of a bad dream. Mummy said, "All the kindness has gone out of his eyes." But at least he could now read without peering past his drooping lids.

In the midst of all this, an absurdly ambitious new project was launching: my mother had found a house in East Hampton, the place where most of her friends went in the summer, and where she'd come to wish she could be instead of isolated in Fairfield. LB would buy the new house—and sell the one in Fairfield—and Mummy would fix it up in her inimitable way so we could all be there together the following summer. How exactly was this going to work? Could people even function without a pericardium?

Yet who dared second-guess Mummy's enthusiasm? And certainly none of us dared voice our acute dismay at the prospect of losing Fairfield.

A day or two after finding her dream house, my mother was brushing her hair, and great clots of it came out. She arrived at the breakfast table shaken and fearful, and said, "The jig is up." "What, they've sold the house to someone else?" Daddy said. "No, my hair is falling out!" "Oh, thank *God*!" he replied, and they both burst out laughing.

*   *   *

My father's lawyer, Paul Epstein, knew a guy who created marionettes that looked like real people if you sent in a photo. So Paul decided to commission five puppets representing the five members of our family, and present them to my parents for Christmas. I volunteered to write a show for the puppets, and I put a team of pals together to pull off the production.

Although the puppets were supposed to look like us, my story had them all playing other characters: there was an evil king in an imaginary kingdom who was plotting to poison the queen so as to acquire some valuable item from her . . . I barely remember the convoluted story anymore.

When Christmas Eve came, the Dakota apartment was chock-full of friends and family. My mother looked beautiful in her Kenneth wig. After dinner, I made everyone sit in the library to watch our show. It was long . . . very long. The audience created a spontaneous break partway through, tearing past us to get to the bar. Lillian Hellman was particularly grouchy. Well, she always groused, but still, I had a sinking feeling that things weren't going well. It reminded me of that night I performed at Erik's: Was I excelling or making a terrible fool of myself?

The last complete family holiday card,
Dakota living room, December 1977.

A few weeks later, Aunt Shirley invited me to lunch. She'd decided enough time had gone by so that she could tell me frankly
what she'd thought of the puppet show.

How was it possible that neither I nor any of my cohorts had
perceived the subtext of my story, in which the Lenny puppet
was scheming to poison the Felicia puppet? Shirley told me people didn't know where to look when it was over. Here I was, an
est graduate, a dedicated shrink patient, priding myself on being
insightful about human dynamics . . . How could I have been so
catastrophically blind? I left the lunch quivering in mortification; I
wished Shirley had never told me.

In January, my mother was well enough to join her husband
in Vienna, where he was conducting Beethoven's *Fidelio* at the
State Opera. She was ambivalent about going on that trip, and

we couldn't quite figure out why she was doing it at all. Mendy went along as her companion—her helper, really; she was very weak. But they had some laughs. Mendy told us that Mummy had adopted the German word *"ausgeschlossen"*—closed, or locked out—to mean anything that was unbearable or impossible. She would stretch her hands in front of her like a traffic cop and proclaim: *"AUS-geschlossen!!"*

Mendy reported that the weather in Europe was persistently freezing and damp, as were the hotels. In Milan, Mummy started to cough in earnest. The people they had to socialize with were stuffy diplomats, fancy folk, and music administrators. It was Mrs. Maestro time at its worst. Why had she agreed to go on that trip?

When Mummy returned to New York, she gradually regained some strength and, with the help of some massive cortisone shots, began picking fabrics, wallpapers, and furniture for the East Hampton house. Sometimes I was conscripted to run out there on various errands in the company of LB's new assistant, confusingly named Jamie. Jeff had arranged for Jamie, his best friend, to take over the job after Jeff himself had received his untimely termination. To reduce confusion, we referred to Jamie as Jet.

The three of us became a triumvirate. Jeff, Jet, and I played music together, and dreamed of forming a band. We even started looking for a loft downtown where we could live and play music. Lofts were cheap in SoHo, and the old cast-iron buildings down there were teeming with artists and musicians.

The music and the loft-hunting were good distractions from the Mummy terrors—but evidently not distraction enough. I came up with the grandest one of all: I was falling out of love with Jeff and falling seriously in love with his best friend, Jet. And yet the three of us were still planning to move into a loft together. The drama of it all was conveniently all-consuming.

My mother endured new rounds of chemo, harrowing episodes of heart fibrillation, a new tumor in her back. She was in constant pain. "We must make it seem hopeful," Daddy kept saying.

"It's been hell," she whispered to me in her darkened hospital room after vomiting all afternoon. Her cough sounded like a thousand sails tearing in a typhoon.

My father and brother resolved jointly to go to Smokenders, which was supposed to really, *really* work. Daddy had gone through several prior attempts to quit, all of them failures. Our family had been particularly beleaguered by a regime imposed by a hypnotist, who'd instructed our father that after dinner he was to close his eyes, count to twenty, and slowly raise his arm in front of him. We had a feeling he hadn't been told to do this *at* the dinner table, but that is what he did. It was a conversation stopper for sure. And it didn't work at all.

For Smokenders, Daddy was told to write down every cigarette he smoked, smoke with his other hand, delay the after-dinner cigarette by thirty minutes. He was also to drop his stubs into a large glass jar, which became a truly odious artifact. I hoped all this would work, but I had my doubts.

One spring afternoon I visited my mother in the hospital, and she discussed her death for the first and only time. She said she was going to ask soon for a priest. She said she wanted her funeral to be "almost Quaker—*no rabbis*." She said there were certain things she wanted certain people to have, and that one of these afternoons we'd sit down together and go through it all.

We never did sit down together and go through it all. She never went through anything, with anyone.

But the priest she was hoping for did come. Father Puma, a friend of her doctor's, came to her bedroom in the Dakota and gave her Communion. The effect was dramatic; Mummy was radiant.

Adolph, Mendy, and LB in East Hampton, a few days
before Felicia's death.

She even ate Chilean empanadas the next day. Daddy was very polite and friendly to Father Puma, but he seemed a bit bewildered by it all. The implication was that the husband had done all he could for his wife. She was turning elsewhere now.

On a Wednesday in late May, in a caravan of cars plus ambulance, we all moved, with Mummy, to East Hampton. The house wasn't ready, but we went there anyway; the sense was that if we didn't hurry up, she might not get to see it at all.

The next weeks were an eerie miasma of extended family and visiting friends, errands and more errands for the house, the "kids" playing lawn Frisbee in the late sunsets, furtive conferring in corners, testy dinner conversations, much drinking. And there I was, in the midst of it all, changing boyfriends midgallop, like some daredevil circus performer. And both of them plucked out of Daddy's own life, for a change.

It had always been true that my mother loved fixing up a new house, while my father only started enjoying the place once everything was settled—which was precisely the moment when Mummy would get restless and start hankering to move to a new place. Now, in East Hampton, my father didn't know where to put himself. His studio couldn't be assembled until the carpeting arrived; he had no place to call his own but the bed in his bedroom—so that is where he mostly stayed. He slept till late in the afternoon, and emerged complaining of problems like noise, or unsuitable lamplight. His main problem was, of course, unfixable.

One morning, Father Puma came out to celebrate Mass in my mother's bedroom. She lay in bed with her mobcap on, her makeup beautifully executed. The altar, at the foot of her bed, was a wicker table covered with a white linen tablecloth, a brass candleholder and white candle, and a small bowl of blue, yellow, and pink flowers. Father Puma put on his white robe in front of us. Outside it was foggy and damp. During the silences, we could hear the morning birds twittering, and the distant roar of the ocean. Mummy was glowing with joy. She read a passage from Song of Songs in a quiet, mellifluous voice. Later, Father Puma spoke in nearly frightened tones of my mother's spiritual energy. She didn't even know she had it, he said.

My father was in the next room, sleeping throughout. And Nina chose not to participate; instead, she performed the indispensable deed of answering the door for the workmen who had arrived at last to lay the carpet in Daddy's studio.

Later that day, my mother had enough strength to give her

husband a haircut. And that evening, as I sat beside her bed, she squeezed my hand and told me that all I needed, all anyone needed in this world, was to be sensitive to others. "Kindness," she said. "Kindness . . . kindness . . . kindness."

Daddy found a stale Carlton Menthol lying around the house somewhere, and he smoked it—on his Smokenders cutoff day. In truth, he and Alexander could not possibly have picked a more stressful time during which to kick the very habit that steadied their nerves.

Mummy started losing her bearings. Daddy said to her, "Isn't it wonderful that Jim Holland's coming out tomorrow?" "Who is Jim Holland?" "He's your doctor." "I don't have a doctor named Jim Holland." "Well, who *is* your doctor?" "Chuck Solomon." She had gone way back.

Then she began rejecting her medication, spitting it out and accusing Elizabeth, the nurse, of trying to poison her. Elizabeth asked Mummy, "Who am I?" Solemnly Mummy intoned, "Savonarola."

She began losing the power of speech. When Uncle BB arrived, her face lit up and she said, "Bee-ba? Bee-ba!" The only words that came out ungarbled were the fillers, like "Oh boy," or "I can't believe it," or "It's wonderful." Alexander said it was as if she were tripping on acid.

One evening, Elizabeth, the nurse, told me Dr. Holland had instructed her to give my mother a Demerol injection every two hours—in other words, Mummy was going to remain asleep. "So you mean this is it," I said. This was it, Elizabeth confirmed. I held Mummy in my arms and soothed her as Elizabeth administered the injection, after which there would be no further consciousness.

Mummy died early the next morning. In the afternoon, my father's friend Rabbi Judah Kahn drove out from New York City to officiate over the coffin in the living room. I remembered how Mummy had said "no rabbis." But at this point it was more for Daddy than for her; I was sure that wherever she was now, she would understand that. Anyway, Father Puma had his turn later that afternoon, when he celebrated Mass right there in the same living room.

The Mass was on the long side, because my father had requested that it be interspersed with a recording of the Mozart *Requiem* in its entirety. As the "Tuba Mirum" movement began, a white moth suddenly fluttered up from the coffin and flew lightly down the middle of the room, past the assembled family, friends, and domestic staff—and out the door. Mendy said later that the white moth was Mummy herself, saying, "That's it—too boring! *AUSgeschlossen!!* I'm getting out of here!"

14

Crawling from the Wreckage

We'd all driven out to East Hampton behind the ambulance; now, three weeks later, we all drove back behind the hearse. Why exactly was Felicia Montealegre going to spend the rest of eternity in Brooklyn? It was a Harry Special. The plot in Green-Wood Cemetery had room for additional family members—plus, Harry pointed out, the cemetery was easily reachable by subway, which would be convenient for the maids to visit. They were the ones, he said, who were most likely to want to visit the grave on a regular basis. Everyone in the family was too stricken to argue.

There was an open-ended gathering at the Dakota. The first person to arrive, and leave, was Mrs. Onassis. After a few hours, Jet and I couldn't take the atmosphere anymore. I left the house with him, wearing skimpy terrycloth shorts that barely covered my backside; Daddy was scandalized. "I'm in mourning!" he protested. As the sorry days unspooled, he was barely functional. He couldn't get out of bed. "I don't *ever* want to get up," he said. I believed him. The combination of loss and remorse had to be an intensely toxic brew—and he didn't have a fresh romance to hurl himself into, like I did. He didn't dress; he didn't shave; it was all Julia could do to get him to eat a few forkfuls of scrambled eggs. Julia herself was a hollow-eyed mess: visibly anguished, but at least able to perform her tasks, unlike El Caballero.

Eventually, Daddy was persuaded to go on a luxury yacht in the Aegean with Shirley and Uncle BB; the latter was himself reeling from his nasty divorce from Ellen. The three siblings managed to comfort one another and even have a laugh or two; Uncle BB told

The Three Apes: Burtie, Shirley, and (a bearded) Lenny.

us things really looked up when "the great god Freon" chose to restore the air-conditioning on the ship.

Nina went back to work at Tanglewood, where she was taken under the protective wing of composer Yehudi Wyner's family; Alexander bounced around between New York and East Hampton; and I stayed in the East Hampton house for the rest of that summer with Jet. I actually loved that house. No one else in the family did—especially my father, who never set foot in the place again.

Things were terrible with Julia. Her despair over losing her beloved Señora mostly manifested itself as rage at us three kids. I was an easy target for her tirades in my new role as "*dueña*" of the East Hampton house. Julia had nothing but contempt for my housekeeping abilities. I'm sure I was not adept, especially compared to my mother, but the greater struggle for Julia was to perceive me, her hapless charge since the age of two, as the *dueña* of *anything*.

Meanwhile, Julia nagged Alexander day and night for his disorderliness, for his sloth, for his smoking (Smokenders hadn't worked for him, either)—but he was going back to Harvard in the fall and would escape her clutches. It was Nina, entering eleventh grade, who was going to be truly and hopelessly stuck with Julia in that cavernous, grief-soaked Dakota apartment. I promised Nina I wouldn't abandon her, wouldn't leave New York as long as she was still living at home. As for our father behaving as any kind of head-of-household, let alone single parent, he couldn't be counted on for much of anything at the moment.

Before the autumn and Real Life kicked in, we first had to get through Leonard Bernstein's sixtieth birthday in late August.

An elaborate, long-planned event was coming up at Wolf Trap, outside Washington, DC: a big-ticket fund-raiser for the National Symphony, bristling with musical celebrities, and televised to boot—a major Harry Special that Daddy felt obliged to honor, despite his being in no mood for celebrations. The extended family and close friends went down to Washington for the occasion. The night before the concert, all twenty-one of us—everyone from Grandma and her sisters to André Previn to Betty Bacall—gathered for a big, raucous dinner at the Watergate Hotel, where we were all staying. Everyone was in dire need of diversion, and alcohol. At the long table we sang songs, performed party tricks, told dirty jokes, and made an unseemly racket—all of which helped us feel a bit more festive.

In the stultifying humidity of Wolf Trap's outdoor venue, Daddy conducted Slava Rostropovich, André Previn, and Yehudi Menuhin in the first movement of the Beethoven Triple Concerto:

a tremendous performance. Later, the entire audience spontaneously broke into a stately rendition of "Happy Birthday to You."
Daddy cried on stage—too shaken, for assorted reasons, to make
a speech.

Before the third section of the concert (the evening was endless),
Lillian Hellman made some controversially bitter remarks that
had to be cut from the TV broadcast: her friendship with Leonard
Bernstein was almost destroyed, she said, by their collaboration on
Candide, and their reconciliation was largely due to Felicia. It was
the only time Mummy was mentioned in the entire evening.

The loss of Felicia had ripped through our family's world with
a seismic shudder. She was so adored, so deeply beautiful . . . and
was gone unbearably too soon, at fifty-six. Heartbreaking cards
and letters arrived by the bushel. I wondered: Was everyone else
more upset than I was? It was hard to attend to my private feelings
when my mother's death was being mourned so intensely by so
many others. I could connect with my own grief only in isolated
spurts. I'd had those nearly mystical private moments with my
mother shortly before she died; after that, I pushed my feelings
down and marched forward—just as I had four years earlier, when
she told me she was going in for the mastectomy.

In September, there was a memorial at Alice Tully Hall. The
audience was thrumming with emotion. Among the speakers were
Mike Nichols, Steve Sondheim, Mendy, Phyllis Newman, and the
host of the event: dear, chivalrous Schuyler Chapin. A performance
of the slow movement from the Schubert double-cello quintet—
Mummy's favorite—wrung us out with beauty and sorrow.

I performed a song of my own: "Pull Up Your Socks!"—the
phrase my mother used on me whenever I was consumed with
melodrama. I had a crushing attack of nerves, my hands trembling
so intensely that I could barely pluck the strings of my guitar.

Halfway through, a faulty connection in the sound system began to make a deafening crackle. I was relieved that something other than myself was messing up my performance.

While LB dragged himself back to Europe to work with the Vienna Philharmonic, Aunt Shirley moved into the Dakota apartment so Nina wouldn't be left alone with the grief-addled Julia. Shirley herself had become ever shriller and more demanding over the years; she wasn't ideal company for Nina at such a delicate time. Alexander said our aunt's multisuitcased arrival was a little like acquiring a case of poison ivy to serve as a distraction from a kidney stone. "But at least you can laugh with Shirley," Nina said. Meanwhile, Mummy's decorator friend Gail Jacobs, who had helped with the East Hampton house, now redesigned Mummy's bedroom into a comfy, handsome studio for Daddy; he was keenly relieved to have his bedroom and studio next to each other again, the way they'd been in the Park Avenue apartment. Apartment 92, meanwhile, was in flux; various of Daddy's friends and assistants came and went, pulling down the little Murphy bed.

With Jeff now out of the picture, Jet and I began fixing up our drafty loft in SoHo. Our days were intense and uneasy. We spent long, bleak hours talking about my family, his family, our relationship; I'm surprised the kitchen table didn't collapse under the weight of all that verbiage. We spent weeks scraping the paint off the brick walls, and when that was done, we undertook the monumental project of building a soundproof music studio, from scratch, into a corner of the living room. As an additional distraction from my mother's death, I was throwing myself back into my music career; writing words had once again taken a back seat.

As always, I longed for Daddy to praise my music, but also I couldn't bear it. He would grasp my fingers and ask me to play him my new songs; when I pulled away, saying, "Tomorrow," he would squeeze my fingers tighter until it was a tug-of-war. He offered me music lessons. He asked me to collaborate with him on an opera. He pushed; I resisted. "Frontal, frontal," he would say every time I turned my head to avoid his attempt to kiss me on the lips. (But that in itself wasn't so unusual; he kissed everyone on the lips.)

Harry, to his credit, had quietly refrained from putting the Fairfield house on the market. Now the East Hampton house was to be sold, and all its contents absorbed into Fairfield. Decorator Gail made the Fairfield master bedroom pleasantly dark and masculine. My father had an unusual piano installed up there: a Bösendorfer upright that sounded wonderful, and allowed him to compose late at night. The piano soon acquired the Mark of Lenny that all his pianos had: a cigarette burn or two on the keys.

Gail's greatest gift—even beyond her decorating skills—was her ability to make the family feel good about all the changes. We could have taken offense, viewing them as attempts to erase our mother from the premises—but instead Gail, who adored our mother, made sure that every alteration was imbued with Felicia's own sensibility. It was almost as if the new rooms for Lenny had been redesigned by Felicia herself.

Whether deliberate or not, it was our mother's masterstroke to have created a separate place in which to die. After she was gone, that place, with all its woe, could be folded up into itself and tidily disposed of—while the Fairfield house, untainted by sadness but full of Mummy's touch, awaited our return, so we could find ourselves there as a family once again.

But for that first fragile Christmas without our mother, the plan was to go somewhere else entirely. The four of us and Shirley, plus Alexander's best friend, Bart, our honorary fourth sibling, went to the splendid Jamaican resort Round Hill. The bright, lazy days seemed to bring my father around. On Christmas night, as we shared a nightcap at the Round Hill bar, Daddy wandered over to a small neglected piano, sat down, and played Gershwin's *Rhapsody in Blue* in its entirety—a brilliant, exuberant performance, just for us and a handful of astonished hotel guests. That was when we knew Daddy was going to be okay.

But his bronchitis seemed to have become a permanent physical state. The coughing was ghastly—and by now I had developed a Pavlovian aversion to the very sound of coughing. After a particularly awful bout, he would look very sad and say, "It just won't go away." And then take a drag of his cigarette.

I imagined saying to him: You know, if you *really* loved us, you wouldn't risk subjecting us yet again to the misery we've all just endured. How about setting aside those goddamned cigarettes?? But then I'd remind myself that the strongest, harshest words I could possibly devise would not make a whit of difference. Nothing would, ever. That was the essence of addiction: to cigarettes, or to anything else.

* * *

Despite myself, the music-making inched forward. I performed my songs at the Prince Street Bar, the restaurant on the ground floor of my loft building. Friends and family came—including my father. For an encore, he accompanied me as I sang "Something's Coming" from *West Side Story*. I felt pretty good about the way things had gone—until the next day, when I bought the *New York Post* and saw the photo of the two of us with the headline "Chip Off the Old Baton." I felt punched in the gut. But after all, what did I *expect*, I told myself savagely.

My next big step was to put together (and pay for) a recording session of two of my songs: a raunchy number called "Hot

Tomato" and a long, complex song, "Gentleman with the Green Eyes," heavily inspired by Jim Steinman's magnum opus for Meat Loaf, "Paradise by the Dashboard Light." "Gentleman" had multiple sections, elaborate backup vocals, and constantly shifting meters—the latter being a trick I'd taken right out of the LB composing playbook.

At Moogtown Sound, I had my first taste of how time and money fly, fly, fly out the window of a windowless recording studio. I also discovered how personalities can chafe against one another in that tight, fraught space. And toughest of all was confronting the disparity between how I heard the songs in my head and how they actually came out.

Trembling with excitement and dread, I played my father the new tape. Afterward he said, "Jamie, you've GOT to do something about the balance! I can't hear the *words*, those Blakeian lyrics! Why are you so self-destructive? Oh, *fuck* the backup band; your *song* is what matters—we've got to be able to *hear those words*!"

Dammit, he was right. I, too, had noticed I couldn't hear all my lyrics in the mix—and yet I'd allowed things to go that way out of some vague desire not to be, well, loud and obnoxious?—during the mixing process. And so much *money* spent! Was it even worth sending this tape around? I cried all the way downtown.

For days, whenever I talked to my father, he'd say: "Come on, couldn't you mix it again? Just bring up the vocal and bring down the guitar." It was a perfectly rational suggestion, but I was infuriated. And I couldn't bear the prospect of spending yet more money. My delays in learning to be financially responsible, combined with the modest trust fund I'd just received on my twenty-fifth birthday, had left me with a paralytic fear of spending any money at all.

A few nights later, at the opening of *Hair* the movie, my father had occasion to meet Moogy Klingman, owner of Moogtown Sound. Who was responsible for "that terrible mix on 'Gentleman'?" my father demanded to know. Moogy said, truthfully, that he'd had nothing to do with it; he just ran the place. But a few days later, I saw two new reel-to-reel dubs of "Gentleman" on my father's desk. Puzzled, I asked him what they were. He told me about meeting Moogy, and that these would probably be remixes, with the voice louder. I was apoplectic. Where did this Moogy, whom I hadn't even *met*, get off making copies and changes on my song without even consulting me?! Secondly—no, firstly—I was furious at Daddy for meddling in my musical affairs.

The next day, he left a rapturous message on my phone machine about how wonderful the new mix sounded, he could hear all the words, how great the song was, on and on. He meant well; of course he meant well. But all I could do was seethe.

Nina's first Mummy-less birthday rolled around in late February, and Daddy tried hard to make an extra fuss over her. On her birthday night, we all attended a preview of Steve Sondheim's new show, *Sweeney Todd*. But the intense static between my father and me marred the evening. As we were walking from our hired limo to the theater, he declared that the chauffeur had been "an asshole" for having the effrontery to ask him what time the show would be over. "It's *his* job to find out," he said. I replied, "You know? You're being a real pain in the ass today." "No, *you're* a pain in the ass," he said, and then *booted* me in that very location as I went in the door of the theater.

The show was breathtaking in its pitch-black brilliance. We knew we had seen something historic. Afterward, we had dinner across the street with Steve. I told him about getting kicked, and Steve pointed out that his competitive pal Lenny was probably pretty anxious about seeing Steve's new show. I hadn't thought of that; my father *was* probably feeling extra-vulnerable—especially so soon after the debacle of *1600 Pennsylvania Avenue*, which he knew Steve hadn't liked. And what was more, my father had probably taken an orange pill to help him get through the evening, which would have exacerbated his erratic behavior.

The next morning, Daddy told me over the phone that he felt he didn't have much time left; he had to make friends, make love, make music, make haste before his time ran out. He apologized for the kick in the ass. "At least with kicking, there's *contact*," he added.

God, he was exhausting.

*　*　*

Nina was having more success than I was in drawing closer to our father. She was studying *King Lear* at Brearley; the real-life father and youngest daughter identified almost mystically with the Lear-Cordelia relationship. So the play was freshly on Daddy's mind when he ran into his old pal Richard Burton on the beach in Puerto Vallarta, a few days after a concert in Mexico City. The two men arrived at the possibly alcohol-fueled idea that my father would direct Richard Burton in *King Lear*, and Nina would be involved in some way with the production.

A few weeks later in New York, my father invited Richard Burton and his new wife, Suzy, to the Dakota, where Nina met them for the first time. Nina told me that after half an hour of chat, Daddy bizarrely announced that he had dinner plans, and would Richard and Suzy please take Nina out to dinner with them. Miserably, Nina went along on this awkward expedition. At the restaurant, Burton began arguing furiously with Nina about the comparative value of words and music. He repeatedly excused himself from the table, returning each time in a yet more combative state. Suzy grew pale and quiet, and finally demanded the check halfway through the main course. The three of them went up to the couple's hotel room, where Suzy poured her husband into bed, explaining to Nina that Richard was taking Antabuse and was not supposed to be drinking—but obviously he'd fallen off the wagon that night.

When Nina told me all this, I wondered whether our father had a clue about the multiple pressures he was inflicting on his seventeen-year-old daughter. In social situations, he was repeatedly putting her in the wife role, even as his own behavior grew more unpredictable. This Lear was demanding an awful lot from his young, motherless Cordelia.

Alexander finally graduated from Harvard, having left partway through and returned to finish a couple of years later. It had been a long, joyless ordeal for him, but he'd done it. When people arrived at the Fairfield house for the celebratory weekend party, they encountered Alexander's Harvard diploma impaled on the front door with a kitchen knife.

One of the features of the party was a string quartet playing outdoors during Sunday brunch. Alexander knew his chamber music, and could regularly astound Daddy with his knowledge of repertoire from Mendelssohn to Schumann to Ravel. When Alexander, Nina, and I were together, we were always playing records and sharing our in-jokes.

"What shall we play now?"

"Let's play 'Shepherd on the Rock.'"

"Okay, I'll be the rock."

This was all in the age-old family tradition. Daddy had endless musical in-jokes with his own siblings, many of them involving special lyrics. For Shostakovich's Seventh, they'd sing: "Jerry Robbins, won't you do, Jerry Robbins, won't you do a new *Petrushka* . . . BRAND-NEW *Petrushka*, BRAND-NEW

Petrushka . . ." For the big tune in Tchaikovsky's Fifth, they'd sing: "Up . . . your leg . . . with a meat hook . . ."

We had our own treatment for that tune: it was one of the many melodies that lent itself to being trilled the way Bugs Bunny sang in the bathtub while soaping his back with a scrub brush. "Tyuhh, tuh-tuh tyuhh, tuh-tuh tyuhh, tyuhh . . ."

One piece Alexander and I doted on was Berlioz's *Symphonie Fantastique*; we'd memorized every note of it by the end of that Philharmonic tour in 1968. Years later, the two of us were driving in separate cars to Fairfield, keeping up with each other on the Merritt Parkway. Suddenly Alexander's window went down as he slid his car perilously close to mine. "Turn on QXR!" he yelled. I did, and sure enough, the radio station was playing good old *Symphonie Fantastique*. For the rest of the drive, we conducted at each other through our open windows, risking life and limb at seventy miles per hour for the Witches' Sabbath finale.

Another beloved piece from our school days came back into our lives when our father passed along a pair of tickets for the Verdi *Requiem*, performed at Carnegie Hall by the LA Philharmonic, with Carlo Maria Giulini conducting. It was unusual for us to be attending someone else's concert—and it was a stupendous performance. Renata Scotto hit one note that was so exquisite, tears literally popped right out of my eyes. (It was the very same pianissimo "*Requi-eeem*" that had given us such fits when sung by Galina Vishnevskaya.)

The gentleman to our left glowered at us throughout; Alexander and I could barely keep still or quiet. Alas, we had inherited some of Daddy's—and Aunt Shirley's—bad audience habits. Both of them were incorrigible. When our father sat in a concert audience, he was essentially still conducting: making not-so-subtle gesticulations and audible comments like, "Oh, why didn't he take that *accelerando?*" Meanwhile Shirley was a compulsive whisperer—except that her whisper was as loud as her talking voice. It was a mortifying torture to sit with the two of them at the theater, and movies, as well; every time they asked a question about the plot, they'd miss the next crucial bit of dialogue during our hurried explanations, resulting in further rounds of questions.

Daddy, Shirley, Alexander, Nina, and I—our new nuclear family—attended a matinee performance of *Cats*, at which Shirley and her brother were particularly audible in their dislike of the proceedings. Afterward, there was a new flavor of embarrassment awaiting my siblings and me at Sardi's, where we all went for dinner. My father had known Vincent Sardi for years, so a great fuss was made over us when we arrived, and we were given a swell table near the entrance (where Vincent Sardi could be sure that everyone who entered his restaurant would behold the glamorous clientele). Alexander had been in the same elementary school class as Paul Sardi, whom Vincent and his wife had adopted. So Alexander nearly had a stroke when Vincent came over to our table to say hello, and my father, after giving Vincent a big hug, said: "And this is my sister, Shirley, and these are my three 'adopted' children: Jamie, Alexander, and Nina!"

It was a kind of cerebral short-circuit that Daddy experienced quite often. Somewhere in the depths of his brain, he *knew* that Vincent Sardi had an adopted son. But this wisp of knowledge had surfaced in the form of an impulsive, lame joke about his own cute little wastrel kids. Vincent blanched, but remained affable. After he'd left the table, Alexander quietly exploded: "Do you realize what you just *did?!*"

Just another night on the town with our dad; we never knew what adventures lay in wait.

But the incident at Sardi's evolved soon enough into a touch-stone of teasing and family hilarity. Our father was generally a good sport about being teased. He knew, most of the time, that he had it coming—and that it was our crucial escape valve for the chronic annoyance of putting up with him.

*   *   *

A year had passed since our mother died. There was a ceremony at the gravesite, which I declined to attend. I was making a decla-ration: I didn't accept that any part of Mummy that mattered to me was in Brooklyn. Daddy took it especially hard that I wasn't there; that was probably my intention.

Father Puma held a memorial Mass for Mummy at his little church in New Jersey; I went to that one. I played a song on the guitar and nearly passed out from fear in that small, unassuming space, with that modest handful of congregants. I could see my scarf bouncing against my chest to the rhythm of my thudding heart. Could stage fright be a genetic trait? It certainly appeared that I'd inherited my mother's malady.

A few weeks later, I had a pair of gigs at a new club called the Fives, way over west on 57th Street. In the days leading up to the first performance, I got a raging sore throat and was drenched in dread. My friends who came to the shows were full of compliments—but as usual, I suspected I'd made a complete fool of myself.

My father didn't come to the Fives; he was touring with the Philharmonic in the Far East. The tour was a smash, but Daddy continued to be out of sorts. He told me on the phone that he was tired—and lonely. There is no moment more lonely, he said, than to finish conducting Mahler's Ninth Symphony and have thou-sands of people screaming at you for twenty minutes while you're up on the stage—then have no one to go to off the stage.

But he wasn't lonely for long. That fall, he did find a source of companionship in a pleasant young guy named Bobby K. Bobby folded fairly comfortably into our family life—though Shirley was resentful, and Uncle BB, never comfortable with his brother's gay side, maintained a careful distance. Alexander, Nina, and I got along just fine with Bobby. He was more or less our age, and seemed almost like a friend. Almost.

But everything was driving me crazy: my family, my boyfriend, my music—everything. To escape, I drove up alone to Martha's Vineyard in my father's little red Fiat Spider, which had never performed correctly for him and which he'd passed along to me. (He now drove a magnificent vintage cream-colored Mercedes convertible sedan; the license plate said "MAESTRO 1," but the *1* was too close to the *O*—it looked like "MAESTROI." Oy.)

I arrived at the funky, briny guest cottage across the lawn from Bill and Rose Styron's house. The rest of the Styron family hadn't arrived yet; there was only Bill in the big house. Upon seeing me, he was boisterous and affectionate, and seemed interested in my music career. He offered to introduce me to his friend, pop artist Carly Simon, who had a house up the road there.

Later in the day, Bill walked in on me in the guest cottage, catching me naked and dripping from the shower. I gasped and made some nervous, wry remark as I hunted for a towel. "Oh, don't worry about me," Bill said, "we're all used to each other's bodies around here," and he slapped my rear end affectionately as he passed by.

The next day, Carly Simon showed up. She was kind to me, and offered generous advice about pursuing a singer-songwriter career. Bill joined us on the porch. He was wearing a bathrobe and undershorts, and sat spread-eagled on the chair, legs wide apart, with his member sticking out the pee flap and one ball sticking out the leg hole. When I told my friend Susanna about her father on the porch, she explained that he sat in that heedless way in front of absolutely everyone. I had to marvel; Bill was as outrageous in his own way as my own father.

No sooner was I back in New York than I was desperate to leave again. I decided to drive cross-country, all by myself, in the little red Fiat. Somehow I had to do this alone; I couldn't explain why. I just let the wheels pull me west, driving hour after hour, day after day, imagining that the left headlight of my car was snorting up the white-painted lane dividers, a continent's worth of cocaine.

In southern Utah, I spent a couple of indelible days with Michael Tilson Thomas, a young conducting colleague of my father's who had become a friend of mine, along with his partner, Joshua Robison. We hiked in Monument Valley, and twirled down the San Juan River on inner tubes. I spent a night in a traditional eight-sided Navajo hogan, got up at six, drove to the Grand Canyon, gawked and gaped, climbed back into my car, drove across the scorching Mojave Desert pouring water over my head from a plastic gallon jug (the Fiat had no air-conditioning)—and at sunset of that same day, my toes were in the Pacific Ocean. I was on the West Coast for the first time in my life.

That night, I unrolled my sleeping bag onto the living room floor of a guy who'd been sitting behind me in the restaurant where I'd pulled in for dinner. I was grateful that he didn't proposition me. If he had, I would have felt compelled to go through with it. I found it hard to say no in those times, because it was even harder to answer the question "Why not?"

At my next stop, in Berkeley, my shoulder bag was stolen out of the Fiat. I now had no wallet, no driver's license, no bank card, no address book. I felt erased from the earth. I would now have to drive all the way back to New York without a license or a speck of ID.

On the eastbound leg of my journey, the temperature gauge in the Fiat began meandering. It would hover near the red danger zone, seeming to indicate that the car was overheating—but then it would subside again. Driving across the vast, empty western landscape, I began to lose my sanity as I obsessed over the little dial. I began to imagine that I could move the needle back down with my mind.

Outside of Des Moines, the Fiat's left rear wheel detached from the axle and rolled across all eight lanes of Interstate 80. My car went scraping horribly into the breakdown lane. Two guys in a camper pulled over to help me. One scurried all the way across the highway and retrieved my wheel in the bushes. The other jacked up the car and pounded out the mangled mudguard while I rooted around in the weeds for the lug nuts. I found three of the four. The guys got my wheel back on, and incredibly, I was back on the road twenty minutes later, shaken to the core but in motion. Even more incredibly, there was a Fiat dealer just ten miles away, where I bought the fourth lug nut for $1.34.

That evening I pulled into Chicago, the Windy City, deranged with relief. A very nice cop took a parking ticket off someone else's car and put it on mine so I could leave my car in the space for a couple of days. He asked me to back up a little, so I got back in and turned the key in the ignition . . . nothing. My car had simply expired, right there in that parking space. I knew exactly how my car felt.

My Harvard friend David Thomas was a wonderful host. We went to the museum, to the zoo, to good breakfast joints. We took long and, yes, windy walks along the lakefront. He slept in the living room and let me use his bed. That arrangement lasted one night. After that, the romance began.

My car started up just fine when it was time to go. But I was heartsick. Here I was heading back to my real life, to Jet and the loft and—what exactly had happened to me in Chicago?

I mailed David a paperback copy of E. M. Forster's *Howards End*. Inside the front cover, I wrote to David: "Still feeling windy." Or, I thought to myself, still feelin' slee.

*   *   *

After my mother died, the fun had gone out of the Dakota for Mendy. He wound up selling his apartment—to Gilda Radner, as it happened—and got himself an enormous loft on what was then a rather neglected corner: 18th Street and Fifth Avenue. Instead of carving up the open space into extra rooms for his visiting grown children, the ever-inventive Mendy created two cubes on wheels that contained perfect little guest bedrooms; they could be pushed around in any configuration he wished. When Mendy had a party, he pushed the two cubes to the side, thereby making room for his guests—and for dancing!

Mendy liked putting on Strauss waltzes. At one party, the "Blue Danube" came on, and my father grabbed me by the hand and dragged me out onto the floor. I knew the piece by heart from having seen *2001: A Space Odyssey* so many times—and Daddy simply knew everything by heart. For once, we were perfectly in sync: anticipating every phrase in Strauss's music the same way, dancing like a single, sentient organism.

But the rest of the time, we were hopelessly prickly with each other. I had developed a bad habit of not letting my father finish his sentences; I knew I did it out of pure annoyance, but I couldn't stop myself. For Christmas, Alexander gave Daddy and me each a pair of bright red Everlast boxing gloves.

Despite the frictions, the Dakota had a centripetal force that was irresistible. The building itself was mesmerizing, with its brass fixtures and carved wooden mantels, the echoing marble stairwells and creepily ill-lit corridors, and the inner courtyard with its fountain of spouting art nouveau metal lilies. It was in that courtyard that the residents held an annual potluck party. And one of those Dakota residents was, incredibly enough, the heartthrob of my girlhood, John Lennon—who now lived there with his wife, Yoko Ono. I invited my school pal Ann to join me for the courtyard party, just in case John showed up. We were breathless with delight to see him arrive with Yoko, plus their baby son, Sean, nestled in a pouch against John's chest. We found ourselves standing next to John in front of the array of desserts. Ann and I felt we could retire from life itself after John mused, in perfect Liverpudlian: "Mmm, I want soomthing mooshy and disgoosting."

It was hard to resist any invitation to join my father and his guests for dinner at the Dakota—and besides, I tried to spend as much time with Nina as I could. But every visit was something of a crapshoot. In the absence of Mummy, Daddy was as untamed as a sail flapping in a squall. The family's preexisting behavioral boundaries were gone; now anything could happen. Three examples:

1. *The dinner with Francis Ford Coppola.* Coppola had an idea for a film musical that he wanted to run by Leonard Bernstein. There were few works of art in those days more beloved than the *Godfather* films, so Alexander, Nina, and I were beyond excited at the prospect of this collaboration. Our guest arrived with an entire case of wine from his Napa Valley vineyard, and proceeded to drink most of it himself. At the dinner table, LB talked obsessively about LB, repeatedly interrupting Francis and reducing us siblings to three microscopic dots of desperation.

After dinner, Francis unrolled a quantity of white butcher's paper and began to draw feverishly on it, all the while explaining his concept for the film with a nearly deranged intensity. Maybe we couldn't blame our father for backing off; we had to acknowledge that there probably wasn't enough oxygen in the universe for those two guys to occupy the same space together.

The one good thing Daddy did that evening was to come up with a grand nickname for Francis: Fortissimo, derived from the starting letters of his first and middle names (*ff*). And Fortissimo did eventually make his movie musical: *Tucker*—a film about a car, with a score by, of all the non-LBs, rocker Joe Jackson.

2. *The dinner with Woody Allen.* LB had been contemplating writing an opera about the Holocaust, and Shirley had arranged the dinner with Woody because she thought, a little oddly, that Woody would be an ideal collaborator for the project. As often happened, Daddy was not ready at the appointed hour. He was getting a haircut in his bathroom and taking his sweet time—maybe on purpose. It fell to the rest of us to make chitchat with Woody and his new girlfriend, Mia Farrow. We knew for a certainty that they had no interest in talking to us; it was a miserable penance to be LB's social placeholder.

When our well-coiffed father finally sauntered into the library a full excruciating hour later, it became instantly apparent that here was a colossal mismatching of personalities. As with Fortissimo, Daddy did way too much talking, and didn't seem particularly interested in what Woody had to say, and anyway, Woody was pretty quiet. At dinner, Woody served himself a single potato. As Aida the maid withdrew the serving tray, she stepped backward directly onto the paw of Julia's little white fluff-dog, Tookie, who let out a blood-curdling squeal. After dinner, we all filed out of the dining room to have coffee in the library. On the way, I overheard Woody say quietly to Mia, "Well, I liked it when she stepped on the dog . . ."

3. *The dinner with the Russian guy.* Daddy had invited a Russian actor who'd been a generous host to him and Mummy in the Soviet Union many years back. Daddy's toast to his dinner guest that night was "May you fuck as well today as you did twenty years ago!" Nina and I looked at each other with the age-old *tierra, trágame* despair. Later, as I left for the evening, Daddy pulled his old trick: kissing me fully on the lips, then pushing his tongue into my mouth.

Daddy tried this tongue-kissing stunt on almost everyone, usually late at night, after much drinking (and possibly also an orange pill). It was a kind of litmus test he liked to spring on people, to find out a few things at once: how accommodating they were, how sexy they were, how much impact he was making. Probably the only ones who were spared Daddy's tongue were his mother and Julia. (But who knows?) It was a disagreeable experience for sure—even more than the mushy, ardent kisses he so often planted on my lips—but my dismay was tempered by knowing he did it to so many others. The intrusion of Daddy's tongue was an occasion less for revulsion and more for weary eye-rolling.

My father's intense physicality and flamboyance had always been there, but now, in the absence of Felicia's calming influence, it became a beast unleashed. It was around this time that Betty Comden's husband, Steve Kyle, died—a shock to everyone, and a terrible loss for Betty, who adored him. She invited her lifelong pal Lenny to be one of the speakers at Steve's funeral.

My father began by describing Betty and Steve in the 1940s, when he'd first met them. "They were both so beautiful," he said, "I couldn't decide which one I desired more." At that instant Betty Bacall, who had been holding my hand, abruptly withdrew her own, muttering, "Son of a bitch."

As people filed out of the funeral home, there was much sotto voce buzzing about Lenny's questionable eulogy. Adolph Green's wife, Phyllis Newman, and her pal Cynthia O'Neal were talking about it as they headed out to Madison Avenue. Suddenly Cynthia felt a blinding pain on her side. She whirled around: a maestro had just bitten her! "Lenny, what are you *doing*?!" she cried. "Gee, I can't seem to do anything right today," he said.

But on the podium, LB was doing very right. He conducted electrifying concert performances of *Fidelio* in Washington, DC, with the soprano Gwyneth Jones and the Vienna Philharmonic. Then they came to New York for a couple of concerts at Carnegie Hall; the audiences went crazy. Best of all was their performance of the "Liebestod" from *Tristan und Isolde*; I had never heard that ravishing music before.

There was, however, a subliminal discomfort in being perpetually brought to a state of ecstasy by one's own father. His musicianship was on such an exalted level; it transported his audiences, and yes, it was erotic. Certainly for him, music-making was a form of lovemaking. For Alexander, Nina, and me, it was a lifelong challenge to figure out how to open ourselves to these immense musical experiences while maintaining some kind of inner equanimity—even chastity.

The *Tristan* that night was to be my father's last engagement for a year; he'd cleared his schedule to be a full-time composer.

What he really wanted to do was undertake a new theatrical work, the first one since the debacle of *1600 Pennsylvania Avenue*. But he still hadn't decided what his subject was going to be—the Holocaust opera was but one of several notions—nor had he settled on a collaborator. He even asked me to collaborate with him, as he was in the habit of doing from time to time. His latest proposal was easier than most to turn down. The plot revolved around an aging rock star who finally admits that of all the groupies and women in his fabled life, the one person he loves is his (male) manager, and as he performs the love song he has written about his manager, his teenage fans storm the stage in fury—and eat him.

* * *

Down in SoHo, the age of cheap lofts for artists was over. Our building's landlord, Gabe, announced he was tripling the rent—and suddenly life downtown was about rent strike, escrow account, lawyers, court hearings. But did I even *want* to stay in that loft—or, for that matter, with Jet?

Did I want to be a responsible person with a stable relationship, or did I want to be, you know, *a rock star*? The latter would require that ever-troubling intensity of self-involvement: it would mean choosing to be more like Daddy. What if I became less *kind*? "Kindness, kindness, kindness," my mother had said to me on her deathbed. Which parent was the better role model? Neither option seemed entirely compelling.

And every now and then, a sense memory of David Thomas in Chicago would leave me rooted to the spot, gazing into space.

I launched into a flurry of meetings with prospective managers, promoters, and record company executives. To send my song demos around, I had to get duplicate tape reels made—a tedious, inefficient process in those days, as was the designing, printing,

addressing, and mailing of invitations each time I performed anywhere. (Today, of course, all of these tasks could be accomplished
with the stroke of a laptop key.)

Every person I spoke to had his or her foolproof theory for making it in the music business. A manager named Ken said my songs
weren't commercial enough. One record company executive said,
"That's not a song; that's *material*." A friend suggested, "Write
something that makes you sick, and it'll be a hit." That was probably the best piece of advice I got, but I didn't follow it.

I hired an energetic young press agent named Tony who set me
up with all sorts of interviews. They all asked the same questions:
Does your *father* give you any advice on your career/songs? Are
you going to collaborate with your *father*? Did your *father* teach
you to play the piano when you were young?

Tony the press agent arranged for an interview with veteran radio personality Joey Adams. Every five minutes Joey said: "I'm
talking with a lovely young lady whose *father* . . ." Joey Adams
even coerced me, despite my desperate protests, to sing a Leonard
Bernstein song, on the air. Grudgingly, I sang one verse of "New
York, New York" from *On the Town*. *Tierra, trágame*.

I hired three musicians, at considerable expense, to be my
backup band at a club called SNAFU. The bass player was fifty
minutes late for the sound check. I was furious, and I didn't want
to feel that way. On the other hand, I thought, maybe I should
"use" it.

Well, I definitely did use it, judging from the reactions I got
afterward. Jet told me there was only one expression on my face:
a snarl. My father's main comment was how *angry* I was up there.
(And Ken the manager was conclusively discouraged by the red
Mylar hot pants.)

The rent strike at the loft was devolving into chaos. Gabe the landlord turned off the water, then the electricity. One day, Jet and I walked into our loft to discover our music studio reduced to rubble. Gabe had gone in with a power saw and destroyed it. Nothing remained but shards of wood, crumbled Sheetrock, severed wires. It was a deep violation; we had worked so long and hard to build that room. Our home, our music-making, our relationship—all reduced to dust. Literally.

As summer reached its zenith, I was down to nothing: I had no loft; I had broken up with Jet; I had no band and no manager; Nina was going off to college (Harvard, of course). Nothing was pinning me down anymore. I began to feel a certain tickling lightness—whereupon I got a call from David Pack, front man for the rock band Ambrosia. Some years back, Pack had played electric guitar in a production of *Mass* in LA, and Daddy had befriended him. Pack had shown up at the awful sixtieth birthday party at Wolf Trap, but beyond that I didn't know him. Still, I'd sent Pack a tape of my songs, just for the hell of it—and now here he was on the phone.

He said he really liked my music, and that maybe we could record some of my songs in his manager's twenty-four-track studio in LA. I said I *was* sort of thinking of going out to LA soon, and he said he *did* happen to have some free weeks in September, and . . .

I was leaping around the room. I called my father to tell him: I could hardly talk for crowing.

I was going to LA! This had to be my big break!

Daddy wrote me a little birthday song, using the best tune from his new piece commissioned by the Boston Symphony, a potpourri of material called *Divertimento*. The song was a quirky seven-legged waltz. His lyrics made fun of the terrible profanities with which Alexander, Nina, and I casually peppered our conversation. He was also making gentle fun of my efforts to make it as a rock musician. And maybe it was a little autobiographical, too:

Shit-a-brick, time is running out on me;
I must get moving fast undoubtedly.
Suck-a-dick, I am sick in heart and soul,
Got to get moving fast to reach my goal:
ROCK 'N' ROLL!
Suddenly I am twenty-eight,
Suddenly everything seems late.
I have to make it big and make it quick,
Shit-a-brick . . .
Su-u-u-ck a dick . . .

Off to LA to be a rock star.

15

The East-West Shuffle

Rockin' it with David Pack.

It was happening. It was all going to happen. And it was going to happen fast. Because it was already happening fast. My record deal was just around the corner from that demo tape that David Pack and I would toss off upon my arrival in LA.

For the first few months, I lived in a briny beach bungalow at the foot of the Santa Monica palisades, where every time I drove anywhere I had to accomplish the hair-raising maneuver of backing out, rear bumper first, into the Pacific Coast Highway. My tiny dwelling had a built-in bed, a minikitchen, and a front room, where my guitar case served as my dining table. I possessed two tape cassettes that I played over and over on my portable player: Ry Cooder's *Bop till You Drop* and Steely Dan's *Gaucho*. I reveled in my sparse new existence. And that weather.

David Pack, together with his bubbly, irreverent wife, Gale, became my surrogate parents—even though we were all the same age. They lived in the upper-right-hand corner of the San Fernando Valley, in a development carved out of a citrus farm. I used to fill trash bags with the clementines off their trees, pack them into my suitcase, and take them home to Julia.

Best of all was the Packs' persimmon tree. Mummy had grown up eating persimmons in Chile, and passed down her love of them to us. In the winter months, the Packs' persimmon tree lost all its leaves, while some of the fruit remained attached, growing ever wrinklier. David and Gale, who had not grown up eating persimmons, made a wide berth around that Martian Christmas tree with its scrotal ornaments.

It was liberating to live in an environment where Leonard Bernstein was as mysterious as a persimmon. The most recognition I could expect from the average Californian was: "Oh, he wrote *West Side Story*? I love that movie." How refreshing! Here, I could reinvent myself, just like people moving to California had done since time immemorial.

But I'd barely been in LA a month when I got my first of several irresistible tugs back into the East Coast net. I was invited to write a song—and sing it on camera—for an upcoming film directed by Franco Zeffirelli. Franco and my father had been friends for years. They enjoyed each other's wit and flamboyance, and their mutual love of opera had led to acclaimed collaborations on both sides of the Atlantic—including that *Cavalleria Rusticana* my father was conducting at the Met when Mummy held her Black Panther fundraiser.

I'd devoured the book *Endless Love* by Scott Spencer, and now here I was, invited to play a small role in the film adaptation, singing a song of my very own. If only this exciting opportunity weren't coming my way through a Daddy connection . . . but how could I say no? I wrote a song called "We Are the Hands," recorded it in New York, then went out to the set on Long Island every day for a week, waiting to shoot the "party scene" where I'd lip-synch to my recording, backed up by a quartet of wriggly high school boys that called themselves the TouchTones. All that week on the set, the five of us shared a Winnebago where we did a lot of sitting around, in a veritable blizzard of cocaine.

The star of the film, sixteen-year-old Brooke Shields, was always kept separate from the rest of the cast, in the company of her protective mother. But we received many visits to our Winnebago from James Spader, the actor who played her brother. I played his girlfriend, Susan, in the film. Jimmy Spader and I took a shine to

With Jimmy Spader on the set of *Endless Love*.

each other, and we would "rehearse" our making-out scene every chance we got. (There was no making-out scene.)

Later, back in LA, I was informed that "We Are the Hands" was being cut from the film entirely. I would now be filming an insert of me singing a brand-new song by R&B star Lionel Richie. First, I was summoned to Devonshire Studios to record the audio of his song titled, like the film, "Endless Love." The lyrics they'd sent me the night before struck me as insipid—so I'd helpfully re-written them. But as I stood in the sound booth the next day with my headphones on, and saw Lionel Richie staring at me through the control room window, a little voice in my head suggested that perhaps I should refrain from springing my "improved" lyrics on the songwriter, midsession.

A few weeks later, when I was summoned to film the insert, I discovered that my own recording from Devonshire Studios had been dumped. Now, my lip synch was to some other, forever unknown singer's rendition of Lionel Richie's song. Five seconds of my face from that insert is what ended up in the "party scene" of the movie. Richie's song comes back under the end credits, in his duet with Diana Ross. (It was the first time a pop "duet" was recorded in separate sessions, on separate coasts.)

The film was a turkey, but the song "Endless Love" was a big hit. I thought it was the worst song I'd ever heard. It dawned on me that for all my sniffing about inferior pop songs, I didn't really have a clue about what a hit was, much less how to write one myself.

Right on the heels of my big nonbreak in film came my big nonbreak in television. In December, my father was to receive a Kennedy Center Honor, and I was invited to write a song for him that I would perform at the grand event, which would subsequently be broadcast nationally on CBS.

If only this promotional bonanza were not so thoroughly tethered to my father. In fact, the whole thing was yet another Harry Kraut Special: he'd arranged with the Kennedy Center folks to invite me to write and sing a song with David Pack backing me up. Harry's thought process undoubtedly went thus: Lenny will love it, and the show will give Jamie's career a boost, while reinforcing her collaboration with Pack, who is going to make her a star. Everybody wins.

The old conundrum: Would I ever catch a Daddy-free break as a musician? And yet who in their right mind would say no to such a gig?

Moreover, wasn't it a shame that I didn't even have a record to promote yet? Launching my career was looking more and more like starting with the World Series and tacking on the baseball season afterward.

David Pack was crushed that he couldn't perform at the Kennedy Center Honors with me; his band, Ambrosia, had a European tour. I wound up putting the performance together with a local band in DC. But Pack and I cowrote the song, called "Thank You for the Big Heart." Writing that song with Pack turned out to be a good way to express the love I truly felt for the Daddy I truly knew existed within that outer shell of erratic behavior. This was a most satisfying triangulation: My father, after all, had introduced me to David Pack, while Pack, in his turn, was thrilled to be helping his idol's daughter with her rock 'n' roll career. And although I resisted a romantic entanglement (for once), the truth was that I had some strong feelings about Pack. Maybe he was having feelings, too. Maybe all three of us—Daddy, Pack, and myself—were triangulating here.

On the day of the Kennedy Center Honors, President and Mrs. Carter hosted a preshow reception at the White House for the honorees and their guests. Leonard Bernstein's retinue was even larger than usual. Not only did he bring along his two siblings, his three children, his secretary, and his manager; he'd also brought down his mother, Jennie, and her two sisters: the vivacious Aunt Dorothy and sweet but slow-moving Aunt Bertha. The trio from Brookline, "the Three Fates," made quite an impression, with their rhinestone-spangled glasses and dubious attire from Filene's Basement in the Chestnut Hill mall.

It was the first night of Hanukkah. My father had requested of President and Mrs. Carter that there be some place in the White House where he and his family could go to light the menorah. He sure had a nerve, I thought, making such demands during a very complicated evening, but incredibly, adorably, Rosalynn Carter arranged for all of us to be escorted to the Lincoln Bedroom, no less, where we placed our little portable menorah on the fireplace mantel and stuck in the two swirled candles: the leader candle, plus one for the first night. We sang the prayers, suppressing

The Bernstein family arrives for the Kennedy Center Honors—LB, Nina, Alexander, Jamie, and Shirley.

giggles over our extraordinary circumstances—and then an aide informed us at the door that it was time to go to the Kennedy Center for the performance.

But what about the menorah? You're not supposed to blow out the Hanukkah candles! Carefully, Alexander carried the menorah to the bathroom, placed it and its two flickering candles inside the sink—and away we went.

At least we didn't burn down the White House that night.

Once down the stairs, we were swept into a mad crush of people, all leaving for the Kennedy Center. Suddenly the Secret Service men were shooing everyone to the side, clearing a path from the elevator to the exit: the president was coming, the president was coming! The band began playing "Hail to the Chief"; the light came on indicating the elevator car was arriving; everyone held their breath. The elevator doors parted to reveal . . . the Three Fates! Aunt Dorothy, Aunt Bertha, and Grandma, beaming at the crowd in all their Filene's Basement sublimity.

Performing my song at the Kennedy Center was exponentially less fun than that moment. As I went on stage, brimful of terror, I experienced a buzzing numbness in my extremities that caused my fingers to curl inward—a phenomenon I later dubbed "dead-chicken-itis." This condition did nothing good for my guitar-playing abilities, while my voice came out in a strangled quaver. But Daddy loved it and wept up in his box—all of which looked very nice on TV a few weeks later.

The morning after the performance, Daddy and I took the Shuffle back to New York. As we got out of the limo in front of the Dakota, we walked past the gaggle of groupies who always hung out by the gate in hopes of glimpsing John Lennon.

I was upstairs in apartment 92 that evening, working out a new song. I liked the Steinway piano up there that Helen Coates had passed along to her former pupil to relieve him somewhat of his Baldwin shackles. As I played, I faintly heard something outside that sounded like gunshots. My hands froze over the keys: What was *that*? A gun going off on Central Park West seemed like a preposterously melodramatic explanation. It must be a truck back-firing, I told myself, and resumed playing the piano. Twenty minutes later, the phone rang. Bart said, "Turn on WNEW! Someone just shot John Lennon."

So, on the very same radio station where I'd listened to Beatles music in the late '60s, I now listened to the announcer I knew so well, Scott Muni, delivering bulletins from the hospital until the final report came in: John Lennon was dead. The shooter was one of those fans outside the Dakota gates; I had walked right past him that morning. John Lennon: my deity, my polestar, my schoolgirl pulse—whose almond-shaped eyes I'd stared into on all those album covers, whose bluesy screams had electrified me, whose lyrics and poetry I'd obsessed over with Daddy . . . I had to see Daddy.

I ran down the back stairs, howling in circles for the seven flights down to the kitchen door. I found Julia inside, very upset; she'd run down to the front of the building when she heard the commotion, and had seen the blood, the ambulance, the inconsolable Cuban doorman, everything. My father took me into his studio and offered me scotch; it was the only time I ever accepted his awful Ballantine's. I sat there remembering how, all those years ago, the grownups cried and drank when horrible stuff happened; now here I was, finally one of them.

* * *

Months trundled by as I waited for David Pack to free up his schedule so we could go into the studio and make that demo that would snag me my record deal. But Ambrosia had rehearsals, tours, an upcoming album; it was always something. Maybe this record-deal thing was going to take longer than I thought.

Still, I saw a lot of the Packs. They initiated me into their Southern California Mexican food rituals: the margaritas, the fajitas, the tostadas—all new to me. Then we'd go back to their house, sit on their sectional couch, and smoke pot till we were silly—and then I would get in my rickety little Fiat and drive back, stoned as hell, over the mountain pass and down to the beach. Gale always made me promise to call them when I got safely home. Sometimes I remembered. Sometimes they remembered that I'd forgotten to call.

The Packs invited me to their New Year's Eve party. When I told one of their friends that I lived alone on the Pacific Coast Highway, he asked me if I carried a piece. "A piece of what?" I asked. Another Pack friend, beyond blasted on coke, expounded to me for twenty minutes on the meaning of the universe. That was the night I started to weary in earnest of cocaine: the drug that made people feel oh so smart, but sound oh so dumb.

In the spring, I moved a couple of miles south to Venice, to live with my New York pals Marjorie and Elliott in a friendly yellow house on a wide, palm-lined street. My new neighborhood was delightfully funky, populated by an expatriate community of East Coasters all trying to make it in the movie business. They were people my age who were writers, actors, producers, mostly Jewish, all college graduates.

In California, my fancy education had often felt like a useless appendage. What good did it do me, anyway, in that perky, sun-bronzed environment, to have impeccable grammar and orthography? To wince when I heard "Beaujolais" pronounced "Boo-jolay"? It did me absolutely no good at all.

So it was a guilty pleasure to talk with the Venice gang about books and lefty politics, and be able to sling around my beloved

Yiddish vocabulary—despite my ambivalence over finding myself back in an environment where Leonard Bernstein had the recognizability more of a peach than a persimmon.

I set up my TEAC four-track reel-to-reel tape recorder in the spare bedroom, and got to work writing new songs. I was making progress, but the pullings-away continued. In New York I met Brian, a songwriter and a columnist for *Spin* magazine. He seemed to know every note, and everyone *of* note, in the New York music scene—and he knew all about world music, too, long before it became a fad. Brian wore only black. He was mystical and soft-spoken—so different, I felt, from my silly, garrulous self. His guitar playing was free-roaming (not clenched like mine), his songs intriguingly cryptic. One day we stood under a tree in the park after a rainstorm, and he rustled a branch and kissed me as the droplets fell all over my face.

And so the bicoastal romance began. It was complicated for me that Brian and I were essentially in the same business. He, too, was a singer-songwriter making demo tapes, pursuing managers, courting record companies. On the one hand, it was gratifying to have a cohort in the trenches. On the other hand, I was jealous and competitive—and disgusted with myself for being so. Whenever I caught myself acting overly ambitious, I was horrified. I was acting like my father! What would Mummy have said?

It was an added complication to be a woman in what was still essentially a man's world. When Brian and I went to a music club, he would schmooze with every musician and music journalist in the room, while I stood there, engulfed in a grease fire of rage at being reduced to the role of insignificant girlfriend. Oh, how I hated that—above all because I feared that maybe that's all I was, all I could ever hope to be: a Stupid Idiot who had no business consorting with that high-powered crowd. Elf's thread: you tyrant, you.

There was another complication: Brian was musically the polar opposite of David Pack. Brian was New York–born, Ivy-educated, a voracious reader. His musical tastes leaned more toward Lou Reed and Talking Heads, as well as the exotic sounds emanating from Nigeria, Bulgaria, India. He had little time for the comparatively stolid, mainstream music that came out of LA. I felt caught in the middle. Brian's edgy musical world fascinated me—even if the coolness quotient was way over my head. But I'd moved to LA and had wed myself, as it were, to David Pack and his pop-flavored, hit-driven musical world. Had I made a mistake . . . ? I fretted and fretted.

This morass of confusion was obviously not enough for me, so I added more, by succumbing to yet another Lenny-connected, soul-compromising career opportunity.

For the tenth anniversary of the Kennedy Center, *Mass* was to be remounted there, in a new production directed by Tom O'Horgan, who had brought the musical *Hair* to Broadway a decade earlier. I was invited to audition for a role in the Street Chorus. (Harry probably engineered that audition, too.) I went to O'Horgan's loft in SoHo and played a few songs on my guitar.

My performance left me feeling uneasy, but I got the part. It reminded me of my murky feelings about getting into Harvard. I would never know for sure whether I'd still have been cast in *Mass* had I been the daughter of, say, Herman Shumlin.

But I loved living and working with my fellow castmates in Washington: being accepted as part of the team. It was actually a relief not to be plugging away on behalf of my own wearisome self. This heartfelt music of my father's sounded better than ever to me. Even the parts that bothered me ten years ago felt less annoying now. Once again, I'd inadvertently found a way to love the most authentic, uncompromised part of Daddy.

My birthday on September 8 brought sweet attentions from my fellow Street Chorus members: funny cards, a cake, a get-together after rehearsal. But things were about to get difficult: the composer was coming to town.

I found LB in an extra-manic mood when I went to visit him in his suite at the Watergate. He was reveling in the fact that now, ten years later, he wasn't feverishly finishing the score of *Mass* for the premiere. This time around, he could enjoy the fruits of his earlier labors and bask in all the attention. The hotel suite was filled with people: cast members, the usual assortment of young men and hangers-on, and Harry Kraut masterminding it all behind his yellow-tinted aviator glasses.

My father was so *on*, and very much aware of the surrounding admirers, the men who breathed in his eroticism like a scent. It was impossible to have a real conversation with him, but I did manage to recount the dream I'd had, in which there was something desperately important I had to tell him, but he was too busy posing in the sun on a cushion tied by a rope to the back of his limousine.

LB summoned everyone over to the piano that the Baldwin company had installed for him there, so he could play the latest special birthday song he'd prepared for me.

He'd written new words to a number from *Mass* called "God Said." In the current production, I played guitar on stage during this song. Now, in front of the suite full of guests, my father made me accompany him on my guitar while he sang the new lyrics in his boozy croak:

Good . . . God . . . Jamie's in Mass
Moving her ass(k)—not—
Why she's in Mass . . .
Movin' her ass, brother,

Movin' her ass, sister,
Movin' her ass, mister,
Movin' her fine, flat ass!

My ass was flat? LB just liked the alliteration. The song had some amusing, raunchy lyrics, and I tried to be a good sport about it all.

Then later that evening, still seated at the piano, with the hangers-on still hanging, he gestured to a crease in his forehead and said to me, "You see this line here that runs right down the middle? That's the Line of Genius. *You don't have one.*"

He was sort of kidding and sort of not kidding.

"Well, ex-cuuuuuse *me!*" I replied, making light of his remark by quoting our old favorite, Steve Martin. But it did seem unusually mean; what had made my father feel compelled to make such a joke at his daughter's expense in front of all those people? Was he simply jealous of my young birthday? Was he turning a wrinkle into a victory point? It didn't seem right to take it literally, to take genuine offense. Of *course* I wasn't a genius. Was I . . . ? I couldn't believe he'd railroaded me into even asking myself such a question.

After the first performance of *Mass*, my father gave me a rib-compressing hug and told me I'd glowed on the stage. The truth was, I loved every minute of performing in *Mass*. I especially loved it during the Fraction, when the entire cast had to remain stock-still for eighteen minutes while the Celebrant had his ranting breakdown. I'd feel oddly safe: just a member of the ensemble, floating in the amniotic fluid of my father's music within the great red womb of the Kennedy Center Opera House.

In the middle of the run, Harry Kraut cooked up a double birthday extravaganza for me and the conductor of *Mass*, John Mauceri. Two hundred people showed up at Pisces disco, including the entire

Mass cast, as well as all Harry's and LB's local pals, mostly gay men. It was at this event that Harry mentioned there was a new "gay plague" going around, making young men mysteriously sick. He said the nickname for the disease was WOG—Wrath of God.

Hours into the party, when everyone was thoroughly inebriated, my worst nightmare came true: the whole Street Chorus, plus LB, got up and sang a surprise rendition of "Good . . . God . . . Jamie's in *Mass*." There they all were, my new friends with whom I'd been feeling so one-of-the-gang, singing my father's icky lyrics at me:

> *She can sing head, yeah!*
> *She can sing chest, yeah!*
> *Oh, what a goddamn chest!*

Later that night I wrote to Ann: "This is the price I pay for riding on the LB train."

Holiday card, 1981: goofing around at the Watergate.

16

Quiet-ish

Stephen Wadsworth Zinsser, a Harvard friend of mine, asked me for an introduction to LB, to interview him for *Opera News* magazine. The interview was never published, but the two of them bonded over music, literature, wordplay, and the intense emotions they shared over having both recently lost a beloved family member: my father had lost his wife at about the same time Stephen had lost his college-age sister in a car crash. In the crucible of their combined grief, they conceived their opera, *A Quiet Place*—a sequel of sorts to LB's one-act opera, *Trouble in Tahiti*, which he'd composed back in the early 1950s.

T in T, as we all called the earlier opera, was a portrait of an unhappy marriage in post–World War II suburbia. My father based the couple on his own parents; he even began by calling them Sam and Jennie, but eventually gave the wife his grandmother's name, Dinah. Perhaps in a superstitious gesture to ward off bad luck, he wrote the opera while on his honeymoon. (I wish there were some record of how his bride felt about that.)

T in T is one of my favorite LB pieces; it's a miniature masterpiece. The opera opens with a jazzy trio huddled around an old-fashioned radio microphone, extolling the virtues of suburbia in their smoothly persuasive harmonies:

> *Our little spot, out of the hubbub,*
> *Less than an hour by train;*
> *Parks for the kids, neighborly butchers,*
> *Saves us the trouble of summers in Maine!*

In old-time radio style, the trio advertises their product: the supposed perfection of postwar middle-class suburban life (white life, that is—and, interestingly, with no specified religion). Sam and Dinah struggle with the widening chasm between the image of themselves that society is selling them and the way they actually feel. Their marriage is a mess, and they can't communicate with each other, except to bicker at the breakfast table:

Sam: Pass me the toast.
Dinah: You might have said please . . .
Sam: This coffee is burned.
Dinah: Make it yourself.

I so admired how my father made the two vocal lines intertwine and overlap in that breakfast scene—a perfect musical evocation of a heated argument, and a perfect example of how music can amplify a libretto. And that libretto: my father managed to make it sound truly, conversationally American. (Stephen would take that approach to the next level in his own libretto for the sequel.)

In the ensuing scenes, Sam goes off to submerge his emotions in the manly, minor victories of office life and the gym, while Dinah seeks solace at her psychiatrist's, and later at the movies. In time-honored fashion, the husband suppresses his feelings, while the wife marinates in hers.

Blending the jazzy trio with Sam's spiky swagger and Dinah's wistful lyricism, my father created a completely personal, wholly American musical vocabulary for portraying his couple in their shiny apple of a perfect world, with its worm of despair hiding within. He also wrote one all-out hilarious, showstopping aria for Dinah—"What a Movie!"—in which she begins by scoffing at the film she just saw, then gets carried away, reliving the exotic, escapist romanticism she secretly couldn't resist:

> *It's a dazzling sight—*
> *With the sleek brown native women*
> *Dancing with the US navy boys*
> *And a hundred-piece symphony orchestra:*
> "ISLAND MAGIC!"

I didn't really get to know *T in T* until my father started working on its sequel with Swoozie (the nickname Daddy coined from Stephen's initials, SWZ). Their plan was to pick up the story many years later, just after Dinah has been killed in a car wreck that appears to have been an alcohol-fueled suicide. The two grown children, Junior (who is mentioned but not seen in *T in T*) and his younger sister, Dede (a new character), drive down from Canada for the funeral with their shared lover, François (also a new character). After the funeral, they all spend the night with grieving Sam in "the little white house" from the first opera, and thrash out their various issues. That was the spine of the story, fleshed out with elements of psychosis, incest, homosexuality, and alcoholism. Yup: just a story about an average American suburban family.

And no political agenda to be seen anywhere. It appeared that after his ambitious attempts to change the world—through *Mass*, through *1600*—my father was now turning inward, to a ravaged psychological landscape, for his subject matter.

The trick was to get him to actually sit down at the piano and compose. There were constant concertizing interruptions; his oath to set aside conducting somehow hadn't come true at all. Also, he was having a harder time than ever getting up in the morning— that is, the afternoon. Four p.m. was a typical LB wake-up time.

Occasionally, Alexander and I shared a meal with him at the Dakota around nine p.m.; our father would be having breakfast.

Yes, he was depressed. He hated getting older, hated his diminishing physicality. But the other part of the problem—and the two were inextricably entwined—was that he was continuing to put prodigious quantities of uppers, downers, and alcohol into a body that was growing ever less efficient at metabolizing all those substances. It fell to the team at the Dakota—Julia; Charlie, the personal assistant; and Ann, the gifted new chef—to kick-start the Maestro every day. And this task also fell to Stephen when the whole household (minus Julia) moved to Indiana University in the dead of winter for a concentrated period of composing and work-shopping. Stephen and Charlie told me later how they would drag LB bodily out of bed and push him to the piano to compose.

While my father was going through his composing torture in Indiana, I was going through a minor musical torture of my own, in a recording studio in New York City. Brian was producing the sessions, and had written one of the songs. I was singing—and paying. Was it his project or my project? The hours and the dollars flew away; I fought a chronic sore throat, hated my singing, gnawed my lips to shreds.

Polygram Records heard the demo tape and passed: "Too smart," they said. I went back to LA, and the drawing board.

By the following summer, the delays on the opera were becoming an emergency; Houston Grand Opera, which had co-commissioned the work, was presenting the premiere the following season. So my father resolved to spend two uncluttered weeks working with Swoozie in Santa Fe. But first, he had a little something to do—in Los Angeles.

LB was having a disagreement with the Tanglewood administration. So he'd decided, instead of going up to Tanglewood that summer, that he would inaugurate the Los Angeles Philharmonic Institute, a Tanglewood-esque initiative with orchestral and conducting students, concluding with some concerts at the Hollywood Bowl.

With a sinking heart, I felt my experience at Harvard repeating itself: Daddy was "following me onto campus." Maybe it was just a coincidence. But now that I was finally building some songwriting

Jamie's first LA demo.

momentum, and making those demos at last with David Pack, it filled me with the ancient ambivalence to contemplate my father's arrival in the distant refuge I'd gone to such pains to create for myself.

He arrived in shaky form: exhausted and irascible. I read the label on his Dexedrine bottle: "One daily." By dinnertime, he was adding scotch to the mix. The combined substances seemed to alter his personality. This father of mine—who reliably helped his struggling friends with "loans" he knew would never be repaid; who was so kind and attentive that even those he met for five minutes reported a deep connection; this father who readily gave his name, money, and time to every worthy organization that requested it—was now prone to throwing lit cigarettes at us across the dinner table or calling people "fuckface."

I'm pretty sure he thought he was being an adorable rapscallion.

My father had once told me a story about a lady—in a book? on a radio show?—called Madame Reformatsky who was always attempting to change and improve the people around her. He'd shared that story to warn me against thinking I could make my boyfriends better—but really, LB was the biggest Madame Reformatsky of them all. One of his rescue cases came along to LA: Ted, a blond, whey-faced young man whom Harry had arranged to be a paid assistant. His duties seemed mainly to consist of annoying the daylights out of chef Ann and assistant Charlie.

In July, Alexander came out to LA for his birthday. At the lavish house in the Brentwood hills where my father had been lodged, the party was an all-day, all-night epic that put tennis court, pool, and hot tub to good use. My housemates, Marjorie and Elliott, brought along their new baby, Sam—my godson! When Daddy finally appeared poolside at four p.m., he was enchanted with Sam; "I feel like a grandfather," he said. "Well, you're a god-grandfather," I told him, a little sadly. Having a kid of my own was not in my immediate plans—after all, I was on my rock star track—but it was hard to suppress the notion while living in a house with a new baby. In any case, I was certain there was something wrong with me, that it would never happen. Maybe I'd done too many drugs. Or maybe I just lacked the instinct; women my age made a fuss over babies to an extent that left me feeling deficient. It seemed somehow unimaginable to me that I would ever have a kid.

Alexander's party concluded in grand form with the EMS coming to pick up Ted after his major vomiting event in the living room.

My father remained miserable throughout his time in LA. I sensed that it pained him deeply not to be at his beloved Tanglewood, that he felt genuinely bad about it. Plus, he wasn't composing his opera, either. He slept around the clock whenever he could. The rest of the time he fueled himself forward with his array of substances. I worried about him; I felt his anxiety as if it were a rash on my own skin.

The hardest feat in the world to pull off was to have a little one-on-one time with Daddy. He was always surrounded by the hordes: the entourage, the fans, the fellows. So it was a minor miracle when he came out one afternoon to visit me in Venice. We sat together on the beach, just the two of us, chatting in the sun for a few hours. We sang pop songs from the '60s together; he remembered all the lyrics to "Paint It, Black," the tune to "Pretty Ballerina," the *bridge* to "Here, There and Everywhere." What a prodigious mind was still in there; I had to marvel.

At the end of my father's stay came the concert at the Hollywood Bowl. I loved that huge amphitheater, dramatically wedged into the surrounding Hollywood Hills: the picnics and wine on the little folding tables, the glow of the stage intensifying as twilight descended, the desert air cooling our arms under the night sky. And all the music.

The first half went beautifully. I was drenched in tears during the final chorale in Copland's *Appalachian Spring*. Nobody could conduct Aaron's music like Daddy did; he was so close to his friend and mentor, he could practically channel him. Then, during intermission, Marjorie and I got stoned. This proved to be a mistake.

The concert was to conclude with Gershwin's *Rhapsody in Blue*, which LB would play, conducting from the piano—as he'd done for decades to perennial acclaim. He'd sounded terrific all week whenever I overheard him practicing in the Brentwood house. But recently he'd developed a new problem: in performance, his fingers turned icy and wouldn't move properly. Harry had arranged for me and my friends to sit in the very front row, directly in front of the piano. Now I writhed in pot-amplified proxy agony as LB garbled passage after passage. The huge crowd at the Bowl seemed to love it anyway; there was a roaring ovation at the end.

For an encore, LB returned to the piano and played a solo Gershwin prelude. He'd played it beautifully for me earlier in the week, but now, in addition to some wrong notes, he also appeared to forget how it went in the middle. *"He's fudging it!"* Marjorie whispered. It was true: for a while there, he was making up the Gershwin as he went along.

What my father needed to do, more than anything, was to wrap it up in LA and go to Santa Fe to work on his opera with Swoozie. But when he finally got there, he came down with such terrible bronchitis that he had to go home. Anyway, that was the excuse; maybe he was crashing from his amphetamine-fueled LA schedule. He even canceled some upcoming concerts in Europe—but not all of them. Nina and I flew over to meet him in Vienna.

Going on the road with our father had been such superb fun when we were kids that Alexander, Nina, and I spent the later years trying over and over to recapture the experience. Yet the truth was, his endless hangers-on and louche habits—what we couldn't help perceiving as the Harryness of it all—were making the touring experience ever less enjoyable for us.

But there could still be magic. On this trip, Nina and I discovered the glories of the Vienna Philharmonic. We were amazed to see them play a Saturday afternoon concert at the Musikverein with LB, then run over to play *Otello* in the pit of the Staatsoper that evening. The next morning at eleven they were back at the Musikverein for another concert with LB, then back to the opera that same night for a performance of *Capriccio*—and then all the next day, rehearsal and video retakes with LB. Their energy and sheer devotion to their work was unlike anything we'd ever seen.

Here at last, Nina and I realized, was a professional orchestra of the highest order that was as passionate about music-making as our father was. They were a uniquely organized cooperative, unburdened by American-style union rules. Back home at the Philharmonic, we'd seen rehearsals where, at the stroke of noon, the Local 802 shop steward in the violin section would stand up and point at the clock, whereupon the musicians would rise out of their chairs midbar, leaving my father fuming on the podium. Such a thing would never happen with the Vienna orchestra; they were willing to rehearse until they got it right, even if they ran over by half an hour. Daddy loved them for that—and the music they created with him was sublime. Harry organized live audio and video recordings of those concerts with the Vienna Philharmonic: all the Brahms symphonies, all the Beethoven symphonies, Mahler, and more. Harry may have been a burden to us, but he gave the world some treasures.

Then the whole gang, orchestra included, went to Munich. After a gorgeous Brahms concert, my thirtieth birthday festivities culminated in an after-party at the Hotel Vier Jahreszeiten, where my father's penthouse suite had its own private entrance to the hotel's swimming pool. Birthday pool party at two a.m.! But so many hangers-on. They were a mixed assortment: a combination of the

LB working team—his audio engineer, his video director, their spouses, his publicist, musical and personal assistants, maybe a doctor or a masseur—combined with the various young men and women who were local, or were friends of Harry's, or had followed along from elsewhere. Daddy never seemed to get tired of the hubbub. In fact, he seemed to need it—desperately.

At such moments, Nina, Alexander, and I would find ourselves thinking the thought we tried not to have: how Mummy would react if she could see the way Daddy was now. She had been such a stabilizing force in his life; now, in her absence, he was a wild child. It had certainly been difficult for both of them. On the one hand, Lenny needed Felicia's steadying influence: *needed* a Mrs. Maestro, as well as someone to tell him not to wear the flocked orange sweater. On the other hand, Lenny needed his other life; he wasn't entirely alive without it, and in the end he couldn't, or wouldn't, suppress it. Felicia found herself forced into the role of an angry scold—and that wasn't fun for either one of them. And of course, there was her terrible curse at the dinner table, the year before she died.

The thing of it was, they'd really loved each other. Maybe that explains why Mummy put up with Daddy's stifling attentions as he stretched himself out next to her on her sickbed. And maybe that explains why, in Munich four years later, LB required his scotch, his multicolored pills, and an entourage filling an entire swimming pool at the Hotel Vier Jahreszeiten to suppress the very same thought that Alexander, Nina, and I couldn't help having.

And maybe even that wasn't enough. A few years later, LB dedicated his recording of the Mozart *Requiem* to his late wife—the very piece he'd insisted on everyone listening to at her funeral Mass in East Hampton. For the album cover, he selected an image of Felicia Montealegre herself, engulfed in a backdrop of flames:

Felicia as Joan of Arc on the cover of Lenny's Mozart *Requiem*.

the very same photo Alexander and I had obsessed over as kids. Our mother had once written to her future husband: "I am willing to accept you as you are, without being a martyr and sacrificing myself on the L.B. altar." But the truth was, she had done exactly that; the role of Joan of Arc was all too apt.

I felt my mother's absence on my thirtieth birthday like an invisible bruise.

* * *

Stephen and LB began workshopping parts of *A Quiet Place* in New York. I heard Act 1 of the opera for the first time in a rehearsal room at the Juilliard School. That whole first act took place at Dinah's funeral, where the freshly bereaved Sam encounters his two estranged children, Junior and Dede, and their mutual lover, François, who have all just driven down from Canada. LB's jaggedly atonal music made an eerie blend with Stephen's idiomatic dialogue, peppered with "ums" and "I means." There were some funny bits, but overall the act was dense, dark, and difficult.

Junior, psychotic and disjointed, makes a disruptive late entrance to the funeral, then sings a truly disturbing striptease number: "Hey, Big Daddy, you're driving me batty . . ." Old Sam, silent through most of the act, at last growls, "You're late . . . you shouldn't have come"—which turns into a hair-raising aria of bitter rage at his children. I couldn't help but wonder to what extent the words that came spitting out of Sam's mouth reflected any of my father's genuine emotions:

None of us can talk to anyone. Not even now . . .
It makes me angry (and guilty) and plenty angry.
(Frightened!) You demean your mother . . .
I could hate you. I fight not to feel it.

At the end of the act, everyone has left the funeral home except Junior, who grieves silently over his mother's coffin, to music so beautiful, so unbearably sad, that I was shaken to my bones.

The plot was disguised, but the pain rang true: all my father's own mad, complicated despair—maybe even beyond what I knew about—was devastatingly manifest in his notes. Whatever would the world make of all this? It was tough stuff; I could barely take it myself, and this was only Act 1.

That same spring, an article appeared in *Harper's Magazine* called "The Tragedy of Leonard Bernstein." Written by Leon Botstein, a conductor and the president of Bard College, it was a deeply dismissive analysis of Bernstein's unrealized potential, couched in an erudite, sneering tone that made me want to hurl the magazine across the room. I hoped my father never read it, but I heard that he did. "What did I ever do to *him*?" my father reportedly said.

Botstein pronounced Bernstein's orchestral works "fatuous and bombastic," the first two symphonies "static and dull." He declared *Mass* to be "endless and flat-footed," and *West Side Story* "a decorative, condescending urban version of *Romeo and Juliet*."

I gasped to read: "Bernstein's Mahler readings are some of his worst." Who *was* this Botstein guy?

I squirmed and swore as I read the article. But some of what Botstein wrote was accurate—and it was the accuracy that was most upsetting of all. He was onto something, I had to admit, when he referred to "Bernstein's need for adulation, for instant and perpetual acclaim." And I cringed to read of "a haze of decadence and mental drowsiness, a mind exhausted by exposure, excessive fame, and wealth." What Botstein had omitted from that list of mind exhausters were the scotch and prescription pills.

To conclude the article, Botstein quoted Gustav Mahler himself— "You must renounce all superficiality, all convention, all vanity and delusion . . ."—and then Botstein hammered his final nail halfway into the coffin: "It is not too late."

So, what with one thing and another, a great deal was riding on *A Quiet Place*; we all felt it, and we knew Daddy did, too.

At least he was making progress on his opera; by contrast, I had precious little to show for myself. David Pack and I were sure Warner Bros. would snap up our new demo tape—but they didn't. "Too Broadway," was the latest aperçu.

Pack said I had to find a manager. I repeatedly underwent the grisly experience of sitting across from a prospective manager, keeping my body still and my face impassive while he or she listened to my demo tape—and then delivered a verdict to my face. "Unshoppable," one manager declared.

In the week before the Houston Grand Opera premiere of *A Quiet Place*, Alexander, Nina, and I rented a car in LA and drove together to Houston, going through canyon country in Arizona, mountains in New Mexico, down to Carlsbad Caverns, across Texas Hill Country. We stayed in poky motels, smoked bales of pot, laughed ourselves into fits. It was the true forging of the entity we eventually dubbed the Three-Headed Monster.

The Maestro's children made a stylish landing at the Four Seasons Hotel in Houston: three grimy, disheveled (and stoned) siblings in a dust ball of a car littered with four days' worth of travel debris. The liveried doormen collected our crumpled napkins and soda cans with majestic solemnity. We were escorted to our very own spacious suite, a designerly fantasy in taupe and chrome. Also, the hotel had a big, big rooftop pool. Let the entourageousness begin.

Between the rehearsals and run-throughs we attended, there was a great deal of downtime. We spent it by that rooftop pool, with the ever-increasing numbers of friends, family, and hangers-on who were descending on Houston for the big premiere. The drinking began before lunch. We didn't see much of LB; he was working hard, surrounded by a humming cloud of colleagues and assistants.

Everyone working on the opera was in a dither. The director, Peter Mark Schifter, had made some choices that particularly baffled and alarmed Stephen, who was himself an opera director. At one point Stephen even tried to write furtive notes directly to the singers. LB saw the typewriter being delivered to Stephen's room and put a stop to it. The director is the director, he told Stephen; you have to let him do his job.

But the directorial choices being made by "Schifty Pete," as LB and Stephen dubbed him, were unpopular with others, as well. For example, while the *Trouble in Tahiti* trio sang about the joys of suburbia (the older opera would open the evening), a surreal parade of actual, full-sized appliances was to float across the stage on a conveyor belt. The parade lasted all of thirty seconds—but in order to create the effect, a team of burly stagehands off stage right had to lift washing machines, hi-fi consoles, and refrigerators onto the belt, one after the other, while a second team of stagehands had to haul them all off into the wings on the other side. No, the stagehands did not love Schifty Pete.

There was a bit of socializing with some culture-minded Houstonians. Lynn Wyatt, the blond, vivacious wife of an oil tycoon, took a shine to my brother: "Oh, Alex-AYN-dah, you're abso-LEWT-ly di-VAHN!" Nina and I took every opportunity to reiterate that tender sentiment in our brother's presence.

Opening night arrived, with its queasy combination of anticipation and outright dread. Alexander, Nina, and I doubled down on our preperformance ritual of kissing both sides of a good-luck penny, then giving it to our father to keep in his pocket; this time, we taped three pennies to a postcard we'd picked up on the road, and lovingly misquoted Junior's "Hey, Big Daddy" aria: "You're driving us *gladdy*!"

The three of us clung to one another in the vast, russet-colored opera house; the occasion seemed to be reopening our collective scar tissue from the *1600* premiere. We loved this music; we knew every note; we wanted the world to love it, too. But we were worried. Maybe the Houston audience wasn't the ideal testing ground for this thorny, profane piece.

The performance began well enough with the older work, *Trouble in Tahiti*. The jazzy, tuneful music, complete with soaring arias

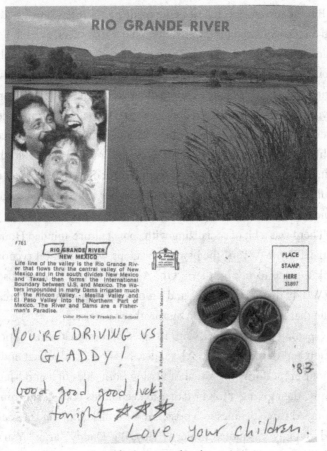

Good luck postcard and pennies.

and the showstopping "What a Movie!" was a natural audience-pleaser. The intermission buzz seemed positive.

Then Act 2 began—that is, all of the new material: two-plus hours of it, presented in one long intermissionless blob that began with that forty-five-minute funeral scene, bristling with new characters and dense, overlapping twelve-tone verbiage. And then, with barely a pause, a scene with old Sam and daughter Dede rereading Dinah's diary on stage right; meanwhile on stage left, Junior has a crazed panic attack while his lover, François, tries to calm him down, partially in French. Torrents of words and plot points and obscenities and complex four-part singing. And then, still with no break, the final scene in the garden the following morning. I fervently hoped the audience around me was noticing the heartbreaking beauty of Dede's opening aria, "Mommy, Are You There?" The daughter singing to her dead mother in the neglected garden always made me cry. But I feared the audience's memory of that aria might have been elbowed aside by the fast-paced multiple singing and plot complexity that followed, including something about a gun that had appeared in the previous act and reappeared in the final act but was never fired, violating one of the hallowed tenets of dramaturgy . . . but that was the least of it. I stewed in my worry: Were the people around me missing crucial sung dialogue? Were the Houstonians appalled by Junior's aria that hinted at incest? Were they distracted by the gun thing and didn't notice how beautiful—*beautiful*—the final music was? It was beautiful music, but it sure wasn't *West Side Story* or *On the Town*. LB was now using his mature musical vocabulary: confrontational, prickly, challenging—especially in contrast to the ear-pleasing *Trouble in Tahiti* at the beginning. I fretted: What if the audience felt they'd been served a slice of chocolate cake, only to have it followed by three heaping tablespoons of cod-liver oil?

Still, it was a premiere, and the audience was appreciative enough, providing standing ovations for the many bows. Afterward, there was an elaborate dinner for the bejeweled patrons and donors, the principal cast, the authors, and all the copious entourage. We dove gratefully into our wine.

Eventually it was LB's turn to go up to the microphone and say a few gracious remarks, as one does at an opening. "I never imagined," he began, "that my little opera would be born in this *cow town*!"

The Three-Headed Monster howled the loudest. "I mean, former! *Former* cow town!" LB yelled over the pandemonium. Waiter, more wine, please! And could you just hand it to us down here under the table?

The reviews of the opera came dribbling in. There were a couple of good ones—Leighton Kerner in the *Village Voice* wrote of "the birth of a powerful new opera"—but the scorn drowned out the praise. Alan Rich in *Newsweek* bemoaned the opera's "dreary psychological quagmire." Donal Henahan in the *New York Times* pronounced the work "as hollow and faddish as *Mass*." Double ouch.

All that work, all that anticipation, all that pressure on Daddy to have a success this time around. I felt sick at heart for him. Yet again.

But already his conductor friend John Mauceri (who had conducted the *Mass* I was in two years earlier) was initiating discussions with the authors about restructuring the opera for its upcoming performances at La Scala and the Kennedy Center. Out of these conversations came the idea of inserting *T in T* into the middle of the opera, as a flashback. And the opera would now have three acts; the audience would no longer be pinned to their seats for two unbroken hours. It was a little wacky, but at least the creative team was moving forward, not moping around. (And it did turn out to be a significant improvement.)

Meanwhile, I went back to my life: more demo tapes, more East-West shuffle, no manager, no record deal—and no serious boyfriend. (Brian and I had parted as friends.)

My friend Marjorie had an expression for a certain kind of high-strung, intense Semitic guy, of which her husband, Elliott, was one: an "electric Jew." I had begun to detect that I was repeatedly attracted to—and entangled with—electric Jews. Nick-oh-Nick had been but one of them.

My father, of course, was the electric-est Jew of them all. "A man with a motor," as Mummy had said long ago. Maybe I was making a mistake even to be looking for a comparable motor.

Was I going to end up like my aunt Shirley, who was never able to find anyone who measured up? She'd remained single—and childless—all her life. My grandmother once said about her daughter, Shirley, "She missed the boat." I remember my mother being outraged by that comment. "How can she say such a thing?" Mummy huffed. "Doesn't she realize that a woman is free to choose a career instead of a family?" That was the modern thinking. But here I was, over thirty, with no momentum in either direction. I wasn't on any boat at all.

17

Redding, Wecord, and
What Was in Between

After four years of hunting for a manager, I finally found one—not in LA but in New York City. Vince had a big friendly smile and was fond of colorful sweaters. Now I had someone actively helping me to shop around my demo tapes. Heartbreakingly, David Geffen declined; he didn't like my voice. Neither did I much, frankly. But there were genuine stirrings of interest from Island Records, a company based, like Vince, in New York.

The gravity seemed to be shifting back East. The David Pack demos and connections had not borne any local fruit—and as it was, I was ambivalent about the whole LA pop music sensibility. So I set my sights on moving back to New York.

My friend Susanna Styron (Bill and Rose's daughter) had a little studio apartment on Jones Street in the Village, which I'd actually helped her move into back in 1977. Together we'd painted the ceiling beams a handsome red. Now Susanna needed to move to LA for her filmmaking career, so we agreed to swap living situations: she'd live in my old room at Marjorie and Elliott's, while I would live on Jones Street, under the ruby red beams.

But before I left Venice, I had a couple of houseguests: David Thomas and our mutual friend Chuck were coming to California for a vacation. David and I had barely communicated since that intense handful of days in Chicago. When the friends arrived, I boldly announced to David that he'd be staying with me in my room, and what did he think of *that*. He was fine with the arrangement, and

David and I picked up our romance precisely where we'd left it off four years earlier. Late at night, joking around about how well we got along, David said, "Let's get married." "Okay," I said. "Okay," he said. We smiled into the dark.

Not only was David Thomas in LA; so was my father, once again doing his thing with the LA Philharmonic Institute. At the big dinner my father arranged for us all in Santa Monica, I noticed how singularly relaxed David was in Daddy's presence. He was up for all the verbal jousting, the musical references, the jokes, the silliness—but there was a gentleness, a relaxed good cheer to David; he wasn't an electric Jew at all, and it was a relief. I could tell my father thought David was terrific. Nina liked him a lot, too, which was no small thing. The pleasure all this gave me was so profound, it felt like the solution to some ancient inner puzzle.

*   *   *

In New York that fall, as my record deal with Island inched toward reality, I was under enormous pressure, above all else, to *write a hit*. I got an upright piano moved into the Jones Street studio, got my TEAC four-track tape recorder all set up—yet all I could do was moon over David Thomas, who was still living in Chicago. I found myself fantasizing about marriage, maybe even children. *Children?* I'd never had such maternal longings before.

Part of the explanation was undoubtedly the simple fact of my being thirty-one, and finding myself newly drawn to some of the more traditional ideas of adulthood than to the—let's face it—puerile notion of being a rock star. But the star-maker machinery, as Joni Mitchell called it, was kicking in at last; wasn't this what I'd always wanted?

Although David Thomas was in the film-rights business, he was quite an accomplished musician. He'd sung in the Harvard

Glee Club; he played the piano beautifully; he could sight-read like the wind—yet he described himself as a dilettante. That made me wince. If David was a dilettante, what did that make me, a dodo?

Sure, I was musical, but I really was a very poor musician. I had no "chops." And why did I have no chops? Because practicing was so painful. And why was practicing so painful? Because I couldn't bear to compete. Yet I couldn't stop competing. It was more exhausting than ever, this combination of craving success and feeling undeserving of success. The old one-foot-on-the-gas, other-foot-on-the-brake.

My New York music attorney was a very tall electric Jew with aviator glasses and a brusque my-meter-is-running manner. He always left me feeling particularly small and foolish. He teased me over lunch when I was too timid to complain to the waiter that the cream cheese on my bagel was speckled with an orange mold. But my attorney was right: I was such a *weenie* about everything. How was I ever going to be assertive enough to make a damn record?

Still, it was heady stuff to be counted among the ranks of Island Records' artists—Bob Marley, the B-52's, Grace Jones—even if the company did seem to be in some disarray. The New York office had a turnover of three different presidents in the course of that year. By president number three, I would walk into the Island offices and not recognize a single face.

But none of it mattered—because I had David Thomas. The trick now was for David to get a job in New York so we could live together. Luckily, his job-hunting visits gave him many opportunities to share in Bernstein events—including a particularly celestial performance of my old favorite, Mahler's Fourth Symphony, with the Vienna Philharmonic on their US tour.

By then this piece had so much resonance for me—starting with the swimming pool in Redding, where Alexander and I had splashed along to the first movement's sleigh bells; then, years later, sitting in the rocking chair at the Dakota crying my eyes out during the slow movement. I thought I'd felt all there was to feel about this piece. But now, with David, I felt something new. My siblings and I had spent a lifetime trying to maintain a delicate equanimity in the face of our regularly received, almost too sublimely intimate aesthetic experiences dispensed by our own father. It was much easier, I was now discovering, to accept Daddy's musical love while sitting with my hand enfolded in David's; this man's quiet ardor and deep musicality allowed us to share the Mahler together on a level that for me, in the past, had felt almost unsafe.

But all too soon, David would go back to Chicago, and for me it was back to write-a-hit at Jones Street. Why was it so hard to crank out a brainless, catchy little number that everybody liked? At one point I even presented a new song to Vince called "Is This What You Had in Mind?"—hoping it was the hit he was waiting for. It wasn't.

Finally I wrote a song that got a rise out of Vince and the Island execs. "Nervous Dancer" went over well, I was grimly sure, because the chorus sounded like Duran Duran and the feel was like the Thompson Twins; both of those bands had techno-pop hits on the radio that I couldn't have cared less about.

Revlon had a magazine ad at the time extolling "a certain drop-dead worldliness." Techno pop aspired to that precise sensibility. "I *hate* drop-dead worldliness," I groused in a letter to Ann. "Maybe I'm a sap like my old man after all, but this music is *cold*."

On one end of the pop music spectrum was the Brit-influenced techno pop, while at the other end was the overblown, overproduced stuff coming out of LA. I couldn't warm up to either of them. As for my old man himself, he had lost interest in pop music—but we agreed on one exception: Michael Jackson. Daddy thought he was a stunning performer, both vocally and as a dancer, and Jackson's androgyny only made him more alluring to both of us.

Other than that, my enthusiasm for what I heard on the radio was at an all-time low. Maybe I wasn't cut out for this racket after all; maybe I didn't even *like* pop music anymore. But I'd picked a hell of a time to be having this realization; I signed the Island Records deal.

David Thomas's New York job finally came through, and together we piled all his belongings into a U-Haul truck and drove from Chicago directly to Fairfield, Connecticut—where David, in adorably courtly fashion, asked my father for my hand in marriage. Daddy danced us both around the kitchen. David and I moved into a little Greenwich Village third-floor walk-up apartment with exposed brick walls. It was just a few blocks from Jones Street, where I still went every day to write-a-hit. A close second in difficulty to that enterprise was finding a wedding date that could be wedged into my father's hectic touring schedule. There were endless contortions and testy exchanges. Uncle Mikey Mindlin teased David: "Why did you bother to ask Lenny for Jamie's hand? You should have gone straight to Harry Kraut."

We finally settled on December 2; there was to be a small morning wedding at the Dakota apartment, followed by a larger party that evening at the freshly renovated Starlight Roof of the Waldorf Astoria. Between my father's address book and my own, our guest list was quickly approaching four hundred.

David was raised Episcopalian, but he agreed to a Jewish wedding ceremony, to please Grandma (and perhaps to please her firstborn son, too, although I guessed my father wouldn't have insisted upon it). We met with a rabbi my father recommended; afterward, I found myself in tears on the subway. I ached for some meaningful spiritual expression, but I knew this expensively dressed, smooth-talking rabbi was not the solution. He did, however, make one astute observation. After I'd described some recent family history, he said, "So in other words, this wedding is the first happy thing that's come along for your family after losing your mother." That was certainly true; it made the event resonate all the more, and maybe even justified the mad, mad expense.

David and I ended up choosing a rumpled, uncharismatic rabbi from the local VA hospital. He didn't solve my spiritual needs; maybe nothing Jewish could. But at least this rabbi wasn't smug.

Shirley was hoping to serve as a mother substitute in helping me plan my wedding, but I feared she would drive me and everyone else crazy. I hurt her feelings when I chose decorator Gail for my wedding planner—but it was a wise choice. Gail's unfettered love for her friend Felicia helped bring my mother's spirit into the proceedings in a way that Shirley's complicated jealousies never would have.

By summer's end, Island approved my record's producer— actually a trio of guys that Vince had put together. There had been great dispute over who was going to produce my record. Many possibilities were floated, vetted, and rejected—including David Pack, who was devastated by the rejection. He felt, justifiably, that he'd earned the right to produce it. I was no longer sure his California pop sensibility was right for me, so I let myself be talked out of going with him. Then I wallowed in guilt and uncertainty. More weenie behavior, and more elf's thread.

I referred to the month of December as "Redding, Wecord, Wecord, Redding." How could two such momentous, long-awaited milestones be happening *simultaneously*? The dual exclamation points oddly neutralized each other; I couldn't exult or concentrate properly over either one.

Amid this excitement, LB had his own momentous recording

project: he was going to conduct the score of his most famous work, *West Side Story*, in a New York City recording studio, with the city's top-level session musicians, and world-class opera stars singing the leading roles. Deutsche Grammophon, LB's new label since he'd left Columbia in the 1970s, was planning a big release— while his video director, Humphrey Burton, would film the whole adventure for a BBC documentary. Harry was very busy, cooking up all those hot deals. As usual, everything was very elaborate, very expensive, and very last-minute.

My father was keen to make the case that his musical could cross the boundary from Broadway to the opera stage, and this recording was going to prove his point. Opera star Kiri Te Kanawa was cast as Maria. Tatiana Troyanos, with her huge mezzo voice, would sing Anita. An up-and-coming American baritone, Kurt Ollmann, would sing Riff.

But who was going to sing Tony? The recording date was fast approaching, and the tenor had not been locked in. Apparently Luciano Pavarotti's name was floated, but LB instantly shot down the idea; how ludicrous would it be for Tony of the Jets gang to have an Italian accent?!

At this point, the story gets a little murky. Did LB hear a tenor he liked at English National Opera, singing *Siegfried*? Or did he hear the voice late at night on the radio, semiconscious from sleeping pills? Whichever way it went, he couldn't remember the singer's name, only that it was Hispanic. And so everyone came to the conclusion, without looking into matters too carefully, that Leonard Bernstein wanted José Carreras to sing Tony on his *West Side Story* recording project.

Carreras was hurriedly booked, and flown to New York straight from his vacation in Greece, one day before the sessions began. LB rapidly grasped that this Carreras fellow was not the singer he'd had in mind, but it was too late to do anything about it. (It turned out the voice he'd liked belonged to a British tenor from Liverpool with the misleading name of Alberto Remedios.)

José Carreras was from Spain. His unmistakable Spanish accent, when he sang in English, was grotesquely wrong for the role of Tony—even worse than Pavarotti's Italian accent would have been. A language coach was hired to work with Carreras to make his voice sound like it was more plausibly emanating from a member of the Jets gang than from the rival Puerto Rican Sharks. But as the Yiddish saying goes, *gornisht helfen*—loosely translated: fuggedaboutit. LB was not pleased—and viewers of Humphrey's documentary would see much glowering from both men.

David and I attended most of the recording sessions. Kiri Te Kanawa was nursing a cold throughout the project, but she gamely sang on. There was great camaraderie in the youthful chorus as the Jets sang "Gee, Officer Krupke" and the Shark girls sang "America." The orchestra itself was brilliant; the composer was extracting lush, powerful performances out of the players. My father said, "I'm falling in love with my music all over again." And so were we all.

But it was the Carreras drama that was most riveting. We loved how he'd pluck the chewing gum out of his mouth the second before he sang into the microphone. There was a take of "Maria" that was going spectacularly well—Carreras was even nailing the American *r* in "Maria"—and as the orchestra surged to the climactic moment featuring Carreras's big sustained B-flat "money note," we all leaned forward in anticipation . . . whereupon Carreras stepped back from the microphone, popping his gum back into his mouth. "I do that part tomorrow," he announced. LB was apoplectic. And all caught on film. Later, Humphrey Burton cursed himself for having turned off his cameras before LB and Carreras were seen walking down the corridor arm in arm—some sort of peace having been restored between the two divos.

Not only was there all the Carreras drama to observe; there was an additional angle of great interest to me. Alexander and Nina had been hired to record several instances of midsong spoken dialogue between Tony and Maria: during "Dance at the Gym," when they first meet; on the fire escape as part of the "Tonight" duet; and in the middle of "One Hand, One Heart," as the couple exchange their make-believe marriage vows in the bridal shop.

Both Nina and Alexander were aspiring actors at the time. Each in their turn had studied with our mother's friend and acting teacher, Herbert Berghof. LB decided it was a great idea to give the dialogue task to his kids (or possibly Harry decided). But it was inherently so embarrassing for the two siblings to speak Arthur Laurents's lines of romantic dialogue that they were in a slow-burning agony of discomfort throughout the recording process—and being filmed to boot.

Everyone thought they did a fine job. Alexander sounded American, which lent needed credibility to Carreras's Tony. And Nina, with her bilingual upbringing, knew how to make Maria sound authentically Latina. But I was squirming right alongside them; I knew all too well about the ambivalent experience of "riding on the LB train." To this day, the three of us still can't quite bear to listen as Nina and Alexander murmur "To love and to honor," "To hold and to keep" to each other on that recording.

What was our father thinking? Well, this was how everything seemed to be back then: big ideas, big doings, and no time to reflect on anything. It's a tribute to the beauty of the music that eventually all three of us siblings were able to fall back in love with "One Hand, One Heart."

The recording sounded wonderful overall, and did indeed

make a strong case that *West Side Story* is as comfortable with operatic voices as with musical theater ones—even if it isn't to everyone's taste (book writer Arthur Laurents, in particular, loathed the recording). And maybe, given all his recent creative failures, LB was grateful to immerse himself in a work of his that was unequivocally admired.

I predicted with great certainty that the Carreras-as-Tony casting fumble was so preposterous that no one would buy the CD. But it sold well and got some good reviews. No matter what the circumstance, I could never spot a hit.

* * *

A hundred people came to the "small wedding" at the Dakota on the morning of December 2. My father had gone to great pains to arrange for the music. "Trust me, I know show business," he'd said when I questioned some of his choices—but he turned out to be right. He walked me (a bit shakily) into the living room, while a piano trio played his artful interweaving of two Aaron Copland songs. It felt right to have Aaron's music at my wedding; he was like a musical godfather to all of us.

David awaited me under the huppah, which was rigged from an opulent Russian blanket Mummy had found on one of her antique-store jaunts—a perfect way to evoke her presence.

After the vows, a chorus of family and friends sang "Almighty Father" from *Mass*. David wore a yarmulke and stepped on the wineglass, like a mensch. (We found out a few years later that his great-grandmother had, in fact, been a Lithuanian Jew. "I *knew* it!" Grandma crowed.)

There were so many people to hug, so many smiles, so much champagne, so much of chef Ann's delicious food. Julia was be-atific. Ever since I'd moved to LA, she'd discovered that she missed me, and we got along much better now—plus, she was bonkers for David.

Later, at the Waldorf, the receiving line alone took an hour and a half. The tables had vases of roses with stems so long that we could see each other across the table beneath them. There was a fifteen-piece band so wonderful that even Grandma danced; in her joy, she forgot all about her painful knees.

Daddy was probably pretty drunk by the time he made his toast. First, he acknowledged that the occasion was also Adolph Green's birthday. "A very big birthday, in fact," he said, nodding to his longtime friend. "But he asked me not to mention how big. So let us simply raise *seventy glasses* to Adolph!"

Daddy concluded his toast by raising his glass to David—"my favorite son." There was a "cow town" strength howl from the family table. I hoped that Alexander was too blitzed at that moment to register his father's heedless gushing.

At ten p.m., after the band had packed up and left, there came a cool woman DJ from downtown who put on the first song, cranked up the volume, and promptly blew out the Starlight Roof's brand-new sound system. I was devastated: No more dancing at my wedding? After a doleful half hour, I heard a strange, rhythmic thumping, growing louder, closer—and into the Starlight Roof bounced a fully costumed Brazilian samba band, loaded with percussion instruments, whereupon everyone tumbled onto the dance floor for a delirious two hours. It was David Pack who had inadvertently saved the day: he'd heard the band at a Brazilian club the night before and hired them on the spot as a wedding surprise.

After our ten happy honeymoon days in southern France, David returned to New York, and I went to Nashville for a month to finish my record in a studio called the Castle. It was, in fact, a replica of a European castle, where the producer trio and I could

Quincy, the Gloved One, LB, JB, and David Pack.

live together and work nearly around the clock. I was feeling so confident that, for a while, I was unbeatable at Ping-Pong.

I abandoned the team for two days to fly to LA, where my father was receiving a special Lifetime Achievement Award at the Grammys ceremony. The night before the show, David Pack granted LB his birthday wish from the year before: to meet Michael Jackson. Pack arranged a private dinner for our whole family, along with Jackson's producer, Quincy Jones, who was a Lenny fan—and the Gloved One himself. There were so many of us, and such fierce competition to sit near the guests of honor, that something inverted inside me; I suddenly couldn't bear my own desire to be near all that pop music greatness. I went and sat at the far end of the table.

Michael was terribly shy. His longest conversation with LB took place, I learned later, when they found themselves in the men's room. LB touched Michael's face where it looked as if he'd applied a great deal of foundation makeup. "What's all this on your face?" my father asked. "You don't need to wear all that." Michael replied in his reedy voice: "Oh, Mr. Bernsteen, didn't you ever have a pimple?"

When I got back to Nashville, I found my producing trio exhausted, grim-faced, burned out. Why weren't they having fun anymore? True, the mixing phase was always the most draining part of the recording process—but I sensed an uneasy, unspoken consensus that the record wasn't coming together.

When we got back to New York and played the tracks for Vince, he was, I reported to David, "heartbreakingly unenthusiastic." This did not bode well for the reaction at Island.

After several postponements, the meeting with Island president Chris Blackwell finally came around, but the producer trio was disinvited. Uh-oh. Sure enough, Blackwell declared that the production was bad, particularly the rhythm section. Rescue options were discussed. Blackwell even suggested going back to David Pack—after all the earlier anguish of Pack's being iced out of the project! I walked out of that meeting past the rows of unfamiliar Island employees, imagining that to those young strivers, my record was of less interest than a dog's leftovers.

Apparently Blackwell felt the same. A week or two later, he simply pulled the plug on the whole project. No record release. Over and out.

How could everything have gone so wrong? Was it because I was such a hopeless *weenie*? I hadn't liked the sound of the rhythm section, either—why didn't I speak up? The voice of Nick-oh-Nick evidently still whispered in my inner ear, warning me against being "loud and obnoxious." My mother's voice was in there, too: "Don't make waves," she used to say.

On the other hand, how could I have dared to second-guess my professional production team when I was, let's face it, such an *amateur*? Yeah: I had it coming, all right. I *knew* I would suck. I *knew* I couldn't write-a-hit. Elf's thread spun its toxic shroud.

I wondered: Did Daddy, too, struggle with elf's thread after he got bad reviews for his compositions? The ambivalent reception for *Mass*. The debacle of *1600*. The Gordian knot of *A Quiet Place*. I knew it had to hurt. But he, at least, had the constant healing balm of his concert audiences, with their euphoric ovations, their tears and flowers—especially in Europe. No wonder Daddy couldn't cut down on his conducting. That was a more potent painkiller than any drug—far better, in fact, because the high came from the gratifying and universally celebrated act of sharing something beautiful with others. He wasn't called a "conductor" for nothing: the energy—music, sublimity, love—traveled through him in a magical circuit from the players to the listeners and back around again. What activity could be more healing—and more addictive?

I never grieved properly over the death of my record. First I was numb, then relieved. Now I could turn my attentions wholly on my husband, David; he would be *my* healing balm. Maybe I could even get pregnant. "Fuck 'em," I wrote to Ann. "There's more than one way to get something made around here."

18

Forward Motion

The fix was in; it had always been in; my existence as a musician was built to self-destruct. And it was just as well: making music was the one activity that reliably gave me that grisly old Stupid Idiot feeling.

I felt I was missing some crucial resource. I called it the Golden Blind Spot: the ability of creative artists to suspend judgment, even common sense, to believe that what they were creating was earthshaking—and to believe it long enough to allow them to complete their creation. I felt mired in gray reality as I struggled on the guitar or the keyboard, writing my songs. The little voice in my head almost never shut up: *You're wasting your time*. Clearly my father had a Golden Blind Spot. Where was mine?

Only one way of making music had stayed fun: oddly enough, I still enjoyed cooking up songs in honor of Daddy himself, songs I could sing to him in the company of my siblings—and now also David. Maybe the built-in guarantee of my father loving anything his daughter made for him erased my need for a Golden Blind Spot.

LB was to be promoted to Commandeur de la Légion d'honneur by the French government in Paris, and his assistant conductor, Michael Barrett, was coordinating the celebratory concert. Michael suggested that as a surprise, maybe I could write something for David, Nina, Alexander, and me to sing. I instantly knew what I wanted to do.

Over the following weeks, I devised "The Maestro Suite": four little a capella songs in four-part harmony. My lyrics were full of in-jokes that I knew my father would love. Writing out the music was a grisly business: my dyslexia for musical notation, combined with my thrice-erased child's scrawl, made every bar a humiliating torture. But I kept at it.

With David's help, I recorded the four vocal parts on my four-track tape recorder. Then I created individualized practice cassettes for each of us. I drilled everyone shamelessly. Where had all this assertiveness been when I was making my record?

With David's true-blue tenor turning the sibling trio into a sturdy quartet, we went to Paris and gave a fine rendition of "The Maestro Suite." The Maestro hugged us black and blue. It was gratifying to have devised a way for all four of us "kids" to express our love to our father, who'd become so difficult to love so much of the time.

He returned from his next long tour thoroughly worn out as usual, but I found myself worrying about him in a new way. I knew how his road life was: in addition to the hard work and relentless travel, he was staying up all night, drinking to excess, pills to sleep, pills to wake up—the usual. But he was older now; it was harder for his body to recover. He was increasingly exhausted and irritable. More and more, he was reminding me of his own description of God that began the narration to his *Kaddish* Symphony:

> . . . *ancient, hallowed,*
> *Lonely, disappointed Father:*
> *Betrayed and rejected Ruler of the Universe,*
> *Angry, wrinkled Old Majesty . . .*

Now that my father was home, his plan, as usual, was to get back to composing. His composing periods were hard-won glades of cleared calendar between conducting jobs. But the older he became, the harder it was for him to switch gears from conducting to composing.

The Maestro would come off the road, manic and drenched in adulation, to find himself at the dinner table with his family. Unlike his fans and acolytes, this crowd was not hanging on his every word and triumphant exploit. We almost felt it was our job to interrupt him, to remind him he was a mortal like the rest of us. He knew it was for his own good, but he'd soon grow irritated. "Everyone shut up but me!" he'd yell, pounding the table. He rattled the silverware, but not us.

Most difficult of all for him was the shift from being constantly surrounded by people while on tour—the orchestra, the entourage, the fans, the patrons, the journalists, the friends, the lovers—to being all alone at his piano, facing a blank sheet of manuscript paper. For my father, that was the most naked horror of all. He hated the lonely, tortured process of composing. Yet it was what he aspired to most—and at some point, despite all the obstacles he put in his own way, he would eventually creep to the piano at some godforsaken hour and wrestle new notes out of the void. This usually started happening after being home for about six weeks—which was just about the time he was scheduled to go back on the road.

By the following summer, LB was acting so demanding and imperious that one night, apropos of some minor altercation, Harry suddenly decided he'd had enough—and quit.

Harry quit! At home, we were gleeful but anxious about Harry's exit, as if the teacher had abruptly abandoned the homeroom: *Now* what would we do?

LB and the New York Philharmonic went off on their US tour, with Margaret Carson, his PR stalwart, filling in for Harry. One of the tour pieces was Tchaikovsky's Sixth; Daddy made up a new lyric for the famous march tune in the penultimate movement: "I'm gon-na quit like Har-*reee* . . ." And sometimes he did feel like quitting. Alexander told me about sitting next to Daddy as he looked through the sheaves of schedules Harry had prepared, some running as far as five years in advance. Daddy pushed them all away with a grimace. "I'm so sick of *Leonard Bernstein*," he said.

But the quitting crisis didn't last long. Amberson, the large, complex machine that Harry had built up for fifteen years, couldn't run without him at the controls. And LB could no longer run his life without Harry. And Harry, of course, had by then devoted his entire existence to Leonard Bernstein. Was it a business relationship, a love obsession, or an evil manipulation? There was no way to figure out any of it. But they all needed one another: Daddy, Harry, and Amberson. Within a month or two, manager and client patched up whatever their disagreement was, and the three-way symbiosis reasserted itself.

By this time, my father had become like an intensely tended-to queen bee, unable to move around on his own anymore. Oh, he's so coddled and insulated, I would think contemptuously; he probably couldn't walk down 72nd Street to buy himself a pair of shoelaces. And then, a moment later, I'd realize the more likely outcome: he'd stroll guilelessly down the block, make friends on the way with five doormen, a couple of cops, and a dozen old ladies—and wind up with six pairs of shoelaces, presented to the beloved Maestro for free.

The Maestro persisted daily in bossing everyone around, roaring at people over the phone, sleeping till five p.m. But there were glades of jollity, usually on the weekends in Fairfield. Shirley, who was almost always along, was a reliable source of mirth. It helped that she and David adored each other. Was it just me, or was David's presence improving the family experience for everyone?

Shirley had taken over my old bedroom across the hall from

my father's. Late at night, the two of them could be found on her bed or his, working side by side on their tricky British crossword puzzles, wreathed in cigarette smoke, chortling in Rybernian—as comfortable and intimate as two siblings could ever be. Shirley, it seemed, had finally achieved her lifelong wish: in their sixties, one widowed and one unmarried, the brother and sister were life companions at last (at least whenever the brother didn't bring his latest lover along).

On those Fairfield weekends, David and I occupied whichever bedroom was available. Sometimes there wasn't one available at all. One family-filled night, we even slept in the back of the station wagon. What were we going to do if we had a kid . . . ?

Wait—not if: *when*. I was pregnant.

* * *

At five a.m. on March 4, 1987, after a long, agonizing labor, my daughter, Frankie, was born, with a perfectly round head under a thatch of dark brown hair. When it was all over, David brought me a fried-egg sandwich: the single greatest meal of my life.

The family came down to the hospital to meet Frankie that evening. I was tired and very sore, but thrilled to be providing everyone with this grand event. My father's kisses were sloppier and more embarrassingly ardent than ever, but I had to admit: it was quite a kick to have presented Daddy with a granddaughter.

After they all left, I leaned back in my hospital bed with my arms behind my head and permitted myself one delicious moment of repose: *I didduhtt.*

If only Mummy could have been there . . . I remembered her stories about giving birth to me: how she'd taken Lamaze classes for natural childbirth, then became so overwhelmed with the pain of labor that she'd yelled for the gas, swearing like a sailor.

Afterward, hordes of well-wishers crammed into her hospital room, where she lay groggily as they swilled booze, smoked cigarettes, and ordered—yes—room service.

Frankie was barely three months old when we took her along to Rome, where Daddy was conducting Puccini's opera *La Bohème* with a young, all-American cast. He fed Frankie a clam out of his pasta. I was aghast: A *clam*? She wasn't even eating solid food yet! But even in Rome, we remained inside the Daddy magic circle: a place where it never rained on outdoor concerts, speeding tickets never got doled out, and food was never poison. So Frankie was fine.

I was so besotted with the marvel of her; I could not begin to express what happened to me when I smelled the top of her head, listened to her milky whimpers, held her dumpling foot in the hollow of my hand. All I could do was clutch the deep feelings to myself, and love my intense, blue-eyed little girl with a secret, speechless ardor. It was even more than I could share with David.

I continued making underslept, half-hearted attempts to revive "my so-called career," as I called it. After the Island Records debacle, I pursued new record company leads with my manager, Vince, but there was little momentum. As for the songwriting itself: after my friend Susanna lost the red-beamed studio on Jones Street, my father invited me to move my songwriting gear into apartment 92, under the rooftop gables of the Dakota. Since his studio was now downstairs, apartment 92 was a place in need of a purpose. So I went up there in my Frankie-free moments—but barely a song came out.

Sitting on the window seat, with Central Park stretched out below me like a fairy-tale kingdom, I felt perched on the pinnacle of an unearned glory: a magnificent nothingness. I'd have been more ashamed of my low productivity if I weren't simply so sleepy. One day when Frankie was about seven months old, I was staggering around the Dakota kitchen downstairs, making her dinner. While something was heating up on the stove, I fastened the bib around her neck. "Oh, am I having dinner, too?" Nina asked. I'd put the bib on my twenty-five-year-old sister.

But one memory from that time remains clear.

We got a memo from Harry, explaining that a lady named Joan Peyser was writing a book about Leonard Bernstein, and that she would be reaching out to all of us for interviews, and that while this was not exactly an "authorized" biography, we should nevertheless strive to be polite, responsive, and . . . Well, Harry's language was so perplexingly circuitous that I got the impression we should actively cooperate. So when Ms. Peyser snagged me at some event and asked if she could talk to my siblings and me, I agreed to round everyone up. And we all went, David included, to Joan Peyser's house one evening for drinks.

She had a lovely town house down on Charlton Street, and was awaiting us wearing a cheerful pink caftan. There was an array of yummy snacks on her coffee table—deviled eggs!—and every sort of alcoholic beverage on offer. Like the wicked witch in "Hansel and Gretel," she was fattening us up for the kill. After about an hour of pleasant questions, when we were all nicely soft and tipsy, she sprang her trap: "So, about your father's homosexuality . . ."

We were caught off guard, but really, it wasn't all that terrible. Over a decade had passed since the worst of the troubles; by now, this was a topic the three of us freely discussed among ourselves, and we really had nothing to hide. Yes, he was gay. Yes, he had lovers. Yes, we were a family that still hugged and laughed and clung to one another. Any other questions?

But once we were out on the street, we gasped to realize how we'd been snookered: how the wicked witch in the pink caftan had plied us with liquor and then pounced.

We put the experience out of our minds, and time passed. Then Joan Peyser's book came out: it was loathsome, prurient, tabloidy stuff. She'd managed to extract a lot of gay gossip from "friends" of Daddy's from his past, including some composers he'd helped, who might have been more gracious. I read the book backward, so as not to ingest it too thoroughly. One thing was clear: Leonard Bernstein had become a Controversial Person—a long, complex evolution from his wunderkind public persona of the 1950s.

And what about Grandma: Did *she* read the book?! Harry had gone to some trouble to make sure she didn't see it, but apparently a friend of hers read her a few passages. Grandma must have been upset, yet strangely, no one seems to remember what her reaction was. I'm guessing her motherly powers of denial were prodigious.

The one person who definitely did not read Peyser's book was Daddy himself. He promised Alexander, Nina, and me "on bended knee" that he never would. The book got mixed reviews and was briefly on the best-seller list, then disappeared. LB managed to avoid most of the blowback by being in Europe, where nearly all his work took place by then. Life went on, but we never did understand why Harry had encouraged Joan Peyser at all. It seemed a high price to pay for a little publicity.

Around that time, there was a premiere of a new LB piece: a song cycle called *Arias and Barcarolles*. The title was a quote from, of all people, President Dwight D. Eisenhower. As my father told the story (and he loved telling it), he and members of the New York Philharmonic had just performed at the White House for President and Mrs. Eisenhower, back in the 1950s. After the concert, the president and his wife offered the musicians tea and cake. It was a decidedly stiff gathering; everyone was longing for something stronger than tea. The president said to my father, "I liked that last piece you played. It had a *theme*."

A theme? My father hadn't the faintest idea what the president meant. But he gamely tried a response. "Oh—I think I understand what you mean; you mean it had . . . a beat?" President Eisenhower replied testily: "No, I mean a THEME. Not like all them arias and barcarolles!"

Them arias and . . . *barcarolles?* Did the president even know a barcarolle was a song sung by Venetian gondoliers? What in the world was he talking about?!

Every time my father recounted this story, he would describe how, at the moment of Eisenhower's gnomic utterance, the tea-cups rattled on their saucers as the Philharmonic musicians tried to maintain their composure.

Three decades later, President Eisenhower's phrase became the title of LB's song cycle. The piece was designed for four voices and four-hands piano—in the style of Brahms's *Liebeslieder Waltzes*. The first performance, in the spring of 1988, was part of a memorial concert for Jack Romann of Baldwin Pianos, a generous gentleman who had died of AIDS. LB, along with his friend and younger colleague Michael Tilson Thomas, accompanied the four singers. The subject matter was love: all kinds. Most of the texts were by LB himself, but one was by a Yiddish poet, describing a demonically brilliant fiddler who played at the poet's wedding. I suspected that the description of the scruffy musician whose maniacal brilliance gave the poet a near nervous breakdown was, for my father, a kind of mirror fantasy.

Another text, "Little Smary," was a bedtime story Grandma made up that her son would beg her to tell him over and over when he was little. (Daddy made sure Grandma got an ASCAP credit for her "lyric.") Much of the music was in LB's later, thorny idiom, and his words, too, were challenging in a number of ways. Alexander, Nina, and I squirmed to hear the text of "The Love of My Life," which featured the line "Tit . . . come . . ." The very clever song "Love Duet" also had some lines that made us uncomfortable:

> *She: What do you think of triads?*
> *He: Triads be real relaxin' . . .*
> *She: What's with this sudden accen' . . . ?*
> *He: Jesse . . . Jackson . . .*

At the time, I couldn't relate much to *Arias and Barcarolles*. Now, all these decades later, it strikes me as one of my father's

Grandma Jennie with Jamie and David at Tanglewood, 1988.

most mature and nuanced pieces: wry and touching and full of delightful surprises—"Tit . . . come" and Ebonics notwithstanding. All I remember from that first performance, though, is my worry about how late it was getting, and how I had to relieve Julia from looking after Frankie.

There was a recording made of the piece later that year, in a new version for two singers. One afternoon, Michael Barrett and his colleague Steven Blier, the two pianists on the recording, arrived at the Dakota with the singers, Judy Kaye and William Sharp, for the CD cover photo session with the Maestro—who was still fast asleep. The group waited several hours. At last he showed up, rumpled and ashen, in his scratchy old bathrobe. And that is precisely how he appears on the cover of the CD.

*   *   *

The really big event of 1988 was LB's seventieth birthday, on August 25. Everyone was excited about the occasion—with the exception of LB himself. He was spooked by the ancient biblical designation of "threescore and ten" as the allotted span of a man's life. Suddenly Daddy felt old. Officially old. He hated that feeling.

Harry cooked up a mega-special: an audience-crammed, star-studded concert in the Maestro's honor at the Tanglewood Shed, the large outdoor venue where LB himself had performed at least a hundred times since the 1940s. The event was to be broadcast live to Europe and videotaped for subsequent broadcast on PBS. Humphrey Burton, Daddy's longtime friend and video director, pulled the whole splashy hodgepodge together.

Everyone from Slava Rostropovich to Midori to Yo-Yo Ma participated. Once again, I wrote a song for the Quartet to sing to Daddy. The last lines of "The Seven-Oh Stomp" could have been addressed to myself:

Don't . . . you . . . wish you could do
A quarter of the things he can do?

Don't . . . you . . . hope you'll have been
Half that cool by threescore and ten?

The concert was long, as such extravaganzas always are, but it was full of highlights—including Bobby McFerrin singing and chest-tapping "Somewhere" from *West Side Story*; and Betty Bacall, perched on an upright piano, huskily delivering a sidesplitting lyric by Steve Sondheim to a Kurt Weill tune: "Poor Lenny, ten gifts too many . . ."

The only person not having fun at the concert was Poor Lenny. To begin with, he loathed sitting passively while others made a musical fuss over him; he would have vastly preferred to be up on that stage, making music himself. But he had to sit there, acting gracious and enthusiastic throughout; the TV cameras were constantly on him, getting reaction shots. In a way, Harry had devised an exquisite torture device for his . . . client? Prisoner? Golden-egg layer?

Worse, my father had recently developed prostate problems. That night, he'd apparently taken a pill that would allow him to pee without difficulty, but it kicked in, with five-alarm urgency, right in the middle of the second act. Unable to excuse himself in the middle of the celebration in his honor, especially with all those video cameras trained on him, he had no choice but to pee, right there in his rattan seat, in the dark of the Shed. The concert concluded with that mother of all grand finales, "Make Our Garden Grow" from *Candide*. All the performers came downstage to sing, while LB's years-back assistant conductor, Seiji Ozawa, conducted the Boston Symphony Orchestra. It was a magnificent climax, and everyone was awash in emotion, but LB was also awash from the waist down. And of course he had to go up on the stage and hug everyone. On camera.

Nina, Jamie, and Betty Bacall rehearsing for Lenny's seventieth birthday at Tanglewood.

His devoted publicist, Margaret Carson, came to the rescue, giving him her long black cashmere shawl. LB draped it around himself, went up on stage, and no one was the wiser. But when the Quartet found out about it later, we shuddered to think of the distress Daddy had endured. That was not an experience to help a person feel good about turning threescore and ten.

The next day, he didn't get up till five, and was nearly mute with gloom as family and close friends gathered at his rented house for the birthday dinner. To cheer him up, we put a big pile of presents in front of him on the dining room table. Daddy liked presents. He began to rally a little. When at last he began festooning his big ears with some of the wrapping ribbon, as was his ancient practice, I breathed a sigh of relief; maybe he was going to be okay.

19

An Arrival

That fall, my father fell head over heels in love with a young aspiring conductor named Mark. Mark appeared frequently at the Dakota dinner table—and at the breakfast table, too. And Mark accompanied LB on tour. We weren't sure what the excitement over this mild-mannered fellow was all about, but it was good to see Daddy animated. Everything had become such an effort for him: his breathing, his insomnia, and all the additional threescore-and-ten indignities. His belly was terribly distended, while the rest of him seemed to be collapsing in on itself.

But he pressed on, wowing his audiences, carousing with his retinue, holding forth on all his big topics: Israel (he was depressed about it), AIDS (he was depressed about it), and President Reagan (he was deeply dismayed).

My father loathed Reagan. That Christmas, he composed a song he called "Xmas Wrap," in which he lampooned Reagan's warmongering policies. He gathered the Quartet around the piano, slapped his new manuscript against the stand, and excitedly played us his new piece, just as in olden times. He explained that he would accompany the four of us singing it on Christmas night at the Styrons' house in Connecticut, and then the following week, back in the city, we'd perform it with him at the annual New Year's Eve Concert for Peace in the Cathedral of Saint John the Divine.

"Xmas Wrap" turned out to be my father's version of a rap song. He was fascinated by hip-hop. I give him credit for intuiting a major new musical genre in the making, but the song he wrote was—how can I say this?—really square. His satire of Reagan fell a little short of hilarious, while the rhythm he'd devised was uncharacteristically leaden. He told us we were supposed to bang pots and pans to that rhythm, a notion that did not fill us with joy. The first lines already had us squirming as he played the song for us at the piano:

Hip-hop Rappaport—rap rap;
Tell me, baby, where it's at . . .

We caught one another's eyes in dismay. At the song's conclusion, we were barely able to choke out the traditional "Hey, that's great!" Did we really have to perform this song in front of the Styrons and all their friends: Mike Nichols, Arthur Miller, Mia Farrow? And then perform it again a week later, for a huge crowd of strangers? We didn't want to let Daddy down, but—really? Our lily-white Quartet ersatz-rapping in front of a massive—and massively diverse—New York City audience? It was a horrifying prospect.

In the car on the way to the Styrons' house, we confessed to Daddy that we had "forgotten" to bring along our music. He was furious and stung, and that made me very sad. He'd thought it would be such fun for all of us to perform his satirical rap song together. But the Quartet felt almost protective about concealing LB's misfire. We managed to worm out of singing the song at the cathedral, as well—although he did manage to rope Michael Barrett into performing it there with him.

It's the only composition by Leonard Bernstein that his family has ever suppressed. No, do not ask to see it.

My father's public loathing of President Reagan was just the sort of thing that would have generated new entries in the FBI's Leonard Bernstein file. But J. Edgar Hoover, Bernstein's personal Javert, was no longer around, and the Freedom of Information Act now permitted citizens to examine their own FBI documents. So Daddy took a look at his.

His dossier turned out to be a staggering eight hundred pages long. J. Edgar Hoover had been obsessing on Leonard Bernstein since the 1940s, when informants started supplying insinuations that Bernstein was a Communist. My father could now read such entries as: "I know that Bernstein is a card-carrying Communist but I have no proof of it but I can tell by the way he talks."

The file had substantially increased in girth during the Red Scare years in the 1950s, when my father had even been briefly denied a passport. In 1970, when the Black Panther business transpired, the FBI became obsessed with Leonard Bernstein all over again; Hoover was deeply paranoid about the Black Panthers. And *Mass* made things even worse; there it all was in the files, about President Nixon's advisers looking into that "secret message" in Latin, designed to embarrass the president.

On Nixon's tapes, the president's voice can be heard reacting to H. R. Haldeman's description of Bernstein at the curtain call of *Mass*, kissing the male members of the cast: "Absolutely sickening." But Daddy was rather proud to have been referred to by President Nixon as a "son of a bitch."

If Nixon thought Bernstein's curtain call kisses were sickening, he would have been freshly appalled at Bernstein's efforts on behalf of AIDS advocacy. LB and Harry were both deeply immersed in that movement. Not only was there no cure, and no money for research, but the disease had such stigma attached to it, mainly due to its association with gay men, that President Reagan wouldn't even acknowledge its existence in public for an infuriatingly long time. Harry told me he'd lost thirty-one friends in a single year. "Such beautiful, sweet young men. What did they ever do to anyone to deserve this?" Harry said to me in a rare moment of emotion. And among many others, my father had lost his own beloved Tommy Cothran, whose original diagnosis of lymphoma had preceded the identification of HIV. But by the time Tommy died, it was clear what had killed him.

By 1989, AIDS awareness had evolved, and my father was now participating in a big-ticket benefit at Carnegie Hall: the first Music for Life concert. David Pack was helping to coordinate the music for the event, and he invited me to cowrite a song with my father for the occasion.

LB accompanying the Quartet at the Music for Life benefit, 1989.

People often asked me if I ever collaborated with my father on music, and my answer would always be a vaguely huffy no. But just around the time Pack asked me about Music for Life, the one record company that had remained interested in me—and had been stringing me along for a year—concluded its negotiations by simply going belly-up. I decided that was an excellent moment to put an end to my so-called career. I parted ways with my manager, Vince, and his colorful sweaters, and that was that.

Suddenly all the stuff I'd fretted about for so long didn't matter at all: the comparisons, the striving for autonomy, the write-a-hit straitjacket—any of it. And so, for the first time since I was seven years old on Martha's Vineyard, I agreed to write a song with my father.

We did it mostly over the phone, while he was vacationing down in Key West. While Julia plied Frankie with tasty food, I stretched the long, curly cord of the Dakota kitchen wall phone around the corner to the laundry room, where I hunkered over the washing machine, scribbling under the overhead fluorescent light as we talked.

On the stage of Carnegie Hall, the Quartet sang the song, accompanied by LB on piano. The pianist himself got one singing line: "Hey, what about me?" The lyrics cited the various ways family members drive one another crazy. The refrain went:

It's written in stone and it never gets better—
It's hard to keep a fam'ly close together.
Mm, mm . . . close together . . .

After Christmas, my father went back to Key West. He'd fallen in love with the place: the warm weather, the picturesque streets, and the island's lively scene of intellectual gay men. He felt unfettered there, and well attended to. While in Key West, he received a call from one David Hampton. This young man recently had been calling him back in New York, claiming to be Sidney Poitier's son and acting wildly flirtatious on the phone. Seduced by the young man's energy, my father took to "shrinking" him over the phone, as was his practice: asking him personal questions and drawing him out—but this time, it was the young man who was drawing *in* the Maestro.

It emerged that this fellow had stolen an address book from a school friend of Nina's, and was working his way through the names. He'd eventually found his way to chatting with Leonard

Bernstein over the private line at the Dakota. A few weeks later, Hampton was calling the Maestro in Key West. And how had he acquired *that* number? He had shown up at the Dakota, that impenetrable fortress, and talked his way upstairs; then he hung out in the kitchen all evening with Julia and Gigi, the maid. From the little round table where they sat chatting, Hampton was able to read and memorize the Key West number scribbled on a piece of paper on the wall next to the kitchen phone. So chummy did he become with Julia and Gigi that they all took pictures together in front of our Christmas tree.

This talented con artist would become, in fact, the inspiration for John Guare's play *Six Degrees of Separation*. And now, on the phone with LB, Hampton announced that he'd arrived in Key West, and was ready to party.

Meanwhile, the parents of Nina's school friend had caught on to the address book deception, and were urgently calling around to warn one and all about David Hampton. When the message finally filtered down to Harry in Key West, he hired detectives and bodyguards. Hampton was chased away, and eventually landed in jail. (He died a few years later, of AIDS.)

Everyone was shaken by the incident. How easily our family had been penetrated; how quick everyone had been to think the best of this attractive, well-dressed young black man. That's what made the con so ingenious; so many families in that address book were, like ours, comprised of well-intentioned liberals who prided themselves on being compassionate, open-minded, and free of prejudice. We were all sitting ducks for that guy.

*   *   *

In the spring of 1989, one of the notations in my calendar was for "amnio": I was pregnant again. I marveled at how, not so long ago,

I'd thought there was something wrong with me: I had no special hankering for children; maybe I couldn't even have them . . . and now here I was, married to David, loving our little girl, and pregnant a second time. It was the double surprise of my life. The test results revealed that a boy was on the way. Julia was euphoric, of course. Daddy named the fetus Spike.

Spike was well into his seventh month in utero when we all trooped up to Tanglewood for my father's annual August concerts. One afternoon, my cousin Karen and I were walking together outside Daddy's rental house when we heard him calling out to us. We

Competing bellies: LB with Jamie, pregnant with Evan.

turned to discover that we were standing in front of his bathroom, where the stable-door-style window was swung all the way open, revealing my father sitting in his favorite place, with a cigarette in one hand and a score in his lap. He said, to us, "I have to tell you what I just discovered about Tchaikovsky!" And for the next fifteen—no, twenty—minutes, Karen and I were pinned to the spot outside the bathroom window while he regaled us with his research and theories about Tchaikovsky's homosexuality, mood swings, and possible suicide encouraged by his Masonic brother. My father was in the midst of a deep immersion in, and rediscovery of, the symphonies of Tchaikovsky. That weekend, he gave a mighty performance of Tchaikovsky's Fourth with "the Kids," the Tanglewood student orchestra. Listeners and critics alike remarked upon LB's increasingly stretched-out tempos—as if he never wanted the music to end.

His seventy-first birthday that year was a study in contrast with the year before: just a pleasant, low-key family day. We took Daddy with us to a local ski area, which in the summer months had an alpine slide. Spike did not deter me from accompanying the gang up the chairlift, then back down the mountain on the little individual sleds that skittered down a winding concrete track. My father and I had always loved rides—and I knew he'd love this one. After several euphoric slides down the mountain, we all went to the snack bar, where Daddy wolfed down hot dogs and sang songs with two-year-old Frankie.

Evan (no longer Spike once he was born) arrived on October 14, 1989. The next day, when we got home from the hospital, Daddy, Harry, and Margaret Carson came over, brown bag of Ballantine's scotch in hand, to meet the new Bernstein boy. I put one-day-old Evan in his grandfather's lap, whereupon Daddy dipped his pinky into his glass of scotch and then popped his

boozy finger right into Evan's mouth. "Daddy!" I yelled, horrified. "He's a *newborn*! That's unsanitary!" As with Frankie and
the clam, there were no ill effects within the magic Daddy circle.
He wrinkled his nose at me: "*That's unsanitary*," he mimicked.

Two months later, LB was in London to conduct a concert
version of his beloved, troubled show *Candide*. There had been
so many versions of *Candide* over the years; songs, lyrics, dialogue, characters, and narrators came and went from production
to production—and at one point Lillian Hellman, the origina-
tor of the project, had been in such high dudgeon over all the
transmogrifications that she demanded her name be taken off the
work henceforward. That was so Lillian: self-defeatingly pure of
purpose—too pure, above all, for the nasty, fly-by-night world of
musical theater biz.

LB had liked a recent version of *Candide* that his conductor pal John Mauceri helped devise at the Scottish Opera, with

"That's unsanitary." LB holding newborn Evan.

Hugh Wheeler's book judiciously expanded by codirectors Jonathan Miller and John Wells. This version had a clever, coherent narration, and managed to include so much of the glorious score that LB chose this one to conduct in concert form at the Barbican Centre, with the London Symphony Orchestra and big-time opera singers—"luxury casting," as Humphrey Burton called it—including Christa Ludwig as the Old Lady and rising opera stars June Anderson as Cunegonde and Jerry Hadley as Candide. Not only was it the first time the composer had ever conducted his show; it would, in effect, be LB's definitive statement on how he'd like *Candide* to sound and be. The performance would also be making the case—as the composer had done for his *West Side Story* five years back—that the work was equally comfortable in a concert hall, an opera house, or a Broadway stage.

Daddy invited all three (four) of us kids to join him, as he so often did—but this time, we all declined. My own substantial excuse was that it was very hard to travel with an infant barely two months old. But the truth was, I just couldn't take the entourage anymore. In fact, all three (four) of us were feeling burned out by the scene on the road. The adulation and postconcert carryings-on seemed to grow somehow louder and more frenetic even as my father grew older and weaker. It was too hard to watch, too high a price to pay—even for the glory of the music. So we stayed away this time. Now we wish we hadn't.

Luckily, my father had Adolph Green along; his old pal was to play the part of Pangloss in the concert—an inspired piece of casting. Adolph could always bring a smile to my father's face, with his perfectly recalled obscure musical references or entire movie scenes quoted from memory. A combination of court jester and zany genius, Adolph was one of the very few people in the world who had known Lenny since his teenaged camp-counselor days.

Adolph knew exactly who Lenny Bernstein really was, under that calcified, complicated exterior. Toward the end, few knew the real Lenny—maybe not even Lenny himself—but Lenny felt the goodness of keeping Adolph close. And now they had this rare and delicious performing opportunity together, so late in both their lives. The pair of concerts were a great success, even though Daddy's tempos were stretched out almost to the breaking point. When it came to his own music, he *really* didn't want it to end.

Then, still suffering from "the Royal Flu" that had seized the entire cast as well as Queen Elizabeth herself, LB flew directly from London to Berlin, where he would take part in one of the truly momentous events in his lifetime: the pulling down of the Berlin Wall. After all the decades of Soviet rule, my father could hardly believe he was witnessing the disintegration of that once immutable oppressor.

The occasion gave rise to the ultimate—and most meaningful— of all Harry Specials. LB conducted a mighty ensemble comprising players volunteering from various orchestras around the world who, along with four soloists and a local girls' chorus, gave a pair of performances of Beethoven's Ninth Symphony: one in East Berlin and one in West Berlin. And to make the performances extra-historic, LB changed Schiller's text in the final "Ode to Joy" movement: now it was "Ode to Freedom." "*Freiheit!*" The word rang out again and again, wreathed in Beethoven's harmonies, and the whole world watched it on television on Christmas Day.

Which is exactly how I watched it.

I'm sorry now that I didn't go to Berlin: what a moment to have missed. Certainly for Daddy, it was the pinnacle of his own lifelong advocacy for world peace and brotherhood—never more eloquently expressed, and never to so many, than through Beethoven's notes in that historic Christmas performance. It may have been his peak performing experience; I wish I'd been there to share it with him. I watched the concert in Fairfield, lying lengthwise on the velvety brown corduroy couch that Mummy had originally bought for the East Hampton house. As Evan alternately nursed and napped alongside me, I couldn't help thinking how grateful I was to be supine, in my sweatpants, with my tiny, beautiful boy—and not in Berlin, suffering the multiple punishments of jet lag, panty hose, entourage gridlock, and small talk with dignitaries. Lying on that couch felt like being swallowed by a great, soft beast; in my half slumber, *"Freiheit"* in Berlin seemed magnificent and very, very far away.

When Daddy got back, he presented us all with chunks of the Berlin Wall that he'd chipped off himself. Then he hightailed it to Key West to recover his health.

He didn't recover it.

20

A Departure

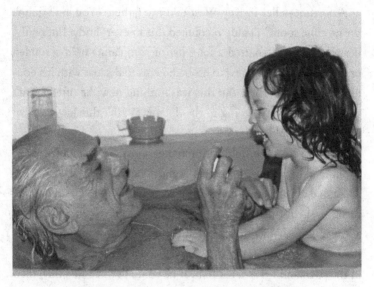

LB and Frankie have bath time fun in Inky West.

With David and our two small children, I went down to "Inky West," as Frankie called it, to spend a few days with Daddy. He was gray, shrunken, still coughing explosively. On the bright side, he was in love—again. Now he was sharing music, poetry, and passion with a brand-new guy; my father called him by his initials, MAT. Mat was a young Democratic speechwriter from Alabama, and he was very, very tall. I inadvertently walked in on the two of them kissing on the living room couch, like high school sweethearts. They sure did make an odd couple: the lanky young southerner and the wizened, white-haired old man cuddled up next to him. My father wasn't really that old—only seventy-one. But all those decades of living at maximum volume appeared to be catching up with him at last; he seemed newly frail. And yet there he was, in love like a teenager.

A fortune-teller in Key West told my father, "You ain't gonna die no time soon." Daddy recounted this to everybody. But really, he wasn't well. I spotted a long list of complaints he'd scribbled onto some notepaper next to his bed: items to discuss with his doctor back in New York. But this was nothing new; he often wasn't well; he was always going to the doctor. Wasn't this just more of the same? Wouldn't this go on indefinitely?

So we were all brought up terribly short a few months later, when Daddy was diagnosed with lung cancer.

Above all, I found myself enraged at him: How dare he put us through the torment of watching a parent go through this disease all over again—just as I'd feared? Also, I was furious that his famous luck had run out. "Oh, I'll never get cancer," he'd boasted in the past, and I'd *believed* him. If he could get sick like this, then there was no magic left in the world.

Oddly, it wasn't the kind of lung cancer associated with smoking; mesothelioma is linked to asbestos exposure. But this diagnostic hairsplitting meant very little to any of us.

Harry was obsessed with keeping the news a secret from the press. My father went through his course of radiation under an assumed name: Franco Levi. He was particularly anxious about hiding the news from Grandma. He didn't want to alarm her—she was ninety-two, after all—but mothers can smell this kind of a rat from a considerable distance. When we went up to Brookline to introduce Evan to Grandma, she'd bizarrely asked her son point-blank: "Lenny dear, are you . . . terminal?"

Daddy denied everything. He did, however, tell his mother that at long last, he was going to quit cigarettes. "Good," Grandma said, and turned to her daughter, Shirley: "Now I'll pray for *you*."

Shirley, meanwhile, had become ultra-protective of her older brother, and was full of grievances about his care. She referred to his doctor, Kevin Cahill, a celebrated author and renowned specialist in tropical medicine, as "that tsetse fly doctor." She meddled, she argued, she criticized, she scoffed—all good ways of not dwelling on the essential fact that her brother was gravely ill, and there was nothing she could do about it.

Dr. Cahill was liberally prescribing pain medication, as his patient complained of constant back and side pain. That spring, my father hauled himself to Sapporo, Japan, for the inaugural of his long-planned Tanglewood-style project, the Pacific Music Festival. He was fearsomely short of breath, though still smoking. (As usual, the quitting thing hadn't worked at all.) His assistant Craig Urquhart told us later that LB had been taking as many as eight Percocet a day in Sapporo—plus two Halcion, two Valium, and all the rest. One day in the hotel, Craig found his boss passed out on the floor and had a frighteningly difficult time rousing him. LB subsequently denied the whole incident, explaining that he'd just been on the floor "looking for something." "Hmm," Nina later mused, "a contact lens?" We got our laughs where we could.

It was something of a miracle that LB could do anything at all in Japan; he was so weak, so diminished. The doctor who had drained LB's lungs of fluid the month before was specially flown over to examine the Maestro. But it turned out the patient was mainly exhibiting junkie symptoms; he was thoroughly addicted to his painkilling medicine. The doctor took away the precious black leather toiletry case; if the Maestro wanted a pill, he had to ask for it. Shirley was livid when she heard about it: "The man is in *pain*! How can they treat him like this?"

Somehow, he pulled himself together for several rehearsals and concerts, but LB was flown home early from Japan: doctor's orders. Four big concerts were canceled; the students in the orchestra were crushed. Once home, my father went through a battery of tests, followed by a powwow with all the doctors. He said it felt like facing a tribunal. They announced that the malignancy hadn't grown since the radiation, and there was no metastasis. One doctor said a spinal test had detected some "hot spots"; another doctor said those could be anything from arthritis to scar tissue. The hot spot doctor, a big Bernstein fan, told my father, "You're a great man. We're really going to miss you."

The tribunal decided to put him on an experimental "mystery drug" to help control his constant pain. It was referred to only as "p.k.," for "painkiller."

We all went out to Fairfield, to try and spend some normal summer days together before the annual Tanglewood doings. Daddy would emerge in the late afternoon, more gaunt and short of breath than ever. Isaac Stern turned up one day with Zabar's shopping bags laden with bagels, smoked salmon, and all the trimmings; you really find out who your good friends are when you're sick.

It wasn't certain Daddy could even make it to Tanglewood, but somehow he did. David and I went up, too, with Frankie and Evan. The usual house wasn't available that summer; the LB entourage wound up in a dark, damp house he dubbed the Mildew Palace. It seemed like yet another sign that the magic Daddy circle was losing its power.

He made it through the first concert—Copland's Third Symphony with "the Kids"—but only barely. Next he had the big concert with the Boston Symphony to contend with—and after that, he was supposed to take the Kids on their highly anticipated tour of Europe, the first time such a tour had ever been organized for Tanglewood's student orchestra.

The big Sunday afternoon concert was sold out, as usual. But in yet another ominous sign, the fabled "Lenny weather" didn't appear; it was cold and rainy. We had to bundle up Grandma with multiple blankets to keep her feet warm. My father got through Benjamin Britten's *Sea Interludes*, but he'd assigned a newly orchestrated version of his own *Arias and Barcarolles* to the assistant conductor, Carl St. Clair. The composer couldn't conduct it himself; his brain was so oxygen-deprived by that point that he couldn't track the complexities of his own music.

Even the rows of oxygen tanks in his dressing room backstage weren't helping. Luckily, he could conduct the last piece on the program, Beethoven's Seventh, from memory—or probably even in his sleep. He was in fact almost unconscious by that point in the concert, from the sheer lack of air in his lungs and brain.

During the third movement, Daddy was racked by a coughing fit so severe that for a while he was sagging against the podium railing, struggling to catch what little breath he had. Phyllis Newman was sitting to my left; we gripped each other's arms in horror. The orchestra played on, rudderless, until my father managed to collect himself and take the symphony the rest of the way to its glorious finish line; there is no greater finale in all the Beethoven symphonies. At the end of the piece, as the audience roared its approval, Nina and I caught each other's eye—we were shattered from anxiety. Our father came out for his bow: tiny, ashen, and nearly lost inside the white suit that now hung so loosely on him, it looked as if it had been tailored for some other species.

That night, for his upcoming birthday, I presented Daddy with an intricate poem I'd devised around a Passover counting song, with lots of in-jokes that I knew would tickle him. But he was so befuddled, I could tell he wasn't getting any of the references. He wasn't getting much of anything. He really did seem to be sleep-walking.

He canceled the tour to Europe with the Kids; he was just too sick. Harry had some terrible damage control to do. Everything was a heartbreaking mess.

Meanwhile, strangely, all the talk became about getting LB into a drug detox program—as if that were the only problem that needed solving. Harry wanted him to go through the detox in the sealed privacy of the Dakota apartment, which struck me as a terrible idea. Surely there were too many ghosts in the Dakota—chief among them the ghost of our mother herself. It was there that she had laid her curse on her estranged husband at the dining room table. I couldn't imagine my father facing that ghost without the help of a very strong painkilling drug.

The day before the Dakota detox plan was to go into effect, my father said he couldn't breathe at all. So instead, he was admitted to the hospital, and that's where he was on his seventy-second birth-day. While Julia looked after baby Evan at the Dakota, the rest of us gathered in the hospital room. Nina, Frankie, and I brought the cupcakes we'd made together. Harry brought silly hats and plastic leis, and Frankie played with the button that made Daddy's bed go up and down.

Detox did, in fact, begin at the hospital. My father complained that the sleeping medicine doses were "for an ant." He told me he'd found himself praying to God to let him die. Once home, he tottered on toothpick-thin legs from the back door to his bedroom, into his blue pajamas, and straight into bed, where he pulled the covers right up to his chin, like a frightened child.

It was David who made the excellent suggestion that we find some wise man—a rabbi, maybe—with whom my father could verbally wrangle. As David pointed out, LB's crisis was as much a spiritual as a physical one.

And so was born the idea of connecting LB to my former psychiatrist, Dr. Samuel Klagsbrun, a very wise man indeed and suitably rabbinical, who now ran a hospital in Westchester called Four Winds. Dr. Klagsbrun initiated a program for LB up in Fairfield, with round-the-clock nurses, various specialists, and physical therapists coming by every day. LB fired them all, leaving only his assistant Phillip, as if everything were back to normal, which it wasn't. Phillip's job was hard. He had to dole out the meds carefully, and resist his boss's pleas for more. He had to persuade him to get up, eat something, move around a little. Each of these tasks presented a gargantuan hurdle. LB just wanted to sleep—and he complained of constant pain.

Uncle BB had a college friend, Dr. Paul Marx, who had started a "pain center" at Sloan Kettering. Shirley got it into her head that her brother should be admitted to the pain center. She would not, could not stop talking about the pain center. When Dr. Cahill rejected the idea, Shirley called the oncologist. The oncologist called Cahill: Please make that lady stop bugging me. Furious, Cahill called Harry: Tell Shirley to stop bugging that doctor. Harry called Shirley. They had such a fight over the phone that they took turns hanging up on each other.

My birthday, two weeks after Daddy's, was up in Fairfield. He came to the dinner table for a few minutes, but couldn't sustain focus on either the food or the company, so he went back upstairs to bed. After he left, Shirley started in again about the pain center. David, usually unflappable, lost his temper. Nina left the table in tears. Julia brought out the birthday cake in the midst of all the screaming. She put a slice of cake in front of me, kissed me wordlessly on the cheek, and moved on.

Just as there is a fog of war, there is a fog of illness. Was Daddy really in as much pain as he said, or was he to some extent augmenting the melodrama? Was the cancer really gone, or was it on the creep, and was his pain related to it somehow? *Might* the pain center be a good idea? Was the substance abuse really the main problem here? Was Daddy simply abysmally depressed? Had he lost the will to live, in which case all our efforts were for naught? No one had the answers to anything. Not even Harry Kraut.

At least we got an answer about the pain center. It turned out it was designed for terminally ill patients, which was probably not what Shirley had in mind. We also found out that the secret, experimental "p.k." drug that Daddy was given to get him off the Percocet was methadone. And where had it come from? The pain center at Sloan Kettering.

The fog of illness pervaded our days. My father went to Dr. Cahill's office and came out with a new prescription for Nembutal. One of his old favorite barbiturates! So, had we tossed the detox plan aside? He was very glad to have "the lovely little pills," as he now called them. Meanwhile, the regular conversations with Dr. Klagsbrun seemed to be helping; Dr. Klagsbrun was very much up to the task of verbal arm wrestling with my father.

There were some slight improvements. Daddy gained a little weight. He even went to the piano one evening and played, in slow motion, an arpeggio from a Ravel piano concerto that Uncle BB had been talking about at dinner. Though he was back to drinking again in the evenings, it was part of Daddy's attempt to be sociable, which seemed like a good sign; we were grasping for any good sign.

But the improvements were short-lived. My father was taking

Nembutal every night—and Percocet had somehow crept back into the mix. He could no longer sleep supine in his own bed; he breathed better sleeping upright in an armchair. A stair lift was installed on the back stairs; an oxygen machine was hooked up in the bedroom. My father could barely sustain the walk from one room to another.

He decided to go back to New York. I accompanied him to his Dr. Cahill appointment. He had to sit down in the elevator from the second floor to the first. All the way across town in the limo, I held his hand while my forefinger skied up and down the arthritic slopes of his knuckles.

The news from the latest scans was not good but, as usual, not precisely clear. The thickening of the pleura *might* be tumor growth, or it *could* be only scarring from the radiation. What was certain was that both of his lungs were in terrible shape. As this information was being delivered, my father lit a cigarette, right there in Dr. Cahill's stuffy office.

A few days later, the press release that Harry and my father had painstakingly devised together was given to the news media, announcing that Leonard Bernstein was retiring from conducting and would devote his remaining time to "composing, writing, and education." Daddy had intended to make no mention of cancer; he was still trying to hide that ultimate piece of bad news from Grandma. But in the end, he called his mother to prepare her for a mention of a tumor in the lining of his lung. Harry summoned Nina, Alexander, and me to his office, where he showed us a list on his desktop computer (he was very modern) of all the close family friends who ought to be called in advance of the press release so they wouldn't learn about it from the newspapers. "My God," Nina muttered, "it's a dress rehearsal for the funeral."

The press release was full of hopeful items about the future projects my father was planning to attend to as soon as he got his strength back: a chamber piece, a recording project, a memoir . . . but at the Dakota, the atmosphere was bleak. Daddy was on oxygen full-time. A wheelchair arrived. I found him sitting in it, poking feebly at Julia's lovingly overbuttered scrambled eggs. In an effort to relieve the grimness, I made a reference to "What Ever Happened to Felicia Montealegre?"—one of our family's elaborate, hilarious home movies from years ago. This one, directed by Steve Sondheim, had been a takeoff on the campy Bette Davis–Joan Crawford horror flick, *What Ever Happened to Baby Jane?* Mummy had played a wheelchair-bound former ballet dancer being tormented by her pianist sister, played by Phyllis Newman. Now, to wheelchair-bound Daddy, I joked blackly: "What ever happened to Lennuhtt?"

"He's gone," he rasped.

*   *   *

For some reason, certain people shine like candles in the dark around the sick and the dying. Mendy Wager was such a person. On a day-to-day basis, Mendy could be flighty, irritable, obsessing relentlessly over opera, Israel, Proust, and his own endless personal melodramas. But he was at Mummy's side all of her last, terrible year, finding ways to make her laugh, sharing books, and watching *Masterpiece Theatre* with her. And as Daddy spiraled into his final ordeal, Mendy was right there again: cajoling, teasing, eliciting the rare smile with his endless supply of Jewish jokes. He spent many nights on the couch in Daddy's studio, formerly Mummy's bedroom; now it was Mendy who was on the other side of the ecclesiastical oaken door. Mendy knew the jig was up before the rest of us did. "He's begging for oblivion," he told me.

October 14 was Evan's first birthday. The party was in Fairfield, outdoors in the sparkling autumn weather. The guests were departing at the end of the afternoon when the phone rang. It was Alexander, shakily telling me the impossible news that Daddy had just died. It was only five days after the press release had gone out announcing Leonard Bernstein's retirement from the podium.

The news shouldn't have been surprising, but I felt as if my hand had gripped an uninsulated wire. I was jangled to the marrow, beyond tears for a minute. Then unearthly noises came out of me. Frankie told me years later she thought I was playacting; she'd never heard me make sounds like that. Nina had already driven off, and there was no way to contact her. Then, amazingly, her car reappeared on the driveway—she'd forgotten something. I told her the news, right there in front of the house. "No, no, no," she cried, reeling in circles and finally crumpling onto the grass.

David was overseas on business, so a friend drove the family station wagon while I sat in the back seat with Frankie and Evan, keeping them amused, keeping that birthday-party feeling going . . . the hardest two hours of my life. Every October 14 since that day, I've reexperienced the cognitive dissonance of that ride in the car.

When we got to the Dakota, Julia took care of Frankie and Evan so I could go into Daddy's bedroom. He was in his bed, in a beautiful pair of cream-colored pajamas. (Julia had changed his clothing.) He looked very calm and small and un-Daddylike—mainly because of the stillness.

Alexander had been there all afternoon; once Nina and I arrived, he filled us in. He'd been in the library watching a football game on TV. Mendy, Dr. Cahill, and Cahill's son Sean were with Daddy in his bedroom. They had worked Daddy into a standing position so that Dr. Cahill could give him an injection in his rear.

Daddy said, "What is this?" and fell forward into Mendy's arms—and that was it.

(Even this horrific moment acquired an indelible built-in punch line for the rest of us: in Humphrey Burton's biography of my father, published four years later, Mendy's last name, Wager, was accidentally misspelled, in a too-good-to-be-true salute to Mendy's opera obsession: "Bernstein slumped in Wagner's arms, dead." Cue the Valkyries.)

Sean Cahill went to the library to fetch Alexander. Alexander found Daddy placed in the red velvet armchair, eerily slumped and limp. Alexander told us how he crouched down in front of Daddy's body, took his father's hand in his own—and then, as sometimes happens with people who have just died, Daddy's mouth suddenly emitted a bizarre, lurching, burp-like sound. Alexander nearly jumped to the ceiling. Some would say that was the moment of the soul leaving the body; others would say it was the famously gaseous Bernstein stomach discharging one final eruption.

Alexander called Adolph Green with the news. "Lenny, Lenny, Lenny," Adolph cried over and over. When he arrived at the door of the apartment twenty minutes later, Adolph was still saying it. In the bedroom, he clutched his oldest friend's hand: "Lenny, Lenny, Lenny . . . *wake up!*"

Alexander and Nina both came down to my place to spend the night on the foldout couch in the living room. We couldn't bear to be alone. We felt like—in fact we now were—orphans, needing to huddle together. We knew that everything coming up next would be unbearable.

First, there were the phone calls: endless numbers of them, just like the "dress rehearsal" five days ago. It fell to Uncle BB to tell Grandma the news. He reported his ninety-two-year-old mother's reply: "This will shorten my life."

In our shocked and weakened states, just as when Mummy died, we turned the arrangements over to Harry, thereby cementing his role as the posthumous leader of everything. (He was in fact a co-executor of the Leonard Bernstein estate, along with Daddy's old friend and colleague Schuyler Chapin and Daddy's attorney, Paul Epstein.) Harry had already assumed the role of family coordinator when Mummy died; that was how she'd ended up at Green-Wood Cemetery in Brooklyn. Now Daddy would be buried next to her in that same plot, just as Harry had planned from the beginning.

The funeral was in the Dakota living room, where I'd gotten married six years earlier. Instead of Mummy's Russian blanket raised on poles as a huppah, there now stood a big, brutish, shiny casket: a sickening intrusion. So much grief was in that room, it felt like a communal drowning.

After the speeches and prayers, the casket was loaded into the hearse outside the Dakota gates. Everyone who had been upstairs piled into a long line of limousines, and the cortege made its way to Brooklyn. The construction workers along the FDR Drive waved their hard hats as we passed: "Bye, Lenny!" Daddy would have loved that.

In our limo, both Shirley and David were smoking. When we got to Green-Wood, there was a delay as the long line of cars snaked its way up the hill to the gravesite. Three-year-old Frankie opened the sunroof to stick her head out. David told her to get down. "But how shall I get the fresh air?" she said. I knew exactly how she felt.

All I remember from the gravesite ceremony is Mendy and the rabbi moaning the multiple "amens" in the kaddish prayer, while Frankie danced among the headstones in the autumn dapple.

21

Life Goes On

Alexander, Nina, and I quickly grasped that we'd acquired a new job for the rest of our lives: to carry our illustrious father's legacy forward. We felt exhausted already by the prospect; it was hard enough to mourn the loss of our father privately, yet here we were with this very public-oriented task to take on. Each of us found different ways to begin doing it.

Nina had abandoned her acting career and was now a trained chef. With Daddy's chef, Patty, she'd started a catering business called Eats of Eden. But in her spare time, Nina set about finding a home for Leonard Bernstein's ultra-voluminous archives. Letters, speeches, essays and poems, music manuscripts, awards, photos, video- and audiotapes—the contents filled one entire floor of a storage facility downtown. Nina recommended that we donate the Leonard Bernstein archive to the Library of Congress because, at the time, they were the institution most advanced in digitizing their collections to be made available, free of charge, online. Nina, who was the tech-savviest among us, knew that was the way of the future.

Alexander, meanwhile, had also set aside acting, and gotten himself a master's degree in education at New York University. He became a full-time teacher, while also undertaking the daunting task of bringing our father's philosophies of education to life. Daddy had been cooking up some notions in his final decade about using the arts to connect disparate subjects across the whole curriculum. Learning about one subject through the lens of another was precisely what our father had done in his Norton Lectures at Harvard, connecting music with linguistics. Leonard Bernstein himself was, in effect, the poster child for his own initiative: a teacher-artist-student who never stopped inquiring, and never stopped sharing what he'd learned.

A year before he died, my father had used the money from the Praemium Imperiale prize he'd received in Japan to launch the Bernstein Education Through the Arts (BETA) Fund. Now Alexander arranged for the project to be developed further at the Nashville Institute for the Arts.

Back in his school days, Alexander had been an ambivalent student: disaffected, resentful of poor instruction methods, and often resistant to Daddy's own relentless pedagogy, as we all were. Nina and I were impressed that our brother seemed to be solving some inner calculus by pursuing his vision for the ideal educational model.

As for me, I collaborated with my father's former assistant Craig Urquhart to create a newsletter that would keep the international community of Lenny fans connected, as well as apprised of Bernstein-related performances and events. We named the newsletter after Daddy's jazzy piece *Prelude, Fugue, and Riffs*.

Craig and I were a good team. He was adept at persuading friends, colleagues, and scholars to contribute articles. For my part, I discovered I had what amounted almost to a disability: my eye snagged on every typo. So I became the editor and proofreader. Also, I wrote "To Our Readers," a few paragraphs on page two of each issue, summing up the contents.

There never seemed to be enough space for all the Bernstein-related news; we had to expand the number of pages as the years progressed. Leonard Bernstein wasn't fading away; if anything, his legacy seemed to be gaining momentum. As I worked on *PF&R* over the years, I began to comprehend my father's impact on the world in a new way.

Harry Kraut had built Amberson into a formidable business engine. But in the physical absence of Leonard Bernstein, the company was no longer coordinating his tours, performances, and new recordings—nor collecting the related fees. Amberson was now mainly in the business of managing the streams of income derived from preexisting recordings and videos, new usage licenses, and live performances of Bernstein works.

In the past, Alexander, Nina, and I had steered as clear as we could of Amberson. But now we were . . . well, we were the owners. We had to be present and alert at the board meetings around the long dining table in the Dakota apartment, absorbing a jumble of new concepts about intellectual property, music publishing rules, artists' shares, grand rights versus small rights, mechanical rights versus performing rights . . . No wonder Leonard Bernstein had never attended a single board meeting of his own company; it was mighty dry stuff.

As the owners, we now had to work closely with Harry Kraut, our inherited Faustian bargain. He seemed glad enough to have us at the board meetings, but perhaps because he'd known us since we were children, that was how he treated us. In truth, we could be pretty infantile, with our in-jokes and perpetual teasing. But Harry wasn't exactly encouraging our maturation as he sat at the head of the table, droning his way inaudibly through item after item on the spreadsheet, while we tried to follow along, squinting at our photocopies in their microscopic font. The subliminal message was: This is all far too complicated for you; let me handle it.

So we were relieved and pleased when Harry invited my husband, David, to join the company, to help run certain aspects of the business. It seemed an exciting prospect: the Quartet taking itself into the real world. David got us off to an encouraging start by pointing out that the company's financial information could be presented in far more accessible ways. Bar graphs! Pie charts! Fourteen-point type!

Harry was not appreciative of David's attempts to demystify business operations, nor did David enjoy working closely with Harry. We weren't surprised to hear that Harry, as a boss, was overcontrolling, critical, even a bully. (I remembered it myself.) The experiment drew to a bitter conclusion five years later.

Our family friend Ofra, with her trademark Israeli accent, accused Alexander, Nina, and me of being "winnies." We knew it was true: we *were* weenies. We could not stand up to Harry. We abhorred conflict and confrontation—just as our parents had. The trio within the Quartet wasn't prepared for the real world after all. Were we ever going to be properly functioning grownups? Would we ever "pull up our socks," as Mummy used to say?

The problem was already in its second generation. The intensity of Daddy's force field had made it hard for his own siblings to grow up, as well. Uncle BB had wound up isolating himself and his family in the depths of Connecticut to increase his sense of autonomy (though he was still only fifty miles away). As for Shirley, not only had she remained single, she'd remained dependent on her older brother in more ways than we realized. For years I revered Shirley as a paragon of women's liberation: an independent woman who eventually owned her own theatrical literary agency, Paramuse. Arthur Laurents, Daddy's *West Side Story* collaborator, had been a Paramuse client, as had Stephen Schwartz, long before *Wicked*. It all seemed impressive, but after our father died, we found out that he, through Amberson, had been infusing Paramuse with a hefty monthly "consulting fee" to keep Shirley's business afloat. Her glamorous office, her snappy outfits—had it all been window dressing? Shirley read her clients' scripts and negotiated their contracts; she followed world events, did the tricky crossword puzzles—and yet some essential part of her had not developed; she was like a child playing a grownup. Alexander, Nina, and I worried: What if we turned out like Shirley, too?

The most visible symptom of our resistance to growing up at that time was our inability to let go of the Dakota apartment. It wasn't that we wanted to live there; all three of us had opted for the funkier ambience of downtown Manhattan. We simply couldn't bear the idea of parting with apartment 23; it would be too physical a manifestation of having lost both parents.

Also, we couldn't bear the idea of parting with the Macy's parade on Thanksgiving morning. And as Alexander likes to say, "The second reason is always the real one."

Harry, Paul, and Schuyler, the executors of the Bernstein estate, tried to talk us into selling the Dakota apartment; they had counted on that sale to pay off the crushing estate tax. But we wouldn't, couldn't budge. We clung to the apartment for a good five years more. So the executors made the best of the situation by turning the place into a tax write-off: Nina's old bedroom, along with our father's bedroom and studio, became offices. Various Amberson assistants worked there—and David, too; he worked in the very room where his father-in-law had died. Julia, meanwhile, still lived in her little room off the kitchen. She made lunch for the gang every day, and was often babysitting Frankie and Evan, who loved spending the night on the foldout couch in the morning room and feasting on Julia's pancakes and bacon the next day.

In the end, it was our desire to infuse money into the BETA Fund that propelled us into selling the Dakota apartment. We engaged Sotheby's to hold an auction, the proceeds of which would go to the foundation.

The dismantling of apartment 23 began—and Julia was having a nervous breakdown. She hated the auction—or "the ocean," as she pronounced it. A world-class hoarder, Julia wasn't happy to throw away so much as a moth-eaten scarf—"Is very good scarf!"—and now here we were, offering strangers the prized possessions of La Señora and El Caballero, the very objects she had fiercely protected for over forty years. I couldn't blame her for being upset; I wasn't too happy about it myself.

Each of the apartment's sixteen-foot-high closets was crammed from top to bottom with half a century's worth of accumulated family belongings. In the kitchen, there seemed to be five of everything—from sets of flatware to rolls of Reynolds Wrap. An entire day was devoted to removing Daddy's "B-52," as he'd dubbed his mighty Bösendorfer grand piano, after the gargantuan military jets that had carpet-bombed Vietnam. The operation required prying off the wooden frame from the living room window, unscrewing the legs from the piano, swaddling the instrument in padding, and sailing it out the window by means of a crane parked on the street below. It was a sickening spectacle, Daddy's B-52 teetering over Central Park West.

Every object in the house—every fork, ashtray, and Otto Perl–stamped coat hanger—got a sticker affixed to it, indicating where it was going next. A rainbow of colors represented the various destinations. Green was for the Sotheby's warehouse; Julia would see a dish or a lamp with a green sticker and cry, "How you can throw that into the ocean?" Other colors indicated the house in Fairfield, or our three respective apartments downtown. Also, there was Nina's recently acquired rustic farmhouse in upstate New York. Coming of age during the family troubles had left its mark on Nina; she was far less sentimental than her older siblings about our past, and that included Fairfield.

There was yet one more colored sticker to reckon with: this

one was for the new, smaller apartment that the three of us jointly bought in the Parc Vendome, a large prewar building on West 56th Street. We'd decided to continue having a "family headquarters": a place for board meetings, social gatherings, and musical events—as well as Alexander's office for the BETA Fund. We furnished the apartment with our favorite items from the Dakota; even the plants moved there, where they thrived in the penthouse sunshine. Nina called the bright, airy new apartment "the Dakota antidote."

But the second (and therefore real) reason for getting "the Dome," as we dubbed it, was to give Julia a place from which to continue in her role as materfamilias.

Julia was already seventy-five; we worried that the trauma of the move might do her in. On the day when every last object was finally cleared out of apartment 23, all that was left was Julia on her step stool in the kitchen; she would not leave. We feared the worst. But she withstood the transition, adapted to the Dome, and enjoyed sixteen more years of cooking daily soups and stews for Alexander, receiving a steady stream of devoted visitors, and doting on all our kids.

Julia Vega had become a proud, active American citizen. She kept up with world events on TV and voted Democratic (a considerable evolution since her days of admiring Richard Nixon's haircut). She even voted for Barack Obama. Julia had seen and done it all: from kissing a pope's ring to dressing a maestro's corpse. What an astonishing trajectory from that farm in the foothills of the Andes.

Although it wasn't our primary purpose, the three of us discovered an additional benefit to maintaining a family headquarters: it gave the spirit of Leonard Bernstein an enduring presence in New York City. At our annual holiday party at the Dome, the guests could feel the reflected warmth of our father as an artist, husband, father, and friend. The Dome kept Mummy alive, too: through her own paintings on the walls, through the grace of her objects, and through us, her children.

When the "ocean" at Sotheby's rolled around, we discovered that Mummy's antique-store finds, while charming, were not excessively valuable. But we knew such items as Leonard Bernstein's batons and capes—and above all the B-52 Bösendorfer with its "Mark of Lenny" cigarette burn—would fetch significant sums. And they did. The BETA Fund was saved, but it was disconcerting to watch our family belongings being oceaned off to strangers. There was one painting from the dining room that I loved—an eighteenth-century Brittany woman with the ribbons of her bonnet blowing in a breeze. Alexander and Nina both wanted it to go into the auction; I relented, but it bothered me. Then I made a side deal with decorator Gail: she bid on the painting and won it—whereupon I gleefully bought it back from her.

*   *   *

When Frankie started preschool, I asked the teachers about their music program. They said, "We don't have one. Would you like to start it?" I wished I hadn't opened my mouth, but I agreed to try. Twice a week, I took my guitar down to Village Infant Center on West 13th Street, to play and sing for the kids. It was the one and only regular music gig I ever had.

At first, I just sang the standards: "Home on the Range," "B-I-N-G-O," "I've Been Working on the Railroad." But soon I was devising ways to get the kids more engaged. I turned "On Top of Spaghetti" into a play. "Who wants to be the meatball? Who wants to be the spaghetti? Who wants to be the bush? Okay, now let's act it out!" I played the soothing lullaby "Rock-a-Bye Baby" at punk-rock speed: belly laughs! Nothing was more gratifying than getting a rise out of this most challenging of all audiences.

But "real" songwriting wasn't that much fun anymore. What used to be the most fun (if agonizing) was showing my songs to Daddy—and best of all had been writing all those songs in honor of Daddy himself. In his absence, it was as if the engine had been extracted from the vehicle. In one whole year, the only song I wrote was "Jump, Little Pumpkin, Jump."

Songwriting was not the only casualty of my father's absence. When he died, I sensed right away that some essential equilibrium in my marriage had been put in jeopardy. David's and my happiness had so much to do with the way he'd fit into the family puzzle—and the way he and my father had delighted in each other. For over six years, the presence of David had made it fun again to be around Daddy, and made the more annoying patches endurable. David, too, I knew, felt my father's death as a catastrophic loss. Our marriage hung on for another decade, but the deep harmony we experienced while Daddy was alive never returned.

Still, there were plenty of bright spots in the 1990s. Frankie was self-possessed, preternaturally verbal, already a writer at the age of seven. Evan was blond and funny, with a mimic's ear and a fierce passion for his videos. The four of us, plus Julia, spent most weekends in Fairfield together: my own childhood in a mirror. Julia's devotion to my kids opened my heart to her; it was the classic transformation between mother and childbearing daughter that I would never experience with my own mother. By the time Julia died in 2009, I realized I'd had her in my life more than twice as long as I'd had Mummy herself.

In a deeply gratifying surprise move, Patty, my father's chef in his last years, volunteered with her husband, Serge, to take care of the Fairfield property. They brought the joy back to the place, raising chickens for fresh eggs, planting flowers and vegetables in profusion, taking up beekeeping and sharing the honey they harvested. All that was missing was Daddy to sample the tomatoes and Mummy to clip the multihued zinnias.

Five years after our father's death, Alexander got married: the first happy family event to come along and pull us out of our collective grief. Nina and I loved our new sister-in-law, Elizabeth, who was fiery and funny, with a dead-aim aesthetic eye like Mummy had.

Alexander had turned into the sweetest, most deeply intelligent and compassionate man we knew. His friends loved him fiercely. Alexander refused ever to whine; it was as if he'd decided that all his lucky breaks in life gave him no right to complain about anything, ever. But I often sensed he suffered silently; as his sister, I knew how hard it was for him to achieve—and maintain— dignity, patience, and strength.

In 1998, Elizabeth gave birth to Anya Micaela. Frankie and Evan were besotted with their new cousin. And Alexander was the happiest dad in the world; he was born to be a dad, it turned out.

Then it was Nina's turn. She married Rudd, a wry, soft-spoken film producer. A few years later, Nina gave birth to Anna Felicia, a peach of a girl. That turned out to be the full complement of cousins produced by the three of us. It felt good to have little kids crawling around under the Passover table again. Possibly no one was happier than Julia. Oh, how she fed and fed her four little ones. (And no gentile on this earth ever made a more authentically sublime matzoh ball soup.)

*   *   *

An inquiry came to Amberson from my father's music licensor, Boosey & Hawkes: Would we be interested in permitting the development of an educational concert, modeled after Leonard

Bernstein's televised Young People's Concerts, but about the music of Bernstein himself? Wouldn't offering this concert to orchestras around the country be an excellent way to promote the Bernstein music catalogue, as well as introduce his music to a new generation of listeners?

That did indeed sound like an excellent idea. Oddly, unaccountably, I volunteered to develop the concert.

What made me think I could do this? I had certainly watched Daddy devise his own Young People's Concerts, and I'd attended nearly every one of them—but I'd been far more focused on the trestle table laden with doughnuts set out for the musicians backstage. Now I was hoping that perhaps by osmosis, I'd absorbed a sense of how those concerts were put together.

And then there was another small issue: How was I going to create this concert when I wasn't a trained musician? I immediately called Michael Barrett, who had worked so closely with my father during his final decade. Michael and I decided to split LB's job in half: Michael would work out the musical details, and I would write the script. As we batted the ideas back and forth, my father's music pushed us forward like a sail catching the wind.

The Utah Symphony agreed to let us test-drive our concert with them. Michael would conduct and I would narrate. Narrate . . . ? I hadn't planned at all to be the narrator—but as I began writing, I heard my own voice. It felt perfectly natural. Why did this all feel so *natural*?

It took Michael and me the better part of two years to prepare *The Bernstein Beat*. My father used to crank out four or five of those scripts per season; however did he do it?

I wrote my script in longhand, then typed it into my very first laptop. When I hit "print" and the pages began their slow march out of the printer, I felt a rare new joy.

We gave our test-drive concert in Salt Lake City. Michael knew exactly how to conduct Bernstein music; the orchestra sounded plush and bright. Our topic, rhythm, had steered us to all the jumping-est Bernstein compositions. I told the young audience they had permission to bop around in their seats if the music made them feel like it. (I myself was incapable of sitting still during those lively excerpts from *On the Town* and *West Side Story*.) But it was a full-length concert, complete with intermission. For little kids. Clearly we had some tweaking to do.

The audience loved the part when I asked nine kids to come up on the stage and represent the beats in a nine-beat bar. I explained how to understand any complex rhythm by breaking it down into bundles of two beats—"hot dog"—and three beats—"ham-bur-ger"—and pretty soon I had the nine kids in formation to represent a tricky nine-beat dance rhythm from LB's *Mass*. Before our concluding excerpt from *West Side Story*, I "rehearsed" the audience in their participatory moment: "Aw, c'mon, you can do it louder than *that*!" We rehearsed it again. Then, when the orchestra played the piece, I held up my big sign at the appropriate moment and the kids roared "MAMBO!" to shake the rafters.

I didn't know it, but my new life had just been born.

One last "Mambo!" during the bows, with Michael Barrett.

22

A New Millennium

One time, in my twenties, I had to renew my passport. Back then it was a brutal errand, involving a visit to the dreaded passport office at Rockefeller Center, where a thick welter of humanity stood in line for hours amid a few grossly inadequate electric fans. Finally it was my turn to approach a window. As the dour civil servant examined my paperwork, she asked if I might be related to Leonard Bernstein. When I told her he was my father, she looked up at me, joy suddenly lighting up her face and turning her into a human being. She told me how much she enjoyed Bernstein's recordings and his Broadway shows: how she'd watched his concerts on television. What a wonderful person he was, she said. And I realized: Daddy himself was the greatest passport of all.

Three decades after that day, Leonard Bernstein was no longer alive—but he was still very much my passport: Michael Barrett and I took *The Bernstein Beat* to Beijing, China.

Any ten-year-old American kid can snap their fingers to the iconic bebop riff in "Cool" from *West Side Story*: "Boy, boy, crayzeee bo-oy . . ." But the China National Symphony had very little experience with twentieth-century American music; my father's notes were pulling them out of their comfort zone. At the first rehearsal in Beijing, when Michael gave the downbeat to the "Cool" ballet, the orchestra began playing a stolid march, one-two, one-two: they didn't know how to "swing." Michael taught them, suggesting they imagine the insouciant gait of a cat.

Michael and the orchestra pulled it together for the performance. The children in the audience were patient and attentive, even with my own narration having to be repeated every few sentences in Mandarin, which lengthened the proceedings. The "hamburger, hot dog, hot dog, hot dog" demo went over nicely ("han-bao-bao, re-gou, re-gou, re-gou"), and the kids were all waving little flags that had been provided by one of the concert's sponsors—incredibly, McDonald's.

The following year, the Lenny passport took *The Bernstein Beat* to Havana, Cuba, where for the first time I narrated in Spanish, my mother's native tongue. It was almost mystically gratifying to combine my parents' worlds in this new way. We were not prepared for the high spirits of the Cuban children, nothing like the quiet, well-behaved youngsters in Beijing. At the end of the concert, the ovation was so prolonged that Michael launched the orchestra into a reprise of the Mambo. The kids were all on their feet, and as usual I couldn't sit still . . . Next thing I knew, I'd hopped off the stage yelling, *"Bailemos!"* The girls and boys came pelting down the aisles, and we all danced together. When the music stopped, they covered me in hugs and kisses.

Nina caught all this on video for a film she was making. When I saw the footage, I knew I was looking at my very happiest self.

*   *   *

Back home, New York's classical radio station, WQXR, sent me up to Tanglewood to prepare and present live broadcasts of concerts by Daddy's beloved "Kids": the Tanglewood Music Center Orchestra.

Tanglewood! My father's old stomping grounds, and scene of many a fraught visit of my own . . . but now it felt very different. It was delicious to drive up to the Berkshires on a summer morning with my new QXR pals. Feverishly we conducted interviews, then cobbled together our preproduced "halftime show" in the hours before the concert. Then came the adrenaline rush of the live broadcast—clapping on the headphones, rolling with the punches—and afterward, the richly earned hangout on the rocking chairs behind Serge Koussevitzky's mountaintop manor, Seranak, where the Tanglewood folks kindly housed us overnight. Under the myriad stars, sharing a bottle of wine with my new friends, I felt useful, validated, competent, comfortable in my skin; my old Stupid Idiot feelings were nowhere in sight.

I realized I still had one foot on the gas pedal, but my other foot wasn't simultaneously slamming on the brake anymore.

I traveled the country narrating *The Bernstein Beat* with other orchestras, other conductors, in places like Fayetteville, Arkansas; Flint, Michigan; San Antonio, Texas. As I introduced my father's music to hall after hall full of kids who knew nothing about him, I felt my age-old discomfort with the Lenny connection ebbing away. This was a job that needed doing, and I was, of all things, uniquely qualified to do it.

Many of the orchestra musicians, it turned out, had watched the Young People's Concerts on television. "That's how I fell in love with music," they would say. Those who had experienced Bernstein firsthand always had a personal story to tell: a moment when they'd had a meaningful exchange with Leonard Bernstein that they never forgot.

Just like the musicians, the parents in the audience had also grown up listening to Bernstein recordings and watching the Young People's Concerts on TV. "He turned me into a music lover!" they'd tell me—and that was why they'd brought their kids to *The Bernstein Beat* that day. The grandparents amazed me even more. So many of them had actually *been there*: Israel in 1948; the first Broadway run of *West Side Story*; the New York Philharmonic back in its old home, Carnegie Hall. I was touched beyond all expectation. Daddy was gone, with all his living complications and maddening excesses—but I marveled at what he'd left behind.

The Daddy I knew seemed in danger of receding behind the Lenny everyone else knew. But an unexpected opportunity came up for me to reconnect with him, in a particularly intense way.

The conductor James Conlon invited me to Cincinnati to be the speaker in my father's Symphony no. 3, *Kaddish*. It was a grand offer, but I still vividly recalled my mother's big, scary actress voice doing the narration on the original recording. Her melodramatic argument with God had left my siblings and me with a lifelong allergy to the work.

And anyway, how could I possibly be the speaker when the very first line of the narration was "O, my Father . . ."? The very thought of the audience wondering whether or not the *F* in "father" was capitalized was, to me, unbearably embarrassing.

But Maestro Conlon wouldn't let it go. To worm out of the situation, I told him I'd ask Harry Kraut whether it was permissible for me to change the text, certain Harry would say no, and that would be that. To my surprise, Harry said: "Oh, sure, go ahead! Lenny used to change that narration all the time." Suddenly, I was stuck with the gig.

A few old demons immediately reared up. There was my old fear of not measuring up to my beautiful actress mother; this narration was, after all, written for *her*—and she'd been a legitimate actress. And didn't I have a nerve to be changing my father's own text? Plus, there was that old bugaboo, my complicated feelings about Judaism. Maestro Conlon's invitation seemed in many ways like the worst possible assignment.

But I became utterly absorbed in the task. As I studied my father's narration line by line, I found myself mentally arguing with him, consumed by an ancient impatience, even fury. Why the complications, the melodrama, the weighty earnestness? This symphony, which so urgently expressed my father's lifelong "crisis of faith," turned out to be the perfect place for me to explore the crisis that had crystallized for Alexander, Nina, and me back in 1976, when *1600 Pennsylvania Avenue* turned out to be such a colossal flop. Who was this flawed, maddening biological creator of ours? It was now my turn to shake my fist at *him*.

Musically, the symphony was a death match between tunes and twelve-tone—a metaphor my father returned to over and over in his compositions to express his fear and anger about existence (dissonance) versus his hope for a better future (melody). But why, I wondered, couldn't the composer just relax and write those *tunes*? Why was he always in such a *dither* about tonality? Still, it was a glorious struggle. When I peeled away my father's narration, I saw how rich and beautiful his music was underneath—despite all its maddening convolutions. Sometimes even because of them.

I remembered Grandpa telling me how the ancient rabbis wrote their commentary in the margins of the Talmud, while a later generation of rabbis wrote *their* commentary in the margins of the previous commentary, and so on for centuries. So maybe my argument with my earthly father, written in the margins of his argument with his spiritual father—which contained much of his rage at his own earthly father, as well—all had a nice Talmudic ring to it. Maybe I was simply adding another generational layer to a long line of chutzpah.

*   *   *

Carnegie Hall's education team asked Michael Barrett and me to develop a family concert about Mozart, in honor of the composer's 250th birthday. It was Michael's idea that I should narrate the concert in the persona of Mozart the kid. "That's a horrible idea!" I said. "I hate when those children's concert narrators come out dressed as Papa Haydn or Uncle Ludwig—so lame!" But then I had a vision of Mozart the kid as a sort of slacker smart aleck who knew he was a genius and didn't care what anyone thought of him. And suddenly my path was clear.

Carnegie arranged for the Metropolitan Opera to lend me an eighteenth-century costume, complete with periwig and little black shoes with silver buckles. It was just a supernumerary's costume—the footman in the corner of some ballroom scene, holding up the candelabra—but the outfit was beautifully made. When I slipped into that cream-and-gold brocade jacket, and

Jamie as Mozart the kid, hugging Julia postconcert.

capered around the stage to the overture from *The Magic Flute*, I felt exactly the way Snoopy looks in the *Peanuts* comics when he dances for joy.

If someone had told me, back in LA in the early 1980s as I strove to be a rock star, that twenty-five years later I'd be a mother of two, dancing around on the stage of Carnegie Hall dressed as a twelve-year-old Wolfgang Amadeus Mozart, I'd have thought that person was smoking something potent indeed.

23

The Venezuela Connection

Scrolling idly through my Facebook feed, I came across a link to a YouTube video showing a very young conductor with unruly black curls leading some Latin American youth orchestra in the good old Mambo from *West Side Story*. I thought: This might be cute to watch for fifteen seconds or so . . . and I clicked on the "play" arrow.

I knew nothing about what I was looking at. These girls and boys looked very young, and they were playing the Mambo as if they were on fire. They were also laughing, dancing in place, twirling their instruments, all without dropping a note. They were wildly virtuosic, all of them—and that young, curly-headed conductor drove them forward in rare style. I found myself laughing, then crying—and certainly not clicking away after fifteen seconds. Who *were* these kids? Why the hell could they play like that? I had never before seen such a joyous spirit pouring out of musicians.

Then I realized: *of course* I had seen that joyous spirit before. This was precisely the same energy that came surging out of my father when he conducted. I had simply never seen it coming out of an entire orchestra. Maybe this was why I'd found myself in tears as I watched: these very young musicians, ablaze in their own playing—it was the embodiment of everything Daddy had ever meant. I was overcome with my longing to share that video with him.

As I watched Gustavo Dudamel and the Simón Bolívar Youth Orchestra of Venezuela for that very first time, on a screen-within-a-screen smaller than the palm of my hand, something seismic happened inside me.

I felt compelled to find out more about those kids—in a way, so as to tell my father all about them. I learned that in the 1970s, a young Venezuelan musician-economist, José Antonio Abreu, developed the idea that a youth orchestra program could provide a safe after-school haven for children living in impoverished, dangerous neighborhoods. Maestro Abreu soon saw that a youth orchestra provided far more than safety; it was, in fact, a template for a successful community. This nurturing daily environment was providing those kids with patience, empathy, self-confidence, focus—the crucial inner resources that would help them pursue whatever they wanted to do with their lives later on. The fact that they were becoming excellent musicians was almost a by-product of what was primarily a social-rescue program.

The program was called El Sistema. By the time I watched that YouTube video, hundreds of thousands of kids across Venezuela were spending their after-school hours learning to play Beethoven, Tchaikovsky, Mahler. The orchestra I saw on the video was El Sistema's all-star team, now touring the world and taking audience after audience by storm.

I had to admit, it sounded way too good to be true. But if it *was* true, I had to know more about it. I had to *see* it—to report about it in my head to Daddy. So I organized a trip to Caracas, Venezuela, with three friends.

Our guides, Norma and Rodrigo, took us to visit half a dozen Sistema sites, or *núcleos*, in the Caracas area. As our van slogged through the endless traffic on the first morning, I fretted: What if El Sistema turned out to be some sort of grimly rigid, Soviet-style experiment?

Well, it wasn't remotely Soviet—or even, for that matter, particularly systematic. The *núcleos* were noisy, chaotic places, bubbling over with the kids' raucous energy. Hundreds of them would cram into undersized, underventilated rehearsal spaces, playing Tchaikovsky and Mahler with a mad exuberance, the string players somehow managing not to poke one another's eyes out with their bows.

The teachers radiated a patient enthusiasm. Many of them had come up through El Sistema themselves; they told us how music had rescued them from the limited options of their neighborhood streets: the gangs, the drugs, the violence. (Maestro Abreu memorably said: "A child who holds a violin will never pick up a gun.")

And everything was happening in Spanish!—my mother's language, the comforting syllables of my earliest childhood. Conversing with the kids, the parents, the Sistema staff, the teachers, I was overcome with a deep sense of wholeness—even though Venezuelan Spanish was so fast and slurred that I missed whole chunks of what people were saying.

I was often fighting back tears in Caracas. Here was a program that synthesized my father's two most heartfelt objectives: sharing the joy of music with young people and making the world a better place. All I could think of was: If Daddy could see this, he would *plotz*.

* * *

When I learned that Gustavo would be coming to New York to conduct my father's former orchestra, I asked the Philharmonic if I could throw Gustavo and his wife, Eloisa, a party. Who was this new me that called the New York Philharmonic brass on the phone? But to my astonishment, the answer was yes; the party was on. As the festivities wound down, Gustavo mentioned to me that he liked dancing: my kind of guy! I organized the posse, and about a dozen of us went straight from the Dome to a gay-lesbian Latino club I knew, on a grimy street behind the Port Authority

Bus Terminal. We caroused until four in the morning. Gustavo, like my father, was most assuredly a man with a motor.

The next day, Gustavo visited the Philharmonic Archives, where he pored over Bernstein's conducting scores, which now reside there. The archivist in chief, Barbara Haws, showed Gustavo a baton of Daddy's; Barbara told me, "When he picked it up, it literally seemed to dance on his fingertips!" She invited Gustavo to use the baton in his final concert with the Philharmonic that weekend. During the last bars of Prokofiev's Fifth Symphony, a particularly vigorous motion caused the baton to snap in half. Gustavo was chagrined, but everyone else loved the incident; after all, a baton used by Lenny, then broken by Gustavo, was a perfect case of value added. Barbara Haws carefully preserves the baton's two pieces at the Philharmonic Archives.

Gustavo went on to conduct all the LB symphonic works in the following years, and my siblings and I attended many of the concerts. Since our father's death, we'd often experienced a what-is-wrong-with-this-picture sensation whenever we saw someone else on the podium. But watching Gustavo conduct was a different, even eerie experience. That energy on the podium, so similar to Daddy's; the unbridled physicality, the tenderness combined with the momentum of a runaway locomotive, all of it carefully calibrated to every nuance of the music . . . it felt so familiar. As I watched Gustavo, I would at one moment feel maternal about this twenty-six-year-old whiz kid; in the next, I would feel as close and proud as a sister; and the moment after that—I couldn't help making the parallel—I would even feel like his daughter, though I was twice Gustavo's age. I kept thinking about how, if my father were alive to see Gustavo in action, he would have enfolded the young conductor in his arms and fractured several ribs with the gusto of his embrace.

Word came from Caracas that I was invited to present *The Bernstein Beat*—*en español!*—with the city's premier high-school-age Sistema ensemble. I'd never in my life been so excited about a gig.

The concert went beautifully, with only one glitch—right at the beginning. For some reason the clarinet player, who had never had this trouble before, added one extra note to his five repeated notes at the opening of the "Times Square" music from *On the Town*, thereby putting himself one beat behind the conductor. This caused some of the players to stay back with him, while others barreled forward with the conductor—creating what musicians refer to as a train wreck. Maestro Dietrich Paredes stopped the orchestra, waited for the clarinet player to collect himself, then started the piece over. The clarinet player did it again: extra note, another train wreck. Maestro Dietrich stopped the orchestra yet again. The hall was engulfed in a sickening silence. The concert began a third time. And the clarinet player did it *again*; his brain had gotten stuck. It happens. This time, Maestro Dietrich just kept everyone going, and after fourteen very shaky bars, things eventually righted themselves. Everything was perfect after that. But it was a tough start for one and all—especially for the clarinet player, who never raised his head again and fled offstage the instant the last note of the concert was played. Between each of our final bows, Maestro Dietrich was frantically asking backstage: "*¿Dónde está Antonio? ¿Dónde está Antonio?*" But Antonio was gone.

After the concert, there was a lunch for us in a hotel dining room. Suddenly the teenage musicians at the long table burst into whoops and applause: Antonio the clarinet player had just been dragged in by two orchestra chums. The young musicians all jumped up from the table and surrounded Antonio with hugs, backslaps, hair ruffling, words of encouragement. He covered his face in embarrassment, but he couldn't resist his friends; soon he was smiling and returning their hugs.

I watched all this with my mouth open; I knew I was witnessing the essence of El Sistema. A staff member said: "You see? We don't build musicians; we build human beings."

*   *   *

On New Year's Day 2010, my friend Elizabeth Kling and I were talking about El Sistema, and how exciting it was to see it becoming a global movement. Elizabeth suddenly said: "I know what: Let's make a film! Let's make a documentary about El Sistema coming to the United States!" "Okay!" I said, the way one does during a New Year's Day conversation with a friend.

But then we actually went and did it.

First we followed Stanford Thompson, an African American trumpet player from Atlanta, as he started his own Sistema-inspired "núcleo" in West Philadelphia. Elizabeth and I had our cameras rolling on day one of the Play On, Philly! program, and we returned there regularly for the better part of two years. We focused on two kids: Raven, an excitable fifth grader who took on the violin, and seventh grader Zebadiah, quiet and quirky behind his dreadlocks, learning to play the viola.

In our third year of filming, we went to Harlem and followed a whole new kid: eleven-year-old Mohamed, who played the trombone in the Harmony Program. Anne Fitzgibbon had launched her program after spending two years observing El Sistema in Venezuela, where even getting kidnapped hadn't dimmed her enthusiasm.

Elizabeth was an experienced film editor and producer, but making a documentary presented its own unique set of challenges—and of course I knew nothing at all. We were in so far over our heads, I'm still amazed that we persevered. The logistics, the expenses, the crises, the crew, the *new* crew, the *new* crises . . . If I'd had any inkling of what I was getting into, I never would have taken on the project. Sometimes ignorance can be a blessing.

When Elizabeth brought in award-winning editor Jonathan Oppenheim, she had no idea that long ago on Martha's Vineyard, Judy Holliday (who had been a member of the Revuers with Betty and Adolph) had brought over her six-year-old son Jonathan to play with me, and that Jonathan's father, David Oppenheim, had been my father's close friend (and lover). This serendipitous family connection fit right in with my urge to show El Sistema to Daddy—and after all, this film was my ultimate expression of that urge.

Jonathan took us a long way, but we ran out of money—despite a harrowing but ultimately successful Kickstarter campaign. We had to let Jonathan go, though the editing was still far from complete. Elizabeth and I talked about giving up.

Then, a miracle. I'd sent a rough cut of the film to my personally appointed godfather, Mike Nichols. Mike called me to say that he and his wife, Diane Sawyer, had watched the film the night before and loved it. How could he help? How about $50,000?

Mike had swept in like the proverbial shining knight and saved our film. He'd been so generous to my whole family as we were growing up; he'd been so kind and thoughtful during Mummy's illness—plus, he could even carve a roast—and now he was doing me such an enormous favor, I could hardly process it.

The premiere of *Crescendo: The Power of Music* at the Philadelphia Film Festival was immediately followed by a live performance featuring a dozen kids from the Play On, Philly! program—including our two local protagonists, Raven and Zebadiah. The crowd went nuts. The film won two prizes straight out of the gate, and won more later on. Netflix bought it, too.

My private joke about the title is that it gave me a permanent opportunity to rant about the universal misuse of the word "crescendo," as in: "The controversy rose to a deafening crescendo." The word, which means "growing" in Italian, is a musical indication for a gradual increase in volume. I strongly suspect the problem derives from the word sounding so much like cymbals making a crash at the end-o . . . Anyway, now I have a built-in excuse to be a perennial corrector—and, my siblings would add, a perennial nuisance. But I like to think my father, ever the grammatical stickler himself, would have enjoyed the finger wagging embedded in my title.

Two months after the opening in Philadelphia, Elizabeth and I organized a private screening of our film at Symphony Space in New York, specially choosing a date that fit Mike Nichols's busy schedule. We couldn't wait to thank him, profusely and in person, for saving our film from perdition. But a week before the screening, Mike died suddenly. No one was prepared. He'd been frail but full of energy, with many projects in the works. It was a sickening, knee-buckling shock to lose him.

We wound up dedicating our film to Mike, but I'll be sad for the rest of my days that I didn't get to thank him, hug him, love him enough for everything he did. I felt I'd lost a father all over again.

24

Lately

Harry Kraut spent more and more time down in Key West. His health was poor; he was the last of the chain-smokers. One evening as he left a restaurant, Harry fell on the steps and hit his head. He never awoke, and died three weeks later. It was a sad, lonely end to an eventful, populous life. But after a bit of time had elapsed, my siblings and I came to realize it was easier in Harry's absence to run what was now called the Leonard Bernstein Office. We weren't quite such "winnies" anymore. Maybe we were even grownups, finally. Nina was using her chef's expertise to work with high school students in tough urban neighborhoods, helping them discover and prepare affordable, nutritious food. Nina was . . . a teacher. As for Alexander, he had helped the BETA Fund evolve into a meticulously devised educational model called Artful Learning, which was successfully running in elementary and secondary schools all around the country. Alexander, too, was an educator. And here I was, writing and presenting educational concerts all over the world. Teaching turned out to be the apple that fell, all three times, close to the Daddy tree.

As for the Mummy tree, here was the surprise: despite both Alexander and Nina having studied acting, the one who couldn't resist the stage—the indisputable ham of the family—turned out to be their pesky older sister.

It's one of life's mysteries that in some families of prominent musicians, the children gravitate effortlessly to music. Rudolf Serkin's son Peter became a celebrated pianist, both of Isaac Stern's sons are conductors, and there are countless other examples—but ours was not such a family. All three of us went in other directions, yet we're deeply, even neurologically tethered to music. Nina, like our mother, is continually tapping out a complex rhythm with her fingers. Alexander does this, too—adding contrapuntal muscle contractions with his hips and knees. On the street, I make rhythm and bass lines to my walking tempo by clicking my fingernails and sliding my teeth against each other. Nina, too, plays tunes with her teeth. And all three of us are perpetually plagued by "earworms": bits of music that play over and over in our heads, sometimes for days—anything from a Tchaikovsky snippet to a tune from *Candide*—or, just as likely, a ghastly TV ad jingle. We're a three-piece band of musical tics. There's but a whisper of difference, it would appear, between a Line of Genius on a forehead and a mild case of OCD.

Around 2008, my concert narrating got an enormous boost from my father's colleague and my friend Michael Tilson Thomas. Since our long-ago hiking days in the Southwest, Michael had become a very important maestro, leading the San Francisco Symphony, as well as founding an orchestral academy, the New World Symphony, in Miami.

I was in the middle of my filmmaking when Michael called me with a proposition: How would I like to design and present educational concerts for adults with the New World Symphony? I would research and write the scripts, then come down to Miami Beach twice a year and narrate the concerts with the orchestra and its young conducting fellow.

I almost turned the job down. It sounded frighteningly demanding—and besides, I was making a movie. But who could say no to MTT? Not me.

First, there was the research part, which I always overdid; that was part of the fun. Then it became a writing assignment: squeezing all that excess information down into a coherent tincture. Then came the dessert: traveling to Miami Beach in the Florida-friendly months of November and February; rehearsing with the brilliant young orchestra in their magnificent new Frank Gehry building; and, finally, delivering my narration at the concert while, on an overhead screen, ingeniously devised visuals accompanied my remarks. Each concert was its own unique, nifty concoction. Yes, it was a lot of work. Yes, it was the best job ever.

By now, I'd been at this concert-writing-and-narrating business for a decade. My unorthodox path to knowledge about classical music was starting to add up. In my narrations, I was learning how to select the engaging detail; how to put an audience at ease by mixing historical information with contemporary references; how to project my persona to the very back row, drawing in my listeners as if we were chatting over cocktails. Maybe I was starting to get good at this stuff. Was this a career?

If so, I was the poster child for life beginning at fifty.

*   *   *

One evening back in the '90s, Michael Barrett and I were walking home from dinner with our spouses when we ran into Michael's friend, the actor Eric Stoltz. "So, what are you up to these days?" Michael asked him on the street corner. Eric began his long list: a film shoot in Canada, a TV taping in LA, a play in Chicago . . . "Man, you are the *giggin'*-est!" Michael marveled.

I stood on the sidewalk thinking about that: about being the giggin'-est. It seemed like a lovely, remote fantasy: to be so full of work, so on the loose. The wistful thought drifted through my mind: Boy, I sure wish *I* could be the giggin'-est . . .

And one day, a quarter century later, it occurred to me that my wish had come true. The concert narrations, the screenings of my film, the performances of Bernstein works I attended all over the world, the conferences and lectures and interviews . . . my nonstop activities kept me on the run full time.

Of course, it was Daddy himself who had *really* been the giggin'-est. But it turned out I had an energy and appetite similar to my father's—not just for sharing the joys of music with audiences, but also for travel, people, intense work, intense play. It took a while, but I'd found my own way to cobble such a life together.

I'd noticed for some time that I wasn't fretting anymore about the LB connection; if anything, it was something interesting to share, but it didn't feel like a burden. When had my father stopped being a burden?

Part of it, I had to admit, was that he was easier to deal with as a posthumous entity. But there was another, crucial reason: I'd stopped fretting about the LB comparisons when I stopped trying to be a musician myself.

It turned out that if I just refrained from making music with my own body, I was much calmer. Oh, the fits I used to have playing music: the worms and spiders spilling out of my fingers onto the keyboard, my scarf bouncing in rhythm to my thudding heart, the dead-chicken-itis crippling my hands. But I could *talk* about music all day, without a tremor. After all, there was no instrument to fumble on, talking presented no pitch problems, and all my words were on a page in front of me. What was there to panic about?

At home, I have a framed student government infraction slip that was served on me in high school: "Offense: talking in assembly." Like Dumbo and his oversized ears, I had eventually found a way to turn my liability into my asset. Loud and obnoxious wins!

It was a good trade-off: I was leading a musician's life minus the music-making part. There were the long, intense rehearsals; the adrenaline of the performance; the fascinating exchanges with audience members afterward. Then the late-night hang with the gang at the hotel bar—trading jokes, gossip, airport horror stories. I'd stumbled into a pretty good compromise; instead of being an accomplished musician, I'd become an accomplished . . . *fan*.

Yes, there was a sadness within it. I'd given up something I loved, that I'd devoted decades of my life to achieve. But making music with my own body had mostly made me a mess. I remembered my long-ago journal entry, about crying because I couldn't be a musician. Well, I wasn't crying anymore. It was okay. I had let the ailing limb atrophy and drop off so that the rest of the organism could thrive.

* * *

You really know you're a grownup when you start losing the grownups. We lost Adolph and Betty, and Dick Avedon. Nanny Helen died at ninety-two. Grandma died at the age of ninety-four, outliving her firstborn son by two years. And it was very painful to lose Shirley. She had a blood disorder that gradually diminished her over the years. When she died I was next to her, on that bed where I'd spent so much time in my teens. As her breathing dwindled, I whispered "Me laudü" in her ear—"I love you" in Rybernian. Without the clangor of Shirley's laugh, our Fairfield dinner table felt eerily subdued. It took us a while to regain the decibels— but they did return. It's hard to keep a Bernstein quiet for long.

Most recently, we lost Uncle BB: that antic, adored non-grownup of my childhood. As Daddy's thirteen-years-younger sibling, he never seemed old to us. But he was eighty-five when he died. Not until he was gone did I realize that he'd been my crucial buffer; in his absence, I have achieved the unwanted status of the eldest Bernstein.

Losing Julia was seismic. For five decades, she had been a complex and indisputable member of the family: raising my siblings and me, seeing our parents through their respective deaths—and, later, doting on our own children. The Dome still reverberates with her former presence—but we simply had to give up on the matzoh ball soup course at our seder.

Everyone clings to a keepsake or a talisman to evoke the people they love and lose. When Shirley died in 1998, we clung to her bathrobes and face creams, and cousin Karen made the felicitous discovery that Shirley's bras fit her perfectly. After we lost Julia in 2009, we couldn't bear to throw away her paring knife with the cracked black handle, or the big, cream-colored teacup stained inside by her oversteeped Lipton tea bags. In Fairfield, we continue to surround ourselves with Mummy's handiwork: her paintings and needlepoint pillows, her hand-restored lamps, her wicker chairs picked clean with dental instruments. But our favorite way to keep Mummy close—and Julia, too—is through the regular use of their most characteristic Spanish phrases. For Alexander, Nina, and me, Spanish serves the same purpose that Rybernian served for Daddy and his siblings: we've adapted it into our own secret, self-referential language. And we still use Rybernian, too; the Three-Headed Monster is trilingual.

When it comes to remembering Daddy, we cling to silly things: a bottle of German Robitussin on the bathroom shelf that says "*Hustensaft*" on the label (expiration date: 1987); a ceramic ashtray with an image of Mount Fuji; a cornflower blue djellaba, still hanging in the closet, that he wore on summer evenings with nothing on underneath.

I also feel Daddy's presence when I have WQXR on in my house or in the car. Not only does it make me smile whenever his name comes up in the back announcements, but also the sound of classical radio gives me the same sense of safety I felt as a kid, lying on someone's lap in the back seat of the car, watching the tops of the trees flash by, the station drifting in and out of reception as we sped under the highway overpasses. My own two kids have no particular interest in classical music, but I wonder whether, after I'm gone, they, too, may gravitate to it for the comfort of their own childhood sounds.

As Alexander, Nina, and I go about sharing the official legacy of Leonard Bernstein, we cling all the harder to the father we lived with: the Daddy who scrubbed his ears so vigorously that the twin mounds of soapsuds slid down his shoulders; the Daddy who

LB in his cornflower blue djellaba.

sucked the last green morsel out of a lobster thorax; the Daddy who taught us the "rubber balloons" routine, played the "Moldy Man" game with us in the hammock, and recited Lewis Carroll on the pool floater.

But nothing conveys Daddy's deepest essence better than his own music. The notes he strung together are as uniquely, identifiably him as a fingerprint. We listen to the wrenching violin solo in the slow movement from *Serenade*, the rollicking "Profanation" from the *Jeremiah* Symphony, or the jagged, propulsive "Rumble" from *West Side Story*, and there he is—in all his tenderness, his raunchiness, his intellectual panache, his agonizing over God, his despair over humanity, his cautious but dogged hope that we're all getting somewhere. When we listen to that music, it's the next best thing to getting a hug from Daddy himself.

Except, damn it all: we still miss the too-tight squeeze that made us yelp, the nicotine-y breath, the scratchy brown bathrobe.

Acknowledgments

I begin my litany of gratitude, as most writers seem to do, with my editor, Jonathan Jao. No one in my whole long life ever pushed me quite as hard as he did, and it turned out I liked being pushed. His talented colleague Sofia Groopman was the "good cop"; her sunny ways cushioned many a blow.

I genuflect to my copy editor, Mary Beth Constant, whose name I didn't even learn until long after she'd swung her scythe. I thought I was good at catching grammatical errors and maintaining consistency of style; Mary Beth taught me how unreliable I actually was. I'm humbled, but grateful.

Enormous thanks to Toby Greenberg, who wrangled the photo credits on a tight deadline—a daunting task.

Then there's my literary agent, Michael Carlisle. He was the one who said, several years ago: You can do this and I can help you. He was the one who pushed the "go" button. I am forever grateful for that crucial first vote of confidence—and I'm grateful as well to Michael's colleague at Inkwell Management, William Callahan, who edited most intelligently those early chapters in preparation for their first exposure to the harsh light of day.

When it came to researching the facts of my father's life and locating documents and photographs, I would have been rudderless without the wisdom and enthusiasm of Mark Horowitz at the Library of Congress, where the Leonard Bernstein Archive resides. Also indispensable was Barbara Haws, archivist of the New York Philharmonic; her brain is an extraordinary repository of facts, all of them brightly illuminated by her enthusiasm and dry Midwestern wit.

The John F. Kennedy Center for the Performing Arts was also very helpful, as were the archivists at the Boston Symphony Orchestra.

But I give particular thanks to Humphrey Burton, whose ambitious biography of my father became a kind of bible to me for checking facts and chronology. (His wife, Christina, has been an invaluable photo resource as well.) My copy of Humphrey's book is splayed, smudged, and infested with Post-its; those pages, like its author, have been a faithful friend.

Various other books on Bernstein were very helpful—especially Nigel Simeone's collection of my father's letters; Barry Seldes's book about my father and politics; Jonathan Cott's *Dinner with Lenny*; and Allen Shawn's fine book about my father from a few years ago. Also invaluable was Alex Ross's article in the *New Yorker* about my father's FBI file.

It will be clear to anyone who reads these pages that I depend on my family for my existence and my sanity. I profoundly thank my siblings, Alexander and Nina, for reading several versions of this story, and for giving me permission to say what I had to say. With all my heart I thank my daughter, Frankie Jay Thomas, for being the most rigorous reader I know; I almost didn't write the book, so anxious was I about her opinion. I'm forever grateful for her encouragement after she read the early, clumsy version. I also salute her husband, Dr. Ian Tattersall, for his felicitous brain-heart balance. And I thank my son, Evan, for having put up with me on a daily basis while I was writing, and for walking the dog late at night: a precious gift.

And I embrace my siblings' respective families: Nina's husband, Rudd, and their daughter, Anna Felicia; and Alexander and Elizabeth's daughter, Anya Micaela. Those two nieces, my "A-girls," are hope and joy incarnate.

I send warm greetings to the family of David Thomas, including his sisters Marilyn and Lisa, and their respective broods.

Deep thanks and hugs to my cousins Karen and Michael, who lost both of their parents, Ellen Ball and Burton "Uncle BB" Bernstein, while I was writing these pages. I was so terrified of my uncle BB's judgment that I didn't tell him for over a year that I was writing this book—and then he was simply gone. His lifelong, near-monastic devotion to the craft of writing left me in awe. I send love to his surviving wife, Jane.

I salute my mother's side of the family in Chile: cousins Patricia, Arturo, Magdalena, and Francisca, and all their copious brood. I hold them close, even with the thousands of miles in between.

Very much in the family category, I add my profound thanks and love to Patty Pulliam and Serge Boyce in Fairfield, Connecticut; they pour honey on our collective soul.

Various longtime family friends have been warm and supportive. Phyllis Newman Green kept an open ear and a ready smile, despite her own maladies. Cynthia O'Neal has been a reliable source of encouragement and hilarity. Beloved family friend Ofra Bikel was always there, and saw it all. Shirley Perle has been an extraordinary presence in my life: sharp, incisive, and full of heart. Amy Greene has remained a direct line to our mother, all these decades hence. Harold Prince and his family have been guardian angels. And "Decorator Gail" Jacobs believed I could do this book thing before I even knew it was a thing. Everyone in this world should have a Gail Jacobs cheering section.

They should also be so lucky as to have a David Pack cheering section. David's devotion and enthusiasm over the years fall into a category all their own. Thanks, Dave.

I send especially grateful hugs to Marjorie David and family, and to Susanna Styron and all her family. And yet more hugs to the families of David Oppenheim, Sid Ramin, and Lukas Foss.

Although he may not realize it, Steve Sondheim has been a steady and loving presence, more precious to me every day. Steve is not famous for warm fuzziness, but by golly, he's been warm and fuzzy to me, and I'm grateful as hell.

I owe an incalculable debt to my English teachers at the Brearley School. All that drill, drill, drilling on grammar; those crushingly lengthy summer reading lists; the papers that came back spider-webbed with red ink—it all added up. Brearley gave me some invaluable skills, such as making outlines, constructing coherent sentences, and keeping my butt in the chair. Thank you, Brearley—and thanks to all my beloved classmates who refrained from tearing me limb from limb when I was "loud and obnoxious." A special thanks to Ann Siegel, Tonne Goodman (and her sisters), Irene Dische, Margot Bradley, and Lucy Watson—each of whom has been helpful in ways they don't even know. And a big shout-out to Lisa Morrison, who will be forever mortified that her second grade teasing provided the title to this book.

They no longer walk among us, but I continue to give deep thanks for all the love from Adolph Green, Betty Comden, Mike Nichols, Betty Bacall, Dick Avedon, Mary Rodgers Guettel, Mendy Wager, Martha Gellhorn, Mike Mindlin, Rosamond Bernier. And I send my love to all their family members.

And all my love and gratitude to Julia Vega who, I realize in retrospect, became my second mother.

More beloved friends who have been rah-rah-rah-ing on the sidelines: Margaret Mercer, Michael Barrett, Cindy Wright (and our lifesaving tennis game), my film co-conspirator Elizabeth Kling, her sister, Kathy Kling, Janis Siegel, Fred Hersch, Amanda Jacobs, Martine Singer, Leslie and Tanya Tomkins and their beautiful mother, Millicent, and George Steel and Sarah Fels with their anagrams games that preserve my sanity.

Equally fervent thanks to Susan Lacy, Marthe Rowen, and Craig Barton and their terrific kids, Amy Burton and John Musto, Leslie Steifelman, Michael Boriskin and Elizabeth Dworkin, Mark Leno, Emily Mann and her sister, Carol Mann, Dennis Gibbens, Stephen Bogardus, the Pisar family, Peter Shapiro and his wife Bryna, James Capozzi, Jesse Ausubel, Susan Dickler, Brian Cullman, Katherine Mosby and Anne Griffin (and our life-affirming dinners), Jonathan Oppenheim, Glen Cortese, Stephen W. Zinsser and "the other Frankie" Faridany, Peter Kazaras, Norma Stevens, Judith Essien, Janis Susskind, Michele Areyzaga, Joy Horowitz, Martita Goshen, Steve Sherman, Jeff Himmel for getting me there and back, Geoffrey Colvin for attempting to explain the other side to me, Ed Schloth, Harold Chambers, Patty Birch, Steve Blier and his husband Jim Russell, Hank Rutter and Susan Fralick and the whole Moab gang—plus Lisa Halasz, Michele Sutter, John Corigliano and Mark Adamo, Jonathan Sheffer, Russ Titelman, Chris Layer, Steven Damron, Bart Gulley, Chuck Weinstock. And thanks to Nicole Mones for her encouragement, long ago.

Extra love to Michael Tilson Thomas and Joshua Robison, who believed in me since the 1970s. And to the wonderfully supportive team at New World Symphony—especially Doug Merrilat, Ana Estevez, Adam Zeichner, and Clyde Scott—who regularly reinforced the illusion that I know what I'm doing.

Special grateful mention to Jeffrey Stock, who put up with a lot.

My discovery of El Sistema gave rise to a whole new crop of adored friends who have been part of the cheering section: Tricia Tunstall and Eric Booth, Norma Nuñez, Rodrigo Guerrero, and Karen Zorn and Wayman Chin at Longy who led me to a salutary new connection to Leon Botstein. Also Anne Fitzgibbon, Jorge

Soto and the Alvarez twins, Deborah Borda on both coasts, the YOLA gang, Leo Granados and his brother Marco, Perla Capriles, and my larger-than-life pal, Stanford Thompson. I send a cheerful wave to Gustavo Dudamel across the perpetually unbridgeable distance—and a sad but grateful wave to the late Maestro Jose Antonio Abreu, whose founding of El Sistema continues to bring life-affirming harmony to the lives of so many people around the world.

Recent friends who have been unfailingly generous in their support include Eric Abraham, Howard Bragman, Carol Oja, Adam Gopnik and Martha Parker, Julie Desbordes, L. P. How, Elaine Lipcan and Sarah Gordon at Opus 3, Tom Angstadt and Nancy Kivelson, and Roxana Sedano and her Peruvian family, who keep my house (and therefore my brain) from descending into chaos, and give me the much-anticipated occasion to shoot the breeze in Spanish every two weeks.

My body and my soul thank Claudio and his restaurant, Le Zie; let no one ever underestimate the healing powers of well-prepared broccoli rabe.

Hey, what about the doctors! I thank them all for keeping body connected to soul—and especially I thank Doctors Dena Harris and Deborah Coady, who delivered my children; Doctors Jeffrey Gimbel and Bobby Cohen for the GP of it all; Doctors Hiram Cody and Larry Norton when the going got tough; and most of all, Dr. Sally Peterson, who has helped me through everything for the past quarter century.

Finally and enormously, I send my deep gratitude to everyone in the Leonard Bernstein Office: Paul Epstein, Craig Urquhart, Mike Sbabo, Marie Carter, Garth Sunderland, Milka de Jesus, Jacob Slattery, Hannah Webster. Thank you for keeping the LB engine running, especially amid the global madness of the Bernstein centennial celebrations.

And thank you, Mummy and Daddy, for giving the Three-Headed Monster such a wonderful existence.

P.S. May the love of a dog never go unthanked: here's to the Henrys, Franny and Zooey, Duffy, Honey, Tookie, Sonia, Georgie, Tabasco, Shiloh, Charlie, Satita, Ziggy, Ozzie, Melba, and Herbie. So far.

Image Credits

Where not otherwise indicated, photos are courtesy of the Bernstein family.

Lenny, Jamie, and Henry the dachshund, page 1: ©Knickerbocker News, Photo by Bob Paley

Felicia as Joan of Arc, page 6: Library of Congress, Prints & Photographs Division, Carl Van Vechten Collection

Jamie and Henry at Carnegie Hall, page 15: Photo by Alfred Eisenstaedt / The LIFE Picture Collection / Getty Images

Adolph, Betty, and Lenny, page 20: Stanley Kubrick for *Look* magazine / Museum of the City of New York. X2011.4.12304.96E. Used with permission of SK Film Archives

Felicia lighting candles in the dining room, page 36: Don Hogan Charles / The New York Times / Redux

Fairfield house, page 42: Photograph courtesy of Kelly Prizel

Lenny, Alexander, and Jamie on tour, page 57: bpk Bildagentur / Bayerische Staatsbibliothek, Munich / Felicitas Timpe / Art Resource, NY

Alexander, Lenny, and Jamie, at Ed Sullivan, page 63: Photograph by Ken Regan

The Family by the Pool, page 69: Library of Congress, Music Division

Felicia Painting in Ansedonia, page 76: Photograph by Ken Heyman

Felicia cuts Lenny's hair, page 78: Photograph by Ken Heyman

Party Scene, page 86: Photograph by Ken Heyman

Jamie wearing McCarthy button, page 91: Photo by Harry Weber / ANL / Vienna, HXBox065_316923

Felicia, Jamie, and Lenny in Lenny's studio, page 101: PHOTOGRAPH BY HENRY GROSSMAN: / © GROSSMAN ENTERPRISES, LLC

Felicia, Lenny, and Donald Cox, page 111: Photo by Stephen Salmieri

Jamie in her dorm room at Harvard, page 127: PHOTOGRAPH BY HENRY GROSSMAN: / © GROSSMAN ENTERPRISES, LLC

Jamie by tree, page 139: PHOTOGRAPH BY HENRY GROSSMAN: / © GROSSMAN ENTERPRISES, LLC

Harry Kraut, Margaret Carson, Helen Coates, and Lenny, page 142: PHOTOGRAPH BY HENRY GROSSMAN: / © GROSSMAN ENTERPRISES, LLC

Lenny and Lauren Bacall, page 160: Photo by Tim Boxer / Archive Photos / Getty Images

The Marquee of 1600 Pennsylvania Avenue, page 182: Library of Congress, Music Division

Jamie, Felicia, Alexander, and Lenny on opening night of 1600 Pennsylvania Avenue, page 184: PHOTOGRAPH BY HENRY GROSSMAN: / © GROSSMAN ENTERPRISES, LLC

Lenny and Tommy Cothran, page 190: Library of Congress, Music Division

Jamie and Lenny on the front page of The New York Post, page 199: Credit Adam Scull/PHOTOlink.net / Courtesy of New York Post

The Last Complete Holiday card, 1977, page 208: PHOTOGRAPH BY HENRY GROSSMAN: / © GROSSMAN ENTERPRISES, LLC

Jamie and David Pack, page 241: Photograph by Peter Cunningham / http://www.petercunninghamphotography.com

Lenny, Nina, Alexander, Jamie, and Shirley at Kennedy Center, page 246: Photo by Ron Galella / Ron Galella Collection / Getty Images

Alexander, Jamie, Lenny, and Nina at the Watergate, page 254: Library of Congress, Music Division

Felicia on the cover of Lenny's Mozart Requiem, page 265: © Deutsche Grammophon

Postcard, front and back, page 270: Library of Congress, Music Division

Quincy Jones, Michael Jackson, Lenny, Jamie, and David Pack, page 286: Photo by Lester Cohen / Getty Images Entertainment / Getty Images

Jamie, Jennie Bernstein, and David Thomas at Tanglewood, page 298: Photograph courtesy of Christina Burton

Nina, Jamie, and Lauren Bacall at Tanglewood, page 301: Photograph courtesy of Christina Burton

Lenny and the Quartet performing at Music for Life Benefit, 1989, page 306: ©Steve J. Sherman

Jamie holding "Mambo" sign, page 341: ©Steve J. Sherman

Index of Names

About the Author

JAMIE BERNSTEIN is a writer, broadcaster, and filmmaker. She travels the world as a concert narrator. Her documentary, *Crescendo: The Power of Music*, is available on Netflix. She lives in New York City.